Someone Like Me

Someone Like Me

EDITED BY
CLEM BASTOW & JO CASE

VERVE BOOKS

First published in the UK in 2025
by VERVE Books Ltd., Harpenden, UK
vervebooks.co.uk
@VERVE_Books

First published in Australia and New Zealand by University of Queensland Press in 2025.

A CIP catalogue record for this book is available from the British Library.

ISBN
978-0-85730-926-6 (Paperback)
978-0-85730-927-3 (eBook)

2 4 6 8 10 9 7 5 3 1

Typeset in 11 on 13.4pt Minion Pro
by Avocet Typeset, Bideford, Devon, EX39 2BP
Printed and bound in Great Britain by
CPI Group (UK) Ltd, Croydon CR0 4YY

The manufacturer's authorised representative in the EU for product safety is Easy Access System Europe, Mustamäe tee 50, 10621 Tallinn, Estonia
gpsr.requests@easproject.com

CONTENTS

CONTENTS

CONTENTS

Please note, this book contains discussion of topics and themes that some readers may find challenging, including: racism, violence, medical misogyny, war, psychiatry, eating disorders, burnout, religion, interpersonal abuse, emotional abuse, transphobia, homophobia, bullying, ableism, the hospital system, the school system, illness, pain, chronic health conditions, the Covid pandemic, climate change, mental ill health, sex, harmful drug and alcohol use, dictatorship, animal death, bereavement.

INTRODUCTION

Dr Clem Bastow and Jo Case

photo credit: Leah Jing McIntosh

DR CLEM BASTOW (they/them) is a screenwriter, cultural critic and award-winning critical Autism studies researcher from Naarm–Melbourne. Clem also works as a neurodiversity consultant for film and TV, and teaches screenwriting at the University of Melbourne. Clem's debut non-fiction book, *Late Bloomer*, was published in 2021. They have contributed to books including *Investigating Stranger Things* and *ReFocus: The films of Elaine May*, and their writing appears regularly in *The Guardian*. They're currently working on a series of critical Autism studies essays and a collection of science-fiction short stories.

photo credit: Sia Duff

JO CASE (she/her) is a writer and editor who lives in Adelaide. Her memoir of autistic motherhood, *Boomer and Me*, was published by Hardie Grant in 2013, and she has contributed personal essays to *Mothermorphosis* (MUP) and *Rebellious Daughters* (Ventura). She is the deputy editor of Books & Ideas at *The Conversation* and has worked in various roles in books and publishing, including as a festival programmer and literary editor. Her writing has been published in *The Age/Sydney Morning Herald*, *The Monthly*, *Meanjin*, *Kill Your Darlings*, *The Big Issue Fiction Edition* and *Best Australian Stories*.

PREFACE TO INTERNATIONAL EDITION

We are delighted that *Someone Like Me* has made its way across the oceans to a whole new audience. As part of this big journey, ably stewarded by Jenna Gordon and the team at VERVE Books, we are also thrilled to include in this edition six new essays from writers based in the UK, Ireland and USA, woven among the existing essays.

Ivy Lin writes about falling in love with the UK, which she found 'quieter… with less pressure to be assertive and outspoken' than her hometown, Brooklyn, after a visit in her early twenties – and taking the leap to migrate there, despite being someone who, like most Autistic people, struggles with change. She finds beauty, though, in the process of crumbling under pressure and piecing herself back together: 'like *kintsugi*, the Japanese art of repairing broken pottery'. We love her embrace of the cracks she's 'fixed from all the changes' she's endured.

'I realised I was weird when I was pretty young,' writes Edinburgh-based Fergus Murray. In a different family, they say, this would have damaged their self-esteem. But Fergus's mother, Dinah Murray, 'had long since come to terms with her own weirdness'. In fact, she came up with the theory of the monotropic brain: 'one in which a relatively small number of interests are aroused at any time, strongly pulling in whatever attention is available'. Fergus's essay is a stirring celebration of Autistic affirmation in families, as well as a fascinating reflection on monotropism.

'Sometimes my attention goes everywhere, a kind of spilling,' muses Pacific Northwest writer Sarah Teresa Cook in her poetic essay. 'What's this *small talk* everyone is speaking of? How do people know what to keep on the inside?' She reflects on the difficulty of knowing exactly how her self has been formed: which parts of her are because she's a writer, which because of trauma, and which are 'the brain-wiring, the cosmic-genetic-happenstance soup'? Sarah's gently looping meditation on eternal questions of belonging and becoming will speak to all who have found themselves in places where they were 'from away'.

Julie Farrell's lyrical ode to stargazing recalls her 'obsessive interest' in the solar system, and her dad's lessons – on freezing Scottish winter nights – teaching her 'to recognise the patterns in the stars and sharing the ancient stories strung between them'. Her deep dive into her intricate, whole-body love of astronomy is a gift to the reader, and a beautiful illustration of Autistic joy in action. 'With every single observation, a *whole new world* unfurls into being before my eyes,' she writes. Being 'eye-to-universe… is who I am.'

It seems unsurprising that *The Lamb* author Lucy Rose grew up to be a bestselling novelist, reading her essay on her all-encompassing childhood ambition to be a fish – specifically, a mermaid. 'Intrusive thoughts of scales hatching from my skin so I can move through the water, where it is heavy and quiet and dark – where my sensory icks can't reach me.' One teacher described her as imaginative 'but he used the word like it was dirty'. Her gorgeous, immersive essay veers widely, describing the pain of being misunderstood and unseen, of being judged as weird and romanticised as a 'manic pixie dream girl'. But above all, it's a complex love letter to finally understanding herself through an Autistic lens.

Irish novelist Naoise Dolan (also a bestseller) opens her brilliantly incisive essay on Autistic writing by sharing the most annoying question she's asked by journalists: how does your Autism affect your writing? She writes, 'The answer I'm tempted to give is: "First, you tell me how not being autistic affects yours."' Perfect. She has two main points. First, she argues interior analysis (tell, don't show) can be an effective way of showing a character's emotion. Relatedly, she argues against the expectation that women writers should foreground bodies – blushing or stomach clenching, for example – to show emotion. If you've read Naoise's work, particularly her brilliant debut *Exciting Times*, you'll know she employs this logic to devastatingly moving effect. But in case you haven't, she uses Jane Austen to make her case.

We hope you will love this expanded edition of *Someone Like Me* as much as we do, and that in its contents you find company, understanding and kindred spirits.

INTRODUCTION

Clem

Whoever said you become more conservative as you get older has apparently never met a critical Autism studies scholar. For me, the process of unmasking – since discovering I was Autistic six years ago – has only led to me becoming more radical in my strongly held beliefs about Autistic culture and community. Nothing radicalises you like first realising that, in fact, you weren't imagining your difference, and then being thrown headfirst into confirming your worst fears about how society, broadly, thinks of Autistic people – people like you. However, it would be incorrect to imply that this radicalisation came solely in opposition to the (neurotypical) status quo; rage can only get you so far. Instead, what has truly radicalised me is immersing myself in Autistic culture.

Key in this has been my interest in and consumption of Autistic creative writing, which was sparked during research I undertook for my book, *Late Bloomer*, and became a blazing inferno during my PhD. Buoyed by the brilliance of Autistic scholars like M Remi Yergeau and Devon Price, and Julia Miele Rodas's groundbreaking critical Autism studies,[1] it became clear to me that so much of what I'd been told was 'wrong' about my writing (including, among other things, the emphasis on information-sharing, repetition, language-partitioning and seemingly beside-the-point segues – all of which I employ in my contribution to this book) was, in fact, determinedly *Autistic* writing.

This is all easy to say now, of course. Ten years ago, it was a very different story. Mainstream narratives about Autism were still overwhelmingly non-Autistic in authorship; even for a media-literate person like myself, it was tough to fight the suspicion that I 'couldn't' be Autistic, since my own experience seemed so different from everything that popular media had told me about Autism. We lived for many years – and, to some extent, still do – in a world, as the late Autistic artist and writer Mel Baggs once put it, 'where an Autistic person's viewpoints are likely to be shoved into the twin oblivions of "But we're not all like that!" and "Thank you for showing me The Autistic Experience™".'[2]

When I published *Late Bloomer* in 2021 it was still necessary to observe my own experience of Autism through a non-Autistic lens and for a non-Autistic audience. I was stumbling into the light, blinking in the immediate aftermath of my 'official' diagnosis as Autistic. I was only a few years into my journey of unmasking; in many ways, I was observing myself through a non-Autistic lens, still desperate to cling to Baggs's 'But we're not all like that!' Discursive evidence of my own and other Autistic people's experiences had to be backed up by – and share sentence space with – clinical literature and hard stats from studies that (with few exceptions) treated us like a problem to be solved. The book was framed as one of diagnosis, when perhaps its subtitle would have been more accurate if it had included just one more word: 'How an Autism diagnosis changed my life *story*'. If I wrote it now, it would be a very different book.

Without having investigated my experiences through that newfound lens of self-knowledge, I certainly wouldn't have come to understand my gender in all its complexities – but, somewhat ironically, given the old chestnuts about Autistic people and nuance, I had to skim over that lest I steer focus away from 'The Late-Life Diagnosis Story'. Regardless, my experience of diagnosis was and still is an outlier for a lot of Autistic people: I am white and university educated, was presenting as a woman, could access a psychologist, and was gainfully employed at the time, so I could pay for it. (As is often the case when the mask crumbles into dust, now I'm just another run-of-the-mill nonbinary 'Level 2' underemployed goblin with a doctorate.) Although my story represented a departure from the 'Rain Man' norm, it quickly came to represent a new status quo.

In the 2010s, it was still commonly believed that women 'couldn't' be Autistic. Those barriers to diagnosis and self-knowledge were – and still are – multiplied by intersections of race, class and coexisting disabilities. Autism is still constructed rhetorically, clinically and in media as an overwhelmingly white, male condition. Things, thank the maker, are changing – if slowly. Non-Autistic people are interested to hear what Autistic people have to say. More Autistic people are carving out niches in screen media, online and in publishing. Gradually, we are chipping away at monolithic notions of The Autistic Experience™ that have persisted for too long. Popular narratives surrounding Autism have great impacts on people's ability to self-identify as Autistic if they don't look like the dominant paradigm, which can bring their journey towards support and self-knowledge to a halt. As disability studies scholar Paul Heilker writes, 'there is a great deal of work to be done to create a more realistic portrait of autism and autistics in our public discourse'.[3]

So, when Jo asked me to join forces with her for an anthology that would throw the doors open to gender-diverse and women Autists, I was thrilled. Evidence, both anecdotal and academic, indicates that rates of gender variance are higher among the Autistic population;[4] many Autistic cis women report discomfort with the expectations of gender norms.[5] Autistic researcher and psychologist Dr Wenn Lawson puts it succinctly: 'The non-autistic world is governed by social and traditional expectations, but we may not notice these or fail to see them as important. This frees us up to connect more readily with our true gender.' Studies have established, distressingly, that young Autistic trans and gender-diverse people are often told their interest in gender affirmation is just another special interest.[6] Autistic cis women who strafe against neurotypical notions of womanhood are socialised to brush their hair, dress nicely, be good girls.

None of this is to say that Autistic men have it easy. As Devon Price has written extensively, that is far from the truth, especially for Autistic men of colour and those with complex support needs.[7] But, faced with diagnostic biases, societal structures and popular discourses that still present young, white, cis men as the pinnacle of Autism, the more voices to the contrary that can be elevated, the better.

What an incredible opportunity to demonstrate that Autistic people have the power to be the authors of their own stories (still a wild notion to some, I know), and also that Autistic writing is as diverse and dynamic as people's experiences of the Autism spectrum itself. And, crucially, it would provide an opportunity for Autistic authors to move beyond writing solely about diagnosis.

As Caitlin McGregor, one of this anthology's contributors, asked in a powerful essay about Autism memoir for the *Sydney Review of Books*: 'What would Autistic storying look like if it wasn't defining itself through and against psychiatry, but establishing itself on its own terms?'[8] *Someone Like Me* is a step towards that utopia: allowing Autistic writers to imagine themselves as separate from the pathologising, the othering and the clinical – and, in doing so, inviting so many other Autistic people to see themselves represented by the stories we tell about ourselves.

Jo

Every time I read a book by an Autistic author, I learn something new about myself. I didn't entirely realise I sometimes cry when I'm overwhelmed until a line in Kay Kerr's *Please Don't Hug Me*, one of her two YA novels with Autistic protagonists, rang a bell. Fiona Wright's exquisite memoir-essay collection *The World Was Whole*, which she wrote (and I read) before she was diagnosed as Autistic, was rich with moments of recognition for me. It helped me, among other things, to be okay with my deep affinity for routine and familiarity. I related so hard, for example, to a passage about quietly panicking when visiting a favourite café that's undergone subtle changes, where her 'food is different somehow' when served. I do exactly this too, and always feel ashamed. Like Fiona, I think: 'I don't want to be the kind of person who resists change.'

And lately, Devon Price's *Unmasking Autism* (a book I first heard of through Clem) has revealed so many small details that help explain how and why I am who I am. For example, that there's a neurotype common to late-diagnosed Autistic people that includes being friendly and socially adaptive, internalising rigid self-taught social rules (like not talking for too long about yourself), being regularly socially 'mothered' into more normative behaviour and often being labelled 'oversensitive' or 'immature' despite our efforts. 'We're social chameleons, and masters at making people like us, but we never let much of our real selves show,' writes Price.

Perhaps it's not surprising that my own essay in this anthology is about the Autistic-coded characters who provided company and inspiration for my bookish younger self, decades before I would even know what Autism was (apart from the limited view provided by Dustin Hoffman in *Rain Man*, a film I loved due to a lamentable teenage hyperfixation on Tom Cruise).

The passionate, socially awkward tomboy and ardent 'scribbler' Jo March of *Little Women* was based on author Louisa May Alcott, whose biographies reveal her as just as idiosyncratic as her much-loved heroine. (Though not more so than her father, Transcendentalist philosopher and experimental educator Bronson Alcott, who is increasingly speculated to be Autistic.) Then there's verbose, high-achieving chronic daydreamer Anne Shirley of *Anne of Green Gables* and blunt, routine-driven people-watcher *Harriet the Spy*, who learns the hard way that sometimes you have to lie a little to get by socially. And, though I didn't discover her until adulthood, Miles Franklin's oddly charismatic, prickly, determined writer Sybylla, in *My Brilliant Career*, is clearly these characters' more complicated, Australian counterpart. (Gillian Armstrong, who directed beloved film versions of both *My Brilliant Career* and *Little Women*, noted the similarities between Sybylla and Jo.)

I was provisionally diagnosed as Autistic in 2007, just over fifteen years ago, by the psychologist, now a specialist in Autistic women, who diagnosed my son. It was a lonely time to be an Autistic woman. I hunted out stories by others like me, but they were few, and rarely resonated with my experience.

Clem's memoir, *Late Bloomer*, was another affirming moment for me because, among other reasons, they wrote about being a pop culture nerd, as I am. I hadn't yet seen that represented in an Autism memoir. Their chapter on the pleasures of echolalia, through their lifelong love of *Ghostbusters*, and their family habit of communicating via *Ghostbusters* quotes made me especially happy. (With my most cherished loved ones, my son and husband, our love language includes quoting *When Harry Met Sally* and *Parks and Recreation*, to the extent that others can get bemusedly annoyed.)

Even better, I knew Clem a little: we both had stints as arts editors at *The Big Issue* (they were music editor; I was books editor) and we were regular segment guests on Melbourne's Triple R in the mid-2000s. My weekly book-review segment was shortly before Clem's 'internet news' shift, and we'd make small talk (yes, I see the irony) in the studio lounge area outside the recording booth. We also followed each other on social media, where I had long enjoyed Clem's incredible passion and detailed commitment to everything they did: making elaborate costumes for Comic-Con, throwing themselves into screenwriting, baking competition cakes for the annual Royal Show – and then, exploring their Autistic identity with an openness I found inspiring.

I liked having Clem for company.

Together

This anthology is about just that: providing company for Autistic women and gender-diverse people. The thirty-one essays in these pages are both highly individual and collective. This dichotomy is reflected throughout the book. As the saying goes, if you meet one Autistic person… you've met one Autistic person. There's a lot we share, but being Autistic is just *one* part of our identities.

As Khadija Gbla articulates in their arresting essay, 'The intersections of personality, abilities, heritage, gender, sexuality, race and so much more make our experiences of the world around us unique.' It is meaningful, they explain, that when growing up with bombs falling around them during the civil war in Sierra Leone, Autism and ADHD were 'not only unheard of but the least of our problems'.

The coexistence of Autism and ADHD is meaningful – and not unusual, both among our contributors and in the general population. Meta-analyses estimate the comorbidity of Autism and ADHD to be anywhere from 40 per cent to above 70 per cent. (Emerging research also suggests what is diagnosed as 'comorbid ADHD' is not necessarily a discrete condition but a manifestation of Autistic executive dysfunction.)[9] Khadija also writes about living with chronic pain and using a mobility aid due to fibromyalgia, chronic fatigue syndrome and hypermobility, conditions that may also be more prevalent among Autistic people than the general population.

Having written extensively about her experience of anorexia, Fiona Wright returns to the subject with a new perspective – her Autism diagnosis in her mid-thirties – for this anthology. Though as many as half of all people with anorexia may also be Autistic, she writes, the medical profession's knowledge of that prevalence has been slow to emerge. Part of the blame falls to diagnostic overshadowing, meaning that when there's an anorexia diagnosis, everything that applies to both anorexia and

Autism – detail-focused thinking, social anxiety, perfectionism, a poor sense of self and intense, engulfing emotions – is explained by the former. But the consequences of this overshadowing, considering the dominant, one-size-fits-all treatment rarely works for Autistic people, are dire.

Adele Dumont addresses the links between her trichotillomania (compulsive hair-pulling) and Autism in her essay about why, as an Autistic person, she flourishes in her role teaching English as a second language – but panics during unstructured gatherings for pizza and beer in the staffroom. Repetitive behaviours like hair-pulling are relatively common among Autistic people due to their strong sensory component, she writes. We often find them highly stimulating or soothing. (Adele finds it soothing.)

Sensory issues are common for Autistic people, and sensory processing can be experienced as hyper – too much – and hypo – not enough. Marlee Jane Ward experiences both: 'I was sure it wasn't normal to be driven to self-harm because the fluorescent lights in my office were so *loud* and they got into my *spine* and *teeth* and *eyes*.' In her essay for this collection, Marlee Jane explores this from a perspective that is rarely represented: an intense enjoyment of sex. While others she spoke to equivocated about sex, she 'could not imagine anything better', and recalls, even now, the details of her first sexual experience, aged sixteen, with 'a razor-sharp focus'.

Similarly, Walbunja-Yuin artist Sara Kian-Judge writes very deliberately against popular understandings of what it is to be Autistic. Their essay is a fierce and powerful ode to autism**DARK**: the opposite of *SPARKLE*, a popular vibe for Autism awareness material and catchword for Autistic joy, obsession and aptitude. *SPARKLE*, she writes, 'makes me feel as though Autism is being used to shove me back into the "helpless little princess" box that I have kicked and screamed my way out of ', watering down (or glitter-gluing over) the messy complexity of her Autistic identity: 'the **FEROCIOUS**, the **FERAL** and the **FREAK**ish'.

'Nature was my stim palace', writes Shadia Hancock in their intriguing essay on their happy immersion in plants, first, then animals, which both remain 'my solace in a world I often find chaotic and confusing'. They memorably compare animal training techniques to the controversial Applied Behaviour Analysis (ABA), which is still considered the gold standard 'treatment' for Autistic people and was designed to 'decrease inappropriate behaviours'. As was the case with Autistic people, Shadia writes, animals were once thought not to possess a wide array of emotions and thoughts. Of course, we know that to be entirely untrue – and Shadia finds real comfort in being able to be their whole self in the accepting and predictable company of animals. As they explain, their dog didn't care that they 'needed to stim, or had meltdowns, or communicated differently'.

Tash Agafonoff expresses a similar idea in her beautiful tribute to one special dog in her life, Bud. 'I was never sure when people were my friends', she writes. 'But animals? All animals were friends. Animals didn't judge me the way people did.' Tash's friendship with Bud provides 'a type of social scaffolding' for a new, years-long friendship with his owner, who she met through a former friend who dumped her for not being interested enough in their romantic troubles. That more stable friendship then provided a structure for Tash's exploration of her Autistic identity, which explained a lot of things about her that others found puzzling. One of those things was alexithymia (an inability to identify and articulate emotions), which is common for Autistic people.

Food writer Jess Ho describes their meticulous flying routine, which gives them 'full control' of their travel environment. It was developed pre-pandemic – applying various high-end skincare products, compression socks, a face mask, and wiping everything down with antibacterial wipes – and regularly has flight attendants erupting in awe ('that's so fierce'). Jess writes: 'It's the 'tism.' Jess's open approach to making the accommodations they need is impressive, especially because so many of us have spent so much time 'masking' – covering up our Autistic traits, often at great discomfort. Many of us have spent time pretending to be someone we're not.

Lauren Metzler beautifully explores this experience in her graphic story about masking, sensory overload, burnout and self-discovery – eventually finding solace and self-expression through art-making. Lauren's gorgeous illustrations are a testament to her journey of self-knowledge.

Kate Gordon and Anna Whateley offer a short, sharp, funny and moving deep-dive into two Autistic brains grappling with imposter syndrome in their parallel monologues. 'Do you think that when everyone else has a conversation, they just… talk?' wonders Kate. 'And when the whole conversation is over, do you think they just… go about their day?'

This idea surfaces in Amanda Tink's gorgeous, poetic fragmented essay – a collage of four Autistic voices (including writers Daniel Tammet and Joanne Limburg), dedicated to the late, great Australian Autistic poet Les Murray. 'We auties [Autistics] often find ourselves staying awake at night and reliving past conversations', someone recalls Les saying during a public talk.

Kay Kerr's wryly moving meditation on the shifting meaning of dance in her life begins with purely joyful living-room dance parties as a child (soundtrack: The Beach Boys' 'Kokomo'). Though dance began as an instinctual pleasure for Kay, it turned into 'a lesson in masking: observe, mimic, practise, repeat' – with unhappy consequences. Now, in recreating the dance parties of her childhood, she embraces the opportunity as an Autistic parent to help her child build the foundations for them to be loved as themselves, in neuro-affirming ways: 'Ours is a home of musical statues, movie soundtrack performances, YouTube choreography lessons and special interest songs on a loop.'

There wasn't much in the way of neuro-affirming care twenty years ago (or ten, or five), writes Sienna Macalister in their excellent essay on their experience of the school system. Rather, Sienna says, therapy was 'compliance training', aimed to cure and make them 'normal' rather than actually assist them with life. They recall, for instance, enduring 'planned ignoring': a behaviour control tactic that meant their attempts at communication – and their very real needs – were ignored, making them feel even more isolated and frustrated. Reflecting on these experiences and more, Sienna powerfully argues for 'inclusion as the norm'.

Caitlin McGregor's bitingly funny (for Autistic readers, anyway) essay about their appointment with a speech pathologist during their Autism assessment brilliantly illustrates Sienna's point about non-neuro-affirming professionals. The teeth-gritting starts when the pathologist explains she's going to identify 'glitches' in their conversation, which she then does based on the firm belief that she knows the 'right' way to react and behave. 'Neurotypical people don't give so many options,' the speech pathologist says authoritatively, explaining that Caitlin has not responded appropriately to an exercise in imagining what people in a photograph might be thinking. 'I just look and know my instinct is right.' Caitlin wonders how – and so do we.

Autistic people have long been accused of not having empathy, though it's increasingly accepted that our empathy just has different triggers than neurotypical people experience. More recently, that divide has been further explained and given a name: the double empathy problem. Caitlin's essay, and several others in this anthology, explore circumstances explained in part by Milton's double empathy problem. The concept, articulated by Autistic academic Damian Milton, explains that because Autistic people experience the world and process emotions differently, and have different life experiences, it is more difficult for us to understand and empathise with non-Autistic people ('allistics').[10] And, crucially, it makes it more difficult for them to understand and empathise with us. It's not a one-way, hierarchical problem to be corrected. It's a communication divide to be addressed by both parties.

Pastor Alison Sampson addresses the question of empathy,

too, in their beautiful essay on religion, a passion for words and coming to accept and embrace the fact they are 'fearfully and wonderfully made'. Autistic people often have the opposite of a lack of empathy; they can experience it more intensely than other people (just differently). When a psychologist tells Alison their empathy is 'off the charts', they articulate a problem: 'how do you establish boundaries with empathy levels like these?' Boundaries can be hard for many Autistic people to establish – even as they're essential for us.

As a pastor, Alison's work is among folk who had left or been kicked out of church. They imagine 'a church that made our trans friends cheer and the atheists laugh and the bishop curl up like a snail'. Alison's flock included Dr Wenn Lawson, who, with Dinah Murray, developed the theory of monotropism: 'Monotropic minds tend to be deeply engaged with a small number of interests at any given time, leaving fewer resources for other neurological processes.' So-called 'special interests' – all-encompassing passions that we focus a lot of attention on – are a defining feature of being Autistic. (Though, as some of us find the terminology somewhat infantilising, maybe we could just call them 'passions'.)

CB Mako in their essay writes arrestingly about their driving passion for robots. It opens in their home country of the Philippines on the brink of a peaceful revolution against dictator Ferdinand Marcos. They are nearly thirteen years old, standing in the street before a military tank, and 'all I can think is one question: could all these military vehicles transform or combine into one giant robot?' They also reflect on their later-in-life Autism diagnosis on the 'leafy, privileged' side of the town where they live today, the only person of colour in a waiting room packed with white people, having taken out a loan for the assessment. This story sharply, poignantly reflects both the obstacles to seeking a diagnosis (part of the reason it's so important to acknowledge the validity of self-diagnosis) and why it's important to be able to access one if needed. They write:

'I am not rich, nor privileged, but I crave a formal diagnosis – solid proof, written down by a person of authority and expertise.'

Ange Crawford's central passion, shared unsurprisingly by many in this anthology, is writing itself. In their exquisite experimental essay, they describe writing as 'a place / for me to go when nothing around me makes sense and the world / feels too much. Which is often.' Writing is a comfort and a vocation, but it's also a compulsion founded on the way their brain works, one that mirrors the way they process life itself: 'I am carefully constructing – editing – / self-editing – editing myself,' they write. 'Noticing never felt optional to me.' They recognise their writing, and the hyperfocused state they enter to do it (both 'a private ritual / comfort' and 'a straight-A / force') as intrinsic to their Autistic self.

For some Autistic people, their passion can focus on people themselves. This might manifest in an intense drive to discover what makes people tick (a useful strategy for social navigation) – or a hyperfixation on romantic interests. And so, in a breezy, hilarious and painfully relatable (for some of us) essay, Jerico Mandybur delivers their shamelessly Autistic guide to romantic longing. Jerico explores how 'maladaptive daydreaming, centred on romantic longing' can monopolise your mental energy, make you 'think and act as if there's an arthouse film camera following you around'; create endless mixtapes (if you're old-school), playlists and journal-scribblings; and 'cultivate a passion so big that just being in your body feels like being on fire'. It's not for the faint of heart.

'You're Autistic, which means a whole lot of things that have nothing to do with numbers or trains, okay?' writes Kai Ash in his clever, funny essay addressing his younger self. Though he warns that he shouldn't tell anyone of his Autism for a few years ('Wait until you're a legal adult and the court can't overrule your healthcare plans'), he gives himself permission to 'leap into maleness'. But he also cautions about some of the struggles ahead, including the challenges of finding work that will suit him as an Autistic person: 'You need to avoid jobs that require you to use a phone, sit in an office, have regular meetings and attend social events.'

LT is a former GP who writes about burning out while working as a doctor – and why the medical profession absolutely did not work for her as an Autistic person. The impossibility of actually keeping to the schedule of fifteen-minute appointments, one after the other, paired with intense preparation for each appointment, checking through a patient's history and trying to anticipate why they may be coming in – which, of course, she rarely could – was her own personal recipe for disaster. Honestly, she sounds like the caring GP everyone dreams of having. But, unsurprisingly, trying to live up to impossible standards broke her. 'I thought everyone cried,' LT writes. 'It seemed the logical response to the conditions.'

This experience of Autistic burnout is something Erin Riley also explores in their valuable contribution. As they say, though Autistic burnout is not widely covered in entry-level Autistic literature, it's a phenomenon Autistic people are well acquainted with: a pervasive fatigue – similar to but not the same as occupational burnout (though they can intersect) – resulting from the cumulative load of masking and operating in a world that is not designed for us. The closer to Autistic burnout you are, the more your Autistic traits emerge. Erin challenges us to see it as an 'opportunity to de-centre ourselves and to connect with the larger, collective world around us – to notice how sick it is too'. Of course, they also recognise that it's not that simple, and we need to balance thinking about how to do things differently with the need to work to pay our bills.

Danni Stewart reflects on some similar themes, including that of 'crip time', which they call 'a re-imagining of what can and should happen within time'. Their fascinating essay explores the various ways Autistic people can experience time differently – including the way operating within a world not structured for us, and having to heed its artificial 'clock time', can be a problem.

Danni is in favour of the 'radical concept' of rest and the time it gives us 'to recover from an overstimulating world'. They also draw on Einstein's theory of spacetime: that all that has ever happened and all that will ever happen exists at once. (Of course, Einstein is widely conjectured to have been Autistic.) 'Multiple psychologists have told me I need to "live in the present", that I spend too much time in the past and the future,' Danni writes. This idea will be familiar to many Autistic people.

On a surface level, Phoebe Lupton's essay is about another common Autistic experience, that of not driving: 'At least one-third of us will receive their full licence by the age of twenty-one – but this is still a minority experience, and I am in the majority.' But the essay is also about time, metamorphosis and so-called 'growing up'. Driving – a sign of maturity, of a coming-of-age in cultures like our own – doubles as a metaphor.

The most amazing thing about editing this collection has been the sense of community we've discovered: the feeling of seeing ourselves in others and being seen. Of not being alone.

We knew this to some extent already. Clem is only half joking when they talk about their 'powerfully Autistic' ancestry with the enthusiasm of a YouTuber tracing the genealogy of royal houses in *A Song of Ice and Fire*. After beginning their process of self-identification, it was Clem's Autistic friends who reacted with joy and relief at the suggestion that, perhaps, Clem might be 'in the club', too (sample text message: lol yes we have had our suspicions about you). And Jo has Autistic friends and family – with new members of the 'Autistic club' emerging all the time.

But there's been something very special about being invited to read the many brilliant essays submitted to this anthology, all intimately engaged with the writers' experience of being Autistic.

This anthology is not an exhaustive catalogue of Autistic experiences – the very notion borders on science fiction. The scope of *Someone Like Me* is limited to the relatively small handful of voices it contains, but even that is powerful. Within this collection of thirty-one voices exist intersections of class, race, culture, disability, gender, sexuality and education that help to complicate the notion of what an Autistic person 'looks like'.

What this collection offers, we hope, is an opportunity to broaden the collective imagination, pushing the door open just a little wider to allow new voices to stream in. There are still many people who, because of the way psychiatry is structured (which is to say, through a lens of carceral white supremacy), do not yet know that they are Autistic. May their own anthologies follow this one.

Spending time with these thirty-one essays, piecing them together, is a first step towards expanding your understanding of Autism – not as a collection of clinical traits, or a series of popular media tropes, but as it manifests in specific Autistic people's lives. Individually they provide fragments of specific Autistic experiences. Together they work towards creating a richer and more complex picture.

We hope you'll find company, discovery and even perhaps enlightenment in these thirty-one essays, as we did. We hope you will experience Autistic joy. We hope you'll make connections, find similarities to and differences from your own life (and to the lives of people you know and love), and be inspired to read further. We hope these essays will generate conversations, even if only with yourself.

Sources

1. Yergeau, MR 2018, *Authoring Autism*, Duke University Press, North Carolina; Price, D 2022, *Unmasking Autism: The power of embracing our hidden neurodiversity*, Monoray, London; Rodas, JM 2018, *Autistic Disturbances*, University of Michigan Press, Ann Arbor.
2. Baggs, A 2010, 'Up in the clouds and down in the valley: My richness and yours', *Disability Studies Quarterly*, vol. 30, no. 1.
3. Heilker, P 2012, 'Autism, rhetoric, and whiteness', *Disability Studies Quarterly*, vol. 32, pp. 193–204.

4. Strang, JF, van der Miesen, AIR, Fischbach, AL, Wolff, M, Harris, MC & Klomp, SE 2023, 'Common intersection of Autism and gender diversity in youth', *Child and Adolescent Psychiatric Clinics of North America*, vol. 32; Warrier, V, Greenberg, DM, Weir, E, Buckingham, C, Smith, P, Lai, M-C, Allison, C & Baron-Cohen, S 2020, 'Elevated rates of Autism, other neurodevelopmental and psychiatric diagnoses, and autistic traits in transgender and gender-diverse individuals', *nature communications*, vol. 11, no. 1, p. 3959; Strang, JF, Janssen, A, Tishelman, A, Leibowitz, SF, Kenworthy, L, McGuire, JK, Edwards-Leeper, L, Mazefsky, CA, Rofey, D, Bascom, J, Caplan, R, Gomez-Lobo, V, Berg, D, Zaks, Z, Wallace, GL, Wimms, H, Pine-Twaddell, E, Shumer, D, Register-Brown, K, Sadikova, E & Anthony, LG 2018, 'Revisiting the link: Evidence of the rates of Autism in studies of gender diverse individuals', *Journal of the American Academy of Child and Adolescent Psychiatry*, vol. 57, no. 11, pp. 885–7.
5. Bargiela, S, Steward, R & Mandy, W 2016, 'The experiences of late-diagnosed women with autism spectrum conditions: An investigation of the female autism phenotype', *Journal of Autism and Developmental Disorders*, vol. 46, no. 10, pp. 3281–94.
6. Strang, JF, Powers, MD, Knauss, M, Sibarium, E, Leibowitz, SF, Kenworthy, L, Sadikova, E, Wyss, S, Willing, L, Caplan, R, Pervez, N, Nowak, J, Gohari, D, Gomez-Lobo, V, Call, D & Anthony, LG 2018, '"They thought it was an obsession": Trajectories and perspectives of autistic transgender and gender-diverse adolescents', *Journal of Autism and Developmental Disorders*, vol. 48, no. 12, pp. 4039–55.
7. Price, D, *Unmasking Autism*.
8. McGregor, C 2023, 'Mad pride: Caitlin McGregor on Clara Törnvall', *Sydney Review of Books*, 13 November, <sydneyreviewofbooks.com/reviews/mad-pride>.
9. Hours, C, Recasens, C & Baleyte, JM 2022, 'ASD and ADHD comorbidity: What are we talking about?', *Frontiers in Psychiatry*, vol. 13, 837424.
10. Milton, D, Gurbuz, E & López, B, 2022, 'The "double empathy problem": Ten years on', *Autism*, vol. 26, no. 8, pp. 1901–3.

OVERSHADOWED, OVERLAPPED, UNSEEN

Fiona Wright

FIONA WRIGHT (she/her) is a writer, editor and critic. Her books of essays are *Small Acts of Disappearance* (2015), which won the Queensland Premier's Prize and the Nita B Kibble Award, and *The World Was Whole* (2018). Her collections of poetry are *Knuckled* (2011) and *Domestic Interior* (2017). Her writing is interested in identity, belonging and place, as well as chronic illness, medicine and the body. She is the 2024 Judy Harris Writer-in-Residence at the Charles Perkins Centre, where she is working on a collection of essays about our narratives about the future and what happens when these fail us.

The final straw, the one that broke this particular camel's back,[1] was my girlfriend's receipt of her autism diagnosis over email. She didn't want to open the report alone and asked if I would read it with her – and when we were done, the only thing I could think to say was: *this is all the things we like about each other.*

It was the final straw, and an important one, but I had been gathering a veritable haybale of such pieces of information, slowly and very much in the background, for the best part of two years by then. It was December 2019. So much has changed since then – in all of our worlds, but also in our conversation around (and understanding of) neurodivergence and gender. It's all happened at a speed that sometimes leaves me reeling. This is a wonderful thing: I often think that no-one, soon, will have to clutch at straws the way I had to.

Psychologists have a term, *diagnostic overshadowing*, for what has happened to so many autistic women, girls and gender-diverse folk, over so many years that the scale of it is horrifying to think about in its entirety. It is what happened to me. But it's not the reason, not quite, that it wasn't until I'd been embroiled in the medical system for something like seventeen years[2] that I

1. Days before I started to write this essay, I was wondering about these metaphors – whether or not, that is, the final straw and the straw that broke the camel's back are the same metaphor, extended, or two slightly different metaphors drawn from different sources. I spent a good hour down this particular research rabbit hole in order to confirm that, yes, the final straw is just a shorter version of the camel metaphor. I'm telling you this not as evidence of solid research or correct usage, but because I want you to know that this is what it's like and this is how my brain works. This is what we're dealing with, after all.
2. It horrifies me to think of this, sometimes. Seventeen years is such a long time, by anybody's reckoning. It's long enough for a newborn to

was diagnosed as autistic, nor that the diagnosis was one I'd had to seek out on my own.

I was diagnosed at thirty-six. But I'd first sought out medical care when I was eighteen years old and developed a very physical, very rare[3] stomach disorder that suddenly saw me throwing up – unintentionally and terrifyingly – whenever I tried to eat. It's a condition that isn't treatable and my attempts to manage it, by avoiding the foods that I thought would make me sick, incrementally and imperceptibly morphed into an eating disorder, fuelled by all the personality traits – perfectionism, a shaky sense of self, Big Feelings – that make a person vulnerable to these kinds of illnesses. My anorexia was, as it so often is, a terribly visible disease. It overshadowed everything that underpinned it, and it dominated the medical care I received across all of the intervening years.

This is often the case. Diagnostic overshadowing happens in part as a result of our attempts to cope with our difference – which we don't understand and can't name but somehow know is there – and with all the ways the world around us isn't built to fit us or make us comfortable. All of these attempts, constant and only half conscious, can and do lead us to some difficult places: anxiety and mood disorders, substance use, compulsions of all kinds, eating disorders like mine. So often, these are such obvious sets of symptoms that they are all anyone – doctor or patient – can see. And so, they are mistaken for the 'disorder'[4] itself: they overshadow what is actually going on.

---

all but come of age; in seventeen years' time it will be 2041. An adage from medical science states that it takes seventeen years for research to be translated into clinical practice – or, for what medicine *learns* to translate into what medics *do*.

3. Far less rare, it turns out, in the neurodivergent – though none of us knew that yet.
4. I can't even tell you how long I spent looking for an alternative word here. My autism has never felt like a disorder: it is just how my brain works and, if anything, it is more orderly than usual, or so I've come to learn. So forgive me for using the loaded, problematic medical term, and know I do

These sets of symptoms are more obvious, and they are often more dangerous as well, so it is usually the case that they warrant more immediate attention; it's only recently that I realised how truly lucky I was to survive my anorexia.[5] But the problem is this: once medicine has decided that you have anorexia, for example, or an addiction, or OCD, everything you say and do becomes the words and actions of an anorectic, or an addict, or an obsessive-compulsive, and nothing else. Medicine knows one thing about you and decides it therefore knows everything about you – or, at the very least, it has a single frame within which it pictures every single thing about you.[6]

This is true of all overshadowing diagnoses, but where disordered eating is concerned there is an added complication: part of the accepted symptomology is a level of denial and deep secrecy. In other words, part of the illness, it is believed, is a disbelief that you have the illness. I recently found an old booklet, from my hospital dietitian, which describes people with anorexia as 'sullen', 'resentful and hostile' and 'devious' in their resistance to any suggestion there might be a problem. (This, I know, is of its time – I hope to god you'd never find a clinician using that language now.) A slightly kinder way of phrasing this is the medical term, in use both now and then, '*la belle indifferénce*': 'beautiful ignorance'. But however you phrase it, the result is the same: you cannot argue that you don't have an illness which is characterised by not believing that you have the illness, because

---

it hesitatingly and utterly begrudgingly

5. Statistically, my doctors would often say, a full third of anorexic patients die of the disease. It has, by far, the highest mortality rate of any mental illness.
6. I'm not going to pretend autism as a diagnosis isn't used as a frame, too. If anything, it happens more, and it is applied by a far wider range of people. I'm not sure why I, by and large, resent this less – perhaps because the diagnosis is still less stigmatised, in that it isn't seen as being somehow our fault; perhaps because it feels a better fit. Probably it's just because I'm older now and have far fewer fucks to give.

anything you say is simply evidence that you have the illness. It's like arguing with a conspiracy theorist: anything you offer is just proof you have been brainwashed too.

The problem, for me, wasn't that I didn't have anorexia, or that I didn't know my eating wasn't *normal*.[7] It's just that I knew my anorexia was atypical – because of the physical condition that sparked it and because I didn't have any of the concerns about my weight or appearance, any of the body dysmorphia I saw plaguing so many of the patients I was treated alongside. But none of my doctors ever believed me. They'd ask the same questions about body image over and again, and then in slightly different ways, as if waiting for me to trip up and let the truth slip from my tongue.

It is, of course, difficult to trust your doctors – as they continually told me I had to do – when it is so patently obvious they don't believe a word you say. But perhaps that's exactly the point: you should not, and you should not have to, trust a doctor who doesn't have faith in your own testimony, your own experience of your mind and body. Yet medicine is built on precisely this imbalance of power and I was so desperate for help I had no choice but to try to trust, however much and however often I chafed against it. Because a doctor can – and many did – refuse to treat you entirely: this too I find unconscionable.

But what my doctors didn't know at the time – because no-one knew at the time – is that there's more to the story than overshadowing. There is also overlap.

In the last eight years or so, researchers have started looking into the commonalities – and finding great co-morbidity[8] – between autism and disordered eating. Before this, it was known that many autistic people do have divergent patterns of eating[9]

7. See above, re. begrudging use of medical language.
8. This term, though, this one I love. It's so deliciously… morbid.
9. This term is mine, not theirs. I like it, and you're welcome to it if it suits you too.

– a preference for milder, 'blander' foods, or for the same small range of foods, an avoidance of certain textures[10] – and that sensory differences and a preference for routine often account for these. But it wasn't until the mid-2010s, when a handful of psychologists who had worked extensively with autistic people coincidentally took positions in an eating disorder clinic in the UK, that anybody thought to pay attention to the similarities in thinking and behaviour between these two groups, or to consider that these might be significant.[11]

What I mean is this: spun one way, eating the same foods at the same times (and in the same place at the table) looks like the elaborate eating rituals that develop when a person is malnourished, or obsessively worried about their intake of food. But it could also be the kind of repetitive behaviour that lends many autistic people a sense of reassurance, safety or simple order. A hyperawareness of cooking smells and intense flavours and textures can be related to an anorectic's concern with bodily purity and containment and to the physical and chemical changes that can happen in starvation, or to the sensory sensitivities of autism; likewise, the great discomfort often felt after a meal. Detail-focused thinking is symptomatic of both conditions;[12] so too are social anxiety, perfectionism, a poor sense of self and, importantly, those immense, engulfing emotions that are so difficult to live with and that under-eating can so quickly and reliably quieten within the body and the mind.[13]

---

10. What the fuck even are you, avocado?
11. One of these researchers is Kate Tchanturia, whose projects and publications can be found here: <kclpure.kcl.ac.uk/portal/en/persons/kate.tchanturia/publications>.
12. See above, re. begrudging use of terms. But also, details are fun and wonderful and curious and telling and I wouldn't have it any other way.
13. In one of the case studies I read, a woman talked about this dampening of emotions – a hungry body simply doesn't have the resources to devote energy to emotion, and there's a stilling and a focus to this that I always felt as a relief – by stating this: 'If it were possible to under-eat and over-exercise without losing weight… I would do it.' I felt this as a blow

Those researchers are now positing that as many as half of all people with anorexia may also (may actually?) be autistic. Most studies now estimate the rate to sit somewhere between 20 and 30 per cent (and by means of comparison, the rate of autism in the general population is around 1 per cent).[14] Either way, it's a hell of a lot of people – almost all women and gender-diverse folk, of course – and I know that every single one of us has suffered, deeply and needlessly, because we have not been seen.[15]

Not being seen is an impossible problem when you do not, yet, exist. Shortly after my autism diagnosis, and more than a year after I learnt about this overlap, I bought[16] a copy of my medical records from the public hospital that had overseen most of my eating disorder treatment. I did this because I was furious, at the time, and in a way that felt righteous and important; I know

---

(and in case there's any doubt, I mean that very literally), because I know this is a sentence that I have said, repeatedly and almost word for word. In terms of straws – as it were – this was by far the biggest in my bundle. (The case study in point is: Brede, J, Babbi, C, Jones, C, Elliott, M, Zanker, C, Tchanturia, K, Serpell, L, Fox, J & Mandy, W 2020, '"For me, the anorexia is just a symptom, and the cause is autism": Investigating restrictive eating disorders in autistic women', *Journal of Autism and Developmental Disorders*, vol. 50, no. 2, pp. 4280–96.)

14. Wentz, E, Lacey, JH, Waller, G, Råstam, M, Turk, J & Gillberg, C 2005, 'Childhood onset neuropsychiatric disorders in adult eating disorder patients: A pilot study', *European child & adolescent psychiatry*, vol. 14, no. 8, pp. 431–7.
15. All of this, of course, assumes that any of these conditions have rigid boundaries and strict delineations in the first place. Medicine, with its systematic categorisations and diagnostic checklists, insists that they do, because everything about it as a knowledge system relies on these boundaries, these precise definitions. But our bodies and brains are rarely this uncomplicated, this neat. Overshadowing happens more often where there's a refusal to see in shades of grey, and where overlapping edges are ignored.
16. Yes, you have to pay for this, even though the information is your own. I can't even begin to wrap my head around this.

I thought that I would scour the pages for evidence of what was always there, but overlooked or simply missed, time and again – those Big Feelings, that sense of difference, my confusion at the strange, unspoken rules within their programs and clinics. I thought I would write something excoriating and damning in response – look, just look, at everything they didn't see.

But I didn't do it. I couldn't do it, in part because it's so hard to look at those records and not just feel bereaved, a whole-body grief that still surprises me with its intensity and ache. But, more importantly, I couldn't do it because I realised what was always there was also entirely beside the point: no-one could possibly have seen what did not yet exist, nor drawn on knowledge that was not yet discovered.

I was, after all, unseen even to and by myself.

What gives me solace, still, is this: those researchers are now discovering something I've known for years but never had a way to understand. The standard, and even the 'best-practice', clinical treatments for eating disorders do not work for autistic people. They were never designed with us and our minds in mind. They do not fit. They did not fit, and I always tried to fit myself to them instead – so it's a no-brainer, really, that it did not help at all.

What I mean is this: these kinds of treatments are almost always group-based – which so often exacerbated my feelings of awkwardness and difference – and involve full-sized supervised meals with no concessions made for disliked foods or physical discomfort, which I often found intolerable, and in a way I know now was particularly, sensorially, extreme. I remember once being penalised for pulling the cucumber slices off a sandwich and swallowing them whole because it was the only way I could stomach them. When I was reprimanded for this, I explained that cucumber makes me gag (What the fuck even are you, cucumber?), and the dietitian's response was, sternly, 'Only babies gag.'[17] This might be true for the neurotypical,[18] but it certainly isn't for the neurodivergent.

So, too, with forced exposure to uncomfortable situations – this doesn't work for us, and it only reaffirms our discomfort or fear – so, too, with the focus on social settings; so, too, with the sets of rules by which each program or ward is run. These in particular I never could make sense of, and the contradictions within them drove me wild. I was always butting up against so much.

I spent years in intensive treatment of this kind. Eight solid years, and a truly horrendous amount of money, too, and I kept at it over all this time because it was the only option I had. I kept at it, and I kept not getting better, and I always thought that was my fault. That I wasn't trying hard enough. I wasn't committed enough, brave enough, strong enough, *surrendering* enough. That I clearly didn't want it enough.

I always thought the problem lay with me.

In many ways, I was primed already for that kind of thinking. If there's one thing that I think every disordered eater has in common, it is the belief that there is something in us, something about us, that is bad or faulty or somehow wrong – and all of our efforts and striving and stringency are an attempt to ameliorate this in whatever small way we can.[19] I know I felt this, deeply and obdurately, but I never could understand why – there was

17. Also, it was cucumber. I still don't understand why it should have been such a big deal: I never met another patient who had any qualms at all about cucumber – it has fuck-all calorific value, after all. Everyone else was in far greater panics about the fact that the bread in the sandwich was buttered or trying to stuff slices of ham into their socks.
18. I don't think it is, but I can't find definitive evidence either way.
19. And it's inevitable, in a culture so obsessed with food and diet and body, that some of this should transfer to these domains. It's the most prevalent metaphor we have. Think of how often food is charged with moral meaning: guilty pleasure, indulgence, clean, wholesome, naughty, bad. Think of how often changing the body is spoken of as self-improvement, or dieting as self-control, restraint.

no reason I could find for me to feel this way, to need to push so hard against it.

What I mean is this: I used to joke, in hospital, that so many of our group therapy sessions ended up looking like a game of *My Shitty Family*, because so many of the patients I met there had powerful hands to play. So many of these people had grown up in families with truly awful pressures or dynamics – controlling or demanding parents, bullying siblings, parents obsessed with weight loss and appearance – if not outright abuse. Many, too, had histories of trauma, especially of sexual assault or violence. None of these are a part of my narrative, my history; this makes me incredibly fortunate. My family is, and always has been, loving and supportive, relaxed about bodies and their functions,[20] untroubled around food. I'd suffered no obvious trauma (at least, I hadn't until I became unwell). There was no good developmental reason, that is, for me to judge myself as harshly as I did, and sometimes still do. To always feel out of place in the world, unlovely and unable to set things right, or to believe that I am odd and strange and different.

But this, in many ways, was the gift of my autism diagnosis: there was no good reason for me to feel that I am odd and strange and different – except for the fact that I am. Or, more precisely, that my brain is different, and always has been, and difference is no deficiency of self. Something clicked into place when I finally had this information. Something, too, was lifted from me – some deep, abiding shame and sense of fault that I didn't fully realise I had been carrying over and across all these years. How heavily it weighed.

I don't know how much of this research is filtering through to clinical practice, nor in which ways – I'm no longer involved enough in (which is to say subjected to) these kinds of settings. I do know the knowledge is there, at last, and the discussion

20. i.e., we love a fart joke.

is happening; and I do know that more and more of the research about what suitable treatment might look like is being undertaken, with autistic people involved right from the early design stages. All of this is revolutionary, and I do not use that word lightly.[21]

Because the thing about this kind of knowledge is that it cannot be un-discovered. Once learnt, it cannot be un-known – and once people like me have become visible, even in this strange and limited way, we will not easily disappear. It is a terrible thing to be unseen, especially by the very people you are asking for insight and trusting for clear vision. But to know that this will happen less and less – that fewer and fewer people will suffer in the particular way that you had to – is a marvel and a wonder. And no small solace, either.

21. Of course I don't use this word lightly; this is how my brain works, and what we're dealing with, after all.

WHEN EVERYONE ELSE HAS A CONVERSATION

Anna Whateley and Kate Gordon

ANNA WHATELEY (she/her) is a Brisbane-based writer. She has worked in literature and education, and holds a PhD in young adult fiction from Queensland University of Technology. Her debut novel, *Peta Lyre's Rating Normal*, was released in 2020, and an autobiographical account was published in *Growing up Disabled in Australia* in 2020. She is currently working on another YA novel, *Tearing Myself Together.* Anna is an 'own voices' author, proudly autistic, with ADHD, sensory processing disorder and Ehlers-Danlos syndromes.

KATE GORDON (she/they) grew up in a small town by the sea in Tasmania. She is the author of numerous award-winning picture books and novels for younger readers, including *Aster's Good, Right Things*, published by Yellow Brick Books in 2020, which won the CBCA Book of the Year for younger readers and was shortlisted in the Tasmanian Literary Awards. *Whalesong* was published by Yellow Brick Books in 2022, following Kate's residency at the Maritime Museum of Tasmania. Kate continues to write novels and picture books from a cottage overlooking the river and the mountain on the eastern shore of Hobart. She has two daughters and a very silly labradoodle.

'We should write a thing about imposter syndrome,' I said to Kate. She's such a real writer and a real mum and why would she want to write with me? I've felt the comfort of family with her since we first wrote to each other, so there's a chance she understands.

Imposter Syndrome. Does it have capitals? Or italics? It's not diagnosable. My first notes were academic, because that's how I wrote for twenty years. I thought: fitting in is the opposite of belonging, and autistic folk are encouraged to work on fitting in, with less thought given to our own sense of belonging, squidging and moulding ourselves into something recognisable to our peers.

Belonging is tightly bound to good mental health and at the same time seems impossible if we are to also strive for authenticity. I assume belonging assuages imposter syndrome, when someone is fully qualified and there are no clear reasons for the sense that they have no right to be where they are.

Perhaps while neurotypical people usually feel a fleeting sense of imposter syndrome that flares in new situations, autistic people are faced with frequent bouts of the condition in everyday life, from early social interactions onwards. The dance between the authentic self and the imposed facade is clumsy and faltering. How do we accept our own inherent adequacy?

'We should write a thing about imposter syndrome,' I said.

Kate replied and we both tumbled honestly through our thoughts and feelings.

Do you think that when everyone else has a conversation, they just… talk?

About the weather or the football or *The Real Housewives of Beverly Hills*?

I talk about *The Real Housewives of Beverly Hills* and *Salt Lake City* too, and *Vanderpump Rules*, and I talk about crows and I talk about my kids and I talk about whales and The Beatles and Andy Warhol and how hagfish absorb their food through their skin because I just learnt that and *how is it possible* and, on that note, how are photographs possible?

I know it's something to do with light and mirrors and I know it makes sense, in the way that our eyes make sense and evolution makes sense, but *how* were we once fish?

And do you think Lisa Rinna will ever come back to *The Real Housewives of Beverly Hills*?

Do you think that when everyone else has a conversation, they just… talk?

About the weather?

And when they're done commenting on the weather, they listen to the other person make their comments and they *really listen*, and then they talk again, *at the right point in the conversation*?

Do you think that when everyone else has a conversation, they just… listen?

I don't know any of these shows or *Housewives* and now maybe you won't like me. I don't belong here. I talk about gaming and YouTube even though I'm forty-six. Like *World of Warcraft* or *Minecraft* or *Baldur's Gate 3*.

Oh! I like crows, and I like the Corvus genus and how they function in mythology and literature, but also how they come and watch me like they know something. I have crows in games too, as pets. I talked over you though and now I have lost the train of the conversation and forgotten to listen because I don't belong out here in the world.

Do other people just… listen? All the time?

Evolution is fascinating, and so is the game *Metazooa* where you 'guess the animal' going by where your previous guess fits on the tree of all life and a warmer/cooler proximity system. It would show you about the fish, and you should play, do you want to play? We played for five hours yesterday. I don't think that's what other families do.

Do people choose what they'll remember when they listen?

Not over the other person.

Not before the other person has finished.

Not just to fill the silences?

And when the whole conversation is over, do you think they just… go about their day?

Go to the supermarket, go to soccer practice, go home and maybe they watch *The Real Housewives of Beverly Hills* too but they only watch it once?

Not over and over, so they know every line and every look, so they think of the cast as their friends?

Surely, they don't follow every Housewife, and every fan account and every podcast. Surely, they don't spend four hours a day listening to podcasts recapping the episodes they just watched. Surely, they don't spend another two hours researching crow funeral rites (all these hours spent, of course, while their babies are asleep, because when their babies are awake they are obsessively playing with their babies and reading to their babies and walking with their babies, because when their babies are awake, that is *all they want to do.*)

Surely.

Surely, when they have conversations, they just talk

Do I live in your after thoughts? Am I an afterthought?

I game with such interesting people. One told me he wants to quit the armed forces and be a barber. Then later, I realised I already knew and felt terrible. It's not like I don't care, honest, I do.

One time. I've been to soccer practice once. I'm impressed you know a popular TV show, and that means you belong more than I do, and you are a more functional human.

I might not be able to listen very well about the housewives show; I might just enjoy your enthusiasm. It's already making me smile. I love people being passionate about things.

I look like I don't care, my face won't be right, but I do care.

Secretly, I wonder how much it has cost you to share your passion with me. What pain will you be in later? None? A lot? Will you worry? Have I reassured you enough? Did I ask the right questions to show I was listening? Did you notice when I wasn't focused on what you were saying? I was trying to stay still, busy enjoying your aura. Am I responsible for your feelings, or your belonging? Do you like me being passionate?

How many times today did

about the weather and when they walk away they just go about their lives.

They don't replay the conversation over…

And over…

And over…

And try to remember how many times they mentioned Lisa Rinna.

Must be nice.

Must be nice to just live now. Not always in before and always in after. Not always in past and future. Not regret and worry.

Must be nice.

Must be nice not to worry if every thought you have and every behaviour is an *autistic thing* and if everyone notices your *autistic things*.

If everyone notices you're autistic.

Must be nice not to second-guess every thought you have, every word, every interaction, not to worry that when your big baby is watching she must be cringing because she is the one with the autistic mum. She is the one whose mum yells after her, as she runs up the school steps, 'Don't leave me! I love you! Remember how awesome you are! You're bloody brilliant.'

Other mums don't do that. Other mums talk about the weather.

I think of the word 'belonging'. It goes over and over and it's the wispy thing I can't get hold of.

Do other people like themselves after they talk with people? Or do they go home with endless regret and wishing with all their heart and soul they were different?

I wish I could be different.

Be able to show them I care, be vulnerable.

It's safer not to risk it, surely.

Block out the things I said, the delayed understanding of what you said. The signals I missed. What didn't I hear?

I can control myself better on Discord, just sitting in a group call with gamers. I can be calm and hear everything properly because of my headphones and volume adjustments. I can move and fidget to shush my body. The game we play is always there to give us a reason and a purpose. Tandem activities, like when you play with a toddler.

Then I remember I don't belong there either because I'm old. They've taught me so much about current culture and what it means to be twenty-something, or a teenager, or thirty-something and I'm none of these things. None are in their *forties*.

Nearly every gamer I know,

Must be nice to talk about the weather.

Must be nice not to cry in bed every night, worrying you're making your babies Just. Like. You.

To watch your babies for signs that they have your traits and feel proud when they do.

'Look! Lenny walks just like me! Georgie has my sense of humour! How cool is that!'

Must be nice not to worry that, one day, your babies won't want to know you Because. You. Are. You.

Must be nice not to worry, every day, that you will lose your career, your family, your house, Because. You. Are. You.

Lisa Rinna never feels like that.

Of course, there are other autistic people and, of course, they must feel like this and maybe even the ones who talk to you online feel like this, but you won't know because you'll never ask them because you're too embarrassed too, and too worried to because if they tell you that they never feel like this, you'll know it's only you.

Do you think that when everyone else has a conversation, they just… talk?

About the weather or the football or *The Real Housewives* I'm sure, is neurodivergent. We all listen when a friend goes off on a tangent about the stats on their armour, or how they've been collecting All The Things. It's normal here. I forget how to behave with real-world people, where we shouldn't do that. Real-world people don't care how much I achieved on *World of Warcraft*. My kids have an idea, from their games.

They know it's not what other mums do.

Other mums tell their kids to get away from screens.

Other mums aren't friends with their kids on Discord and don't swap memes to communicate.

They might? I've never asked. I'd have to go to the school gate to find out what mums do now, and I don't go.

I'm on a break.

Fifteen years of pretending to be a *normal* mum, school pick-ups and drop-offs full of anxiety. I listened to all their lives, and they would come to me when things went wrong because I'm the one who knew what it was like. Getting divorced? Ask Anna. Mental health issues? Ask Anna. But having a girl's night out? Don't invite Anna. She's not really one of us.

They'll go out with their

of Beverly Hills?

I talk too much, lately, about crows.

I worry the other school mums are whispering.

I worry my daughter is cringing. That my baby already sees how weird I am. I worry that when I smile at her, she thinks I look like a witch. I worry she'll become scared of me. That I'm scary.

I worry I'll fail her.

I worry everyone who loves me will leave me.

I worry about whales and children in war zones and people who don't have homes and the Voice Referendum and the wallabies who come to our garden and all the people who are hurting.

I'll probably tell you all about it, tomorrow at the school gates.

I'll see your eyes glaze over.

I'll see your jaw become tight.

I'll feel like I am in a constant spiral of my brain gaslighting itself, a constant feeling of being an imposter in my own life, but you can't be an imposter, can you, if everyone sees straight through you.

Do you think that when everyone else has a conversation, they just… talk?

–Kate Gordon

'friends' and I'll realise I wasn't at the event they'll talk about later because that's not me.

Covid said I didn't have to play that game anymore, so I'm taking a break.

My youngest is proud to be autistic. Now it's cool in her year level to be neurodivergent and when one goes for an assessment they all cross their fingers. How did that happen?

Will she feel like an imposter? Or be better at accepting difference than we have been?

They don't even tease redheads anymore. Relentless teasing when I was young because of course they would tease me and my red hair.

Not of course, my kids say. What? I ask and they look bemused. Why would you tease someone for having red hair? They say.

The world can change.

My world doesn't but theirs does. That's good, right?

Do you think that when everyone else has a conversation, they just… listen?

–Anna Whateley

FACTS ARE THE ONLY FEELINGS

Dr Clem Bastow

DR CLEM BASTOW is a co-editor of *Someone Like Me*.

I was forty-two when I learnt I had – Have? Have had? Am having? – a body. In a series of sessions with an occupational therapist, I discovered how to notice, say, that when I have been painting for five hours straight my hands might be sore. Where's my heartbeat? Don't know! It turns out I don't notice anything about my body unless the intensity is set to 'maximum overdrive'. (It also explains my love of extremely loud and fast things.) For most of my life, the day-to-day experience of being a person is best described – like most aspects of my life – associatively. Do you know that sensation during a long-haul plane trip when something shifts in the atmosphere and you feel – just for a moment – like you're suspended in space, in your seat? That's what being in my body is like.

When I am on a plane and I experience that sensation alongside everybody else, it's a rare moment of normalcy: *ah, we're all feeling this at the same time*. Everybody shares glances that say, 'Wow, didn't that feel weird?' The moment of collegiality always passes too soon. As I feel the smile slipping off my face like a tablecloth trick when everyone returns to their chicken or beef, I often turn to the in-flight safety card for a good laugh. Not because I like to laugh at the thought of mid-air catastrophe (although, at 38,000 feet, you might as well), but because I find the little pictograms used to illustrate them intensely amusing. There's something about the shrug of a little figure's shoulders as they book it off the inflatable slide that really speaks to me – maybe because every day of my life I imagine some sort of misfortune befalling me.

Because, when you really think about it, have you ever seen a pictogram having a good time? You know, pictograms: those little guys* with circles for heads.

[*I am using 'guys' in its gender-neutral mode,
like kids do with Sylvanian Families,
or Legos, aka 'my guys'.]

SLIPPERY WHEN WET, UNSTABLE CLIFFS, SUDDEN DROP-OFF, STRONG CURRENTS, SUBMERGED ROCKS, COVID SYMPTOMS, CROCODILES, FALL HAZARD, DEEP WATER, SHALLOW WATER; these guys can't catch a break. Wouldn't you love to see a pictogram just kicking back with a piña colada?

Like so many things I have a deep and abiding interest in, it is difficult for me to choose a favourite example of pictogrammic misfortune, but some that I have enjoyed of late include a trio I saw affixed to the temporary wall of a demolition site: TRIPPING *[guy tripping over a brick]*, FALLING *[guy falling off a ledge]* AND IMPACT *[a variety of objects falling on a guy's head]* HAZARDS PRESENT.

I have been socialised to ask at this point: am I going too fast? Do you know what the hell I'm talking about? Are you exhibiting physical or verbal signs of interest? Today, I do not wish to 'check in'. Instead, I point to Steacy Easton's words on Autistic communication: 'Instead of the small and tightly contained essay – what happens if everything known pours out? What if the act of being concise is no longer a virtue? If language is a kind of commerce, what are the implications of excess?'[1]

Deep breath.

You might be familiar with the DOT pictograms, referred to by some as 'Helvetica man' due to their omnipresence. They were developed by the US Department of Transport after extensive research, tabled in the evocatively titled 1974 report by the American Institute of Graphic Arts (AIGA) *Symbol Signs: The development of passenger/pedestrian oriented symbols for use in transportation-related facilities*. Or perhaps you have seen the ISO 7001 pictograms, introduced in 1980 with remarkably few amendments since then, devised and dictated by the

International Organization for Standardization, one of those truly Kafka-esque government bodies that you're not entirely sure isn't a work of satire.

The AIGA report assessed pictograms according to three basic dimensions: semantic, syntactic and pragmatic. For example, 'The semantic dimension refers to the relationship of a visual image to a meaning. How well does this symbol represent the message? Do people fail to understand the message that the symbol denotes? Do people from various cultures misunderstand this symbol?'[2]

[That one photograph of a staff sign in a diner:
IS IT HOT? DOES IT LOOK GOOD?
ARE YOU PROUD TO SERVE IT?]

Pictograms and labelling related to hazardous chemicals have their own organising standard, the GHS – the faintly utopian-sounding Globally Harmonized System of Classification and Labelling of Chemicals. That utopian name is even funnier when you look up the absolutely devastating pictograms: for example, GHS09, ENVIRONMENTAL HAZARD, which looks like the remains of the Green Place in *Mad Max: Fury Road*; or GHS08, SERIOUS HEALTH HAZARD, which looks like a person collapsing inwards like the house at the end of 'Bad Dream House' from the first *Treehouse of Horror*.

There is a groaning folder of pictogram photographs in my phone, as I snap a shot every time I see one that speaks to my experience of being in the world. They are commonly understood as graphical symbols designed to convey meaning through their visual resemblance to *physical* objects, yet to me they convey emotion due to their visual resemblance to *feelings*.

As a result, I often employ this formal language when I am trying to communicate what I am feeling. Beset by the vagaries of modern life? NO PEDESTRIAN ACCESS *[guy being whacked on the head by a boom gate]*. Disappointed in love again? PLEASE

STAY ON MAIN TRACK *[guy falling headfirst off a crumbling cliff face]*. Working in the neoliberal university? SUBMERGED ROCKS *[guy diving underwater only to collide with rocks, complete with 'headache' dashes emanating from guy's head]*.

This associative mode of visual communication feels, to me, in line with what Julia Miele Rodas observes as 'the partitioning of language with parentheses and semicolons [...] an aspect of autistic expression at once playful and logical'.[3] Or, as Autistic writer Bev Harp puts it, 'I propose (if one is allowed to do so) that parentheses (as well as the semi-colon) are a natural form of presentation for autistic (as opposed to NT [neurotypical]) thought.'[4] Seeing an image and reaching into my internal visual archive is a way of joining and nesting ideas. If (feeling), {then} [image]. No, I don't know how to code. What do you think I am, some sort of savant?

How do I feel? I don't know, but I can dip into the vast fact repository of my mind and pull out something that – to me – explains things perfectly clearly. Such is life when you are an intensely visual, associative thinker for whom identifying and describing emotions is extraordinarily difficult. This mode of explaining my feelings is prone to engender confusion in some when I, say, point to a photo of a seal immersed in a mud puddle and say 'Same, bro', but perhaps my love of a pictogram is, in part, due to their (alleged) universality as a visual language.

In September 2012, Kanye West went on a Twitter spree. It was, as Rawiya Kameir wrote of Ye's slide into right-wing reactionary mode, the beginning of his 'visionary streams of consciousness' era, which in turn led to his support of Trump and less visionary and more actively objectionable streams of consciousness[5], the most recent of which redefine 'rock bottom' in their bald-faced attempts to shock. (Ye, like so many other famous dickheads whose behaviour has come under fire, having previously alluded to 'signs of autism', announced in early 2025 it was definitively 'a case of autism that I have'.) Sprinkled among his vaguely philosophical ejections in the fall of 2012, however, was one that stayed with me: 'Feelings are the only facts.'

It stuck with me because my experience of life is the opposite: faced with the insurmountable challenge of describing my emotions, I turn to facts, images, quotes, information. This rates me somewhere around a 'What the hell are they saying?' along the communication spectrum of 'Normal' to '????'. Returning to Easton: 'The translation of autism is about the ability to note when non-verbal signals are given by the autistic person.'[6]

Reaching out to other people through facts is my preferred mode of communication. I drive my car with the windows down and the stereo up in the hope that someone will notice and nod; I wear badges and T-shirts designed to prompt conversation. When those connections are made – not between seemingly disparate data points in my own mind (Hey, did anybody else notice that the spaceship Tripoli in *The Expanse* was the same shape as Max in *Flight of the Navigator*?), but between people – I feel like I've won the lottery. Alas, in this increasingly atomised society, those moments seem few and far between.

Sharing information is also my way of reminding people I exist. Is there a term for someone else's object permanence? I remember everyone; it's whether or not they remember me that is the problem. Without a steady stream of facts and images, where am I? Who am I? To paraphrase the great philosopher Billie Eilish,* I share, therefore I am.

[*Just kidding. Of course I know who originally said 'I think, therefore I am': it was Pris, Nexus-6 replicant 'basic pleasure model'.]

Sending you a link, or an article, or a photo I think you might like is my way of saying 'I'm thinking about you', and I pride myself on knowing what you will like. Perhaps it is my knack for pattern recognition. *This* friend likes cute dog videos, but *that* friend prefers this specific dog breed. *This* friend likes offbeat anarchist memes, *that* friend likes miniatures, *this* friend likes nightmare comedy, *this* friend likes the intersection of cute dog videos and nightmare comedy, and so on.

As a result, when someone sends me a video or meme with no clear thought as to whether – based on an exhaustive temperature-taking of the memes I share – I will like it, it makes me physically angry. Why would I laugh at a mid 'humour' video with no clear Venn diagram overlap between our respective interests? [Extremely Tim Curry as Darkness in *Legend* voice:] Don't you *know me*, boy?

People have on occasion told me I should be employed by intellectual property lawyers because of my seemingly uncanny knack for spotting 'My Sweet Lord' moments, but not only would that be a depressing line of work, my fondness for shouting 'Listen to this!!' before cueing up two sound-alike bridges or breakdowns or chord progressions isn't because I want, say, Bernard Fanning to be sued to kingdom come for that moment in 'Wish You Well' that sounds a lot like Sweet's 'Stairway to the Stars', but because in sharing those moments of pattern recognition – in laying two transparencies over the top of each other and seeing where they match – I am, once again, offering you something. I noticed!

> [When I was learning to DJ – a generous term for 'playing CDs and records at rock clubs' – I was advised to play 'two for them, one for you', so strong was my desire to follow those synapse links from bassline to snare sound to production technique until I'd bored everyone stupid.]

I can't really read music; I don't know how to do much other than sing; my favourite thing to sing is the harmony; but; surely those 'Hey, isn't that—' moments are proof of musicians' own surrender to associative pleasures. Like 3'35" in the *It's Too Late to Stop Now* version of Van Morrison's 'Listen to the Lion' where Jef Labes seems to start riffing on 'Levon' on the piano. Was he really paying tribute to Elton John in the middle of one of the North of Ireland's most ecstatic soul voyages? Maybe, maybe not, probably not, but when I hear that little riff a light goes off in my mind.

Even though I can't play music, the synapses that fire when I make connections between (seemingly) disparate data sets feel like, I imagine, Morrison and co. felt while blasting their way through what would eventually become *It's Too Late to Stop Now*. To Easton, again: 'exchanging facts, exchanging the taxonomic list, becomes an act of solidarity and intimacy'.[7] Not only is the passion of information-sharing one of my favourite aspects of Autistic culture, to me it's like a jazz odyssey. Yes! Tell me about that light-switch design / sixth-scale-miniature / cool geology fact! Now we are really jamming! Which is, in a way, why I feel so sad when I see someone's eyes begin to glaze when I tell them about [insert topic of 'circumscribed interest' here], or share a Fun Fact that abuts, asides or segues in a sort of ouroboros kind of way back to where we originally started talking. Would your eyes glaze at 'Listen to the Lion' if you had a front-row seat? How about The Isley Brothers playing 'It's Too Late' at the Bitter End? Holst's *The Planets* at its premiere?

This notion of the tedious Autist, ignorant to their companion's boredom persists in spite of information sharing being an intentional form of communication. Anonymous Autism Warrior Parents share despairing op-eds about their Autistic children's endless *Thomas & Friends* quoting; 'best practice' 'therapies' grind those *Thomas & Friends* quotes into dust to make the child say 'good morning' and 'I love you'. But what if quoting *Thomas & Friends* is saying 'I love you'? I ask that because I have heard that non-Autistic people like to be prompted into empathy by way of a hypothetical. But it isn't hypothetical, of course: quotes, facts, infodumps are all acts of love.

[Or, as another famous dickhead once said, there are cathedrals everywhere for those with the eyes to see.]

Goddammit all to hell. I told myself I would write this essay without situating my experience through the lens of the non-Autistic, but isn't it always the way? DANGER: SEA SNAKE SIGHTING *[guy's legs underwater, being bitten by a ringed sea snake]*. For whose benefit do I spend hours in therapy trying to identify my feelings: mine, or those who can't – or won't – understand what I am trying to say through facts instead? *'How well does this symbol represent the message? Do people fail to understand the message that the symbol denotes?'*

Contrary to what dogshit TV series might have suggested to you about Autists being unfailingly allergic to playing fast and loose with the truth, I was actually lying in this essay's opening gambit: I have seen pictograms having a good time. My all-time favourite is the pictogram for translation services, in which three guys stand next to each other: the translator, the speaker and the listener. The speaker's mouth is represented by a triangle, which I love because it represents both the act of talking and happiness at being understood. I have also seen pictogram guys in hammocks, on vacation, sipping tropical drinks, getting spray tans, spending time with family, gazing at the horizon from a lookout.

And yet, these utopian pictograms seem too good to be true. If life has taught me anything, it's that surely soon the next pictogram arrives: of a coconut concussing the guy in the hammock, or the tropical drink becoming toxic, or the cliff giving way under the lookout. Sooner or later the inflatable slide comes for us all.

Sources

1. Easton, S [A] 2013, 'Autism: An anecdotal abecedarium', *Kadar Koli*, vol, 8, pp. 98–107.
2. American Institute of Graphic Arts (AIGA) 1974, *Symbol Signs: The development of passenger/pedestrian oriented symbols for use in transportation-related facilities*, US Department of Commerce, <ntrl.ntis.gov/NTRL/dashboard/searchResults/titleDetail/PB239352.xhtml>.

3. Rodas, JM 2018, *Autistic Disturbances: Theorizing autism poetics from the* DSM *to* Robinson Crusoe, University of Michigan Press, Ann Arbor.
4. Harp, B 2007, 'On the (autistic) use of parentheses', *Square 8: Talk About Squares, Autism, and the Number 8*, 23 March, <8square8.com/2007/03/on-autistic-use-of-parentheses.html?m=1>.
5. Kameir, R 2016, 'Maybe we shouldn't be surprised that Kanye and Trump are "friends"', *The Fader*, 13 December, <thefader.com/2016/12/13/kanye-west-donald-trump-friends>.
6. Easton, S 2013, 'Autism'.
7. ibid.

BUILDING AN INTERSECTIONAL LEGACY

Khadija Gbla

KHADIJA GBLA (she/her/they/them) is a renowned, award-winning, intuitive speaker; human rights activist; and compassionate thought leader. Born in Sierra Leone, Khadija came to Australia as a refugee at the age of thirteen. Khadija is determined to build a more inclusive, culturally aware, safe and accepting society, no matter our differences, through heart-centredness.

I pay my respects to and acknowledge Aboriginal and Torres Strait Islander autistic people on whose sovereign lands I now call home as a former autistic refugee. I acknowledge their intersectional experiences and ongoing experiences of colonisation and its impact.

To my child
This is dedicated to you.
You are loved beyond measure and perfect in every single way!
You inspire me to make the world a better place every day.

Growing up with bombs falling around us during the civil war in Sierra Leone, autism and ADHD were not only unheard of but also the least of our problems. We were fighting for survival every day, and I had no time to reflect or even take notice that I was unlike my peers. If I had, my mother would certainly not have had the time or energy to deal with it.

I was ten years old when we fled Sierra Leone for Gambia. My father was killed in the war, and I stayed at an unofficial refugee camp with my mum, my little sister and many other families.

We were all traumatised from the fear of being killed in the war, so I can imagine us children displayed some unusual behaviour, but I was pointedly different from my friends. If I'm being honest, I didn't really have any. I preferred to play alone and found it a struggle to interact with others. I loved nothing more than reading everything the library had on offer; every encyclopaedia I got my hands on was read from cover to cover. I loved learning and was rarely found without a book in my hand; I even took a book into the shower and read while eating my meals. I was obsessed with anime and loved *Sailor Moon* – I still do.

The main complaint teachers and my family had was that I was 'a strange child', due to my preference for solitude. At home I hid if we had visitors, but I'd be forced to say hello. I would always sneak away again until they left. I became expert in avoiding people. If they didn't want to discuss my special interests, there was no point in chatting. On the flip side, teachers would discipline me for being hyper and talking too much in class. My behaviour had two distinct sides, and looking back now, knowing all about autism and ADHD, it's obvious I had both. But I also had many physical challenges, some that directly relate to autism and ADHD.

Every morning when I woke up to go to school, I would tell my mum: 'I feel like someone has beaten the shit out of me.' I was in constant physical pain, always tired, but my concerns were dismissed. Because we were running on adrenaline after fleeing a war-ravaged country, the general attitude was: *If bombs are not dropping on you, you are fine.* There was no room for a disabled child. My pain was a burden. I was being 'too sensitive'. I needed to pray more, and I learnt to mask the pain in my own home.

But I could not stand it and, at the age of thirteen, I began taking myself to doctors. They were confused, and perhaps a little amused, by this young girl attending appointments on her own and trying to translate through eight different languages to get answers to why she was in constant physical pain.

Only years later, in the tranquillity of our haven of Australia, did I learn that this pain had names. I was diagnosed with fibromyalgia, chronic fatigue syndrome and hypermobility – physical conditions that go hand in hand with autism and ADHD. This has led me to be a mobility aid user.

My autism and ADHD diagnoses followed my child Sammy's. But the difference between me and Sammy and every other neurodivergent person I knew in Australia was that we were black and they weren't. In our community, neurodivergence is not spoken about. But, despite that, now I am questioning, on every platform I jump on: 'Where are all the autistic black people?'

Why are we not getting diagnosed or speaking up about it? I know I'm not the only neurodivergent black person in Australia and, since I spoke out about it recently, I have met a few others on social media.

Because African autistic people are not seen in society and the media, I don't see myself represented – and that can feel isolating and lonely. My disabilities are not understood by my African community in Australia, and most of my neurodivergent peers are white, so they do not understand the nuances attached to being black and neurodivergent.

Being autistic in Australia can be dangerous for me. If I display autistic behaviour, such as having an autistic meltdown, I can be labelled as an 'angry black person' or, worse, be racially profiled and injured by police. The world is not safe for black people with autism, but I am adamant about dismantling this system to make the world that my son has to step into as a young adult a safer place. To pave the way for Sammy, who is nine years old now, I am stepping outside of the safety zone and taking down my mask: I want the community around me to see what ADHD and autism look like. I will raise the profile of black neurodivergent people and help others understand us better. I will advocate for more accommodations and accessibility, which will lead to a safer, more understanding world for all of us.

Sammy's and my diagnoses were the best things to happen to both of us. It helped me put the supports in place that we need to live comfortably in a neurotypical world. Our journeys to ADHD and autism diagnoses started with a conversation with Sammy's kindergarten teacher. Sammy's teacher spotted that some of their behaviours were different to their peers, and I followed up with my GP for support, which led to an assessment. As parents we may feel scared or anxious to do this follow-up as it can be daunting to be told your kid is not like other kids.

However, I'm glad I took those steps and got ADHD and autism diagnoses for Sammy.

As an undiagnosed autistic person, I noticed that Sammy's behaviour was similar to mine, so for years I didn't question my own. My job as a parent is to adapt to my child. But I was delighted that the kindergarten teachers picked it up and we both received diagnoses. It meant we could put early intervention processes in place to support Sammy so they can thrive and have the accommodations they need.

To allow me to continue my work as an award-winning human rights activist, model, inspirational speaker, facilitator, entrepreneur and philanthropist, I also put some strong non-negotiable boundaries in place to make the environment around me adapt to my needs.

I reached out to Amaze's Autism Connect helpline for information that would help us, which they supplied. I felt seen, supported and understood. I also asked them for information on autism and black people and they provided me with a lot of information on that topic too. The most important gift Amaze gave me was the language I needed that empowered me to say: 'I am an autistic person, and this is what I need.'

I now have a team of people around me to help me succeed, and I clearly state my needs to them and to my clients who book me for keynote speaking or modelling opportunities. I send a list of what my requirements are to allow me to do the work. For example, if I am speaking on a panel on stage I need wheelchair accessibility and a comfortable chair, not a stool, in case I am having a fibromyalgia flare-up. I need a lapel microphone due to hand mobility issues and my need to use my hands to express myself and burn up some of my hyperactive energy. And I need the air-conditioning to be on a cool setting because I run hot, which makes me extremely uncomfortable. I need to have a room where I can escape to if I need to regulate my overwhelm, and I need someone to explain the order of events so I can be prepared and not have to deal with anything unexpected.

Usually these conditions are met, but I do emphasise that they are not an option – they are a requirement.

I also let everyone around me know that I prefer texts or emails to phone calls, and I have my voicemail set up to send me messages and emails. My friends and clients need to book in calls, and I need to know the context of them. When the phone rings, I begin catastrophising. I imagine the worst-case scenario and feel panicked if I'm not prepared for it and don't know what it is going to be about. I feel like I'm being put on the spot – and I also have a delayed processing disorder, so it could take minutes, hours or even weeks or months to digest that information.

Since I started seeking support and putting professional advice into action, I have gained the strength in my voice I needed to state my needs. I now have a list of things that impact Sammy and me, so we can try to create an environment that gives us peace and calm and a community around us that understands our needs and differences.

Neither Sammy nor I like strong smells or loud or repetitive noises; we avoid bright lights; and we must have our drinks freezing cold or piping hot – nothing in between. My list extends to non-sensory things, such as despising clutter, unclear plans and being interrupted when completing a task or in hyperfocus mode. I cannot make eye contact with people – it feels physically aggressive and unsafe to me – but I don't mind if someone looks at me while in a conversation. I let people know that I will not be giving or returning eye contact, so they don't mistake this for rudeness, which often happens. I feel I explain my autism and ADHD quite a bit, but having people in our lives who understand us makes everything easier and reduces misunderstandings.

The diagnoses of autism and ADHD for me and my son were life changing. While I always had an awareness that I was different, this helped me understand in what ways and what we both need to thrive.

They say it takes a village to raise a child, but what happens when you don't have a village? You make your own, right? And, with my support team behind me, I am creating the village I need to help raise Sammy in a completely different way to how I was raised. His differences will never be ridiculed or dismissed. They are accepted and celebrated.

My journey to diagnoses was gruelling, which is an experience many of us share. It took a lot of time and energy fighting to overcome the psychologist's ingrained biases, but when I got the diagnoses I was relieved and felt vindicated. *See, I am not just lazy – I actually do have to work three times as hard as others on tasks*, I thought to myself. On the other side, I thought about the potential risk of prejudice in the workplace or socially when revealing my diagnoses.

But after settling into the fact that we both have autism and ADHD, I continued to reach out for as much support as I could get my hands on for our little family. Eventually, the shame disappeared, and I became empowered to own it. Now I am shouting about it from the rooftops every opportunity I get. This is because I am genuinely proud of myself for thriving through autism, ADHD and a truckload of physical disabilities every single day. Some days I am thriving, and other days the weight of it all breaks me, but I am working through it day by day. I am using my platform and voice to raise awareness and understanding of autism and ADHD, and to help others who may still carry that shame to shake it off and embrace every part of themselves.

I cannot say that there aren't some days I regret speaking out and wish I could take it all back and put my mask on and continue to fake it to fit in. Sometimes it seems easier than showing all my cards to the world. I do get vulnerability hangovers, but they are worth it. While I don't owe my medical history to anyone – and it would be far more comfortable to keep it to myself – I am sacrificing this in exchange for social change. I have outed myself in every way, and I do this purely to help other people like me be proud of who they are and make society understand that people with disabilities do not need to be silent about who they are and what they need. We need to keep dismantling the systematic barriers and ableism in our ableist society until we are seen and treated as equals to everyone else.

Everyone's experiences with autism and ADHD are different. The intersections of personality, abilities, heritage, gender, sexuality, race and so much more make our experiences of the world around us unique. Different parts of our identities do not exist in isolation. For example, you cannot separate my blackness from my autisticness, and you cannot separate me being non-binary from me being black or autistic. These aspects make me who I am. I'm not just a carer – I'm an autistic and disabled carer. I'm not just a parent – I'm an autistic parent to a child who is also autistic.

There are parts of autism and ADHD that are not understood well: rejection sensitivity disorder, pathological demand avoidance and being non-speaking. I often experience these, which confuses people around me who are convinced I am 'high-functioning'. I believe terms like *high-functioning* and *low-functioning* are ways of segregating members of our community, and I don't support that. My presentation and needs change on a day-by-day, hour-to-hour basis, which can lead to misunderstanding. I have dynamic, complex, multi-system disabilities, so my support needs also fluctuate. We need to be inclusive of all support-level needs and ensure we don't leave anyone behind!

As part of my late autistic and ADHD diagnoses, I also found out that I have been experiencing what is known as situational mutism. I have always experienced this, just never had a name for it. Growing up, it was not uncommon for me to be called 'rude' or 'disrespectful' because in my culture, when your elders speak to you, you are meant to respond, and if you don't respond you are rude and disrespectful. So, being quiet is punishable and usually ends in discipline. But for me, simply put, in situations where I am overwhelmed and anxious, as a trauma response my brain can decide that not speaking is the best course of action.

I have always known over the years that sometimes I just can't speak, not because I don't want to, but because I *can't* – especially in situations where I feel extremely stressed, anxious and unsafe; that is just what happens. I can go days without talking to people. I didn't always know why this was happening, I just knew that it was obviously something that upset my family and people around me. You can't win: it's either, 'You talk too much!' or, 'Why is she not responding to me? Why is she being so rude? She's snobby. She thinks she's all that.'

It took being admitted to the emergency department and everyone there realising that I couldn't talk. I have never been more vulnerable as a black person in those moments. I couldn't even communicate the fact that they were touching me too hard and it was causing me pain. And the lights were too bright, and it was too loud, and they were minimising the notes I had made. Two professionals, social workers, came all the way down to the hospital, but it still didn't change or stop the medical racism.

I am well known for my voice: my powerful voice as a human rights activist, my powerful voice as somebody who speaks up, as somebody who uses their voice in a very pronounced way. Most of the compliments I get are connected to that. In fact, I don't think I ever get a compliment that does not somehow apply to my voice. As somebody who has so many intersecting identities, and who is racialised and marginalised, being able to speak for myself is very important. It's very important to be able to express my experience of the world. So, imagine being in a medical setting, being that unwell and not being able to communicate with the people who are providing care. (This is on top of medical racism and on top of misogyny as a non-binary person; there are a lot of things happening there already.) At the very least, I can usually count on being able to speak for myself, but I couldn't.

And I know, I think it's simple for people to see me as somebody who does use their voice and speak up, and for them to think it just comes natural to me. But it doesn't come any more natural to me than other people. I speak up because the things I believe in require me to speak up. And that comes also at a cost. Think of how, even in your neurodivergent spaces and disabled spaces, the same voice is still not given to us, the black and Indigenous people, in our expression of our own autism, our expression of our neurodivergence, here in this space. It's still racism. It's still the expectation of a white expression of autism.

There is a fine line I constantly feel like I walk in my pursuit of representation and visibility, and the importance of that, especially for my little one and how much I want them to have it different to what I had. And I think of all the other people in my community and all the vulnerable people, and the power that knowing that you're not alone has, and knowing that the people you look up to, the people you think are superheroes or the people you think are just smashing it, how they're also human and fallible, and they bleed, they get sick, they're disabled. When we're able to see ourselves in them, it's a reminder that we are not broken; we're perfectly imperfect, but we're not broken, and we don't need fixing. But those struggles we have, especially the ones that hold so much shame and stigma, also hold so much vulnerability when we have intersectional identity – especially racialised identity, because I want to be very clear that being Afro-African Indigenous is my primary identity. And that racism, you know, is the greatest threat. Racism via white supremacists is the greatest threat to me.

There are no words to explain the vulnerability of experiencing situational mutism. Not speaking gets taken differently when you're black: you're defiant, and that connects to how black children are more likely to be diagnosed with oppositional defiant disorder than autism. We don't get softness; we don't get gentleness; we don't get protection. We are treated as aggressive and a threat, instead. I think of what that looks like for my child at school. I think of what it looks like for them everywhere they go. My little family is intersectional. I don't care about the disability-rights flag; I don't care about the autism 'levels'. I care about my baby not being killed because they show distress, because they're black.

I like to include everyone in society when I am fighting for human rights. Human rights are exactly how they sound: rights for every human on the planet. So, when helping all humans thrive, it is important to consider how abilities, gender, race, culture and physical environment can see some people needing extra support.

For example, me being a carer in a major Australian city is difficult enough, but what about Aboriginal carers living in remote communities? They are often disadvantaged due to being far away from the city and the services it offers. Then I see myself as a black parent advocating for my child and my experience of this could be more challenging than a white parent. I often feel self-conscious when advocating with the school and relevant health systems. I feel aware that I may be seen as the stereotypical 'angry black woman', but this is not felt by everyone using these systems. We need to be aware that people who may appear to be in the same boat as us from the outside could have higher hurdles to jump because of who they are and the way they are viewed in society.

While I am fully aware of how my neurodivergence, my disabilities, my blackness and my gender and sexual identity can be hurdles, I am also acutely aware of my privileges and how others may not be as fortunate as I am to have my skills, abilities and social capital that helps me thrive – or, at times, survive. Not everyone who has the same disabilities as me has such a strong voice – they may even be non-speaking, which I am sometimes – or has the platform and system literacy that I have. And for them, I will fight even harder. I will use my voice twice as hard for those who are more vulnerable than me and have been left out, whether that is due to disability or oppression.

I am asking others to do the same. I am calling on community members to support their neurodivergent peers. Read up about neurodiversity, learn about it, listen to what we need and help us fight for our needs and our rights. We need your support. Before I received diagnoses for my disabilities and before I became a parent to a neurodivergent child, I cared and advocated for people with disabilities, and I would like more people without disabilities to become allies and help us dismantle the current system, which is limiting our potential and ability to thrive.

The sky is the limit for me and Sammy. We do not just want to be happy. We want to reach every goal we set for ourselves, no matter how out of reach it may seem. But far too often I see a low bar being set by others – sometimes even by parents of neurodivergent children.

Let's not underestimate our potential. I am living proof that despite my disabilities or difference – such as being non-binary; a black person in Australia; a neurodivergent and disabled, demisexual, pansexual person; and a parent and carer of a complexly disabled child – I have had a solid twenty-three-year career as a leading human rights activist. I did this despite being raised in a household where my disabilities were not accepted, and I wasn't allowed to be disabled. I had to constantly mask and act able-bodied, which was truly exhausting and prevented me from being me.

Too many people wait until disability is at their doorstep before they care, but why not care before that happens? Why not advocate with us and create a fairer environment for everybody? Let's create an environment where people with disabilities feel confident in who they are, feel confident to use their voices to advocate for themselves and others, and see no limit to what they can achieve in life. But, most importantly, help dismantle everyday ableism and systems of oppression that harm us! We are all the solutions to the challenges our families, communities, nation and world are facing. We are the change-makers!

IS CHANGE A CONSTANT?

Ivy Lin

IVY LIN (she/her) is a programmer originally from New York City. After graduating with a degree in media communications and computer science, she worked at an extracurricular coding school, where she was trained to teach children on the Autism spectrum. That training eventually led to her own Autism diagnosis after she moved to the United Kingdom. In her spare time, she travels, draws, writes YA romance novels featuring Chinese Autistic characters and spends time with her husband and dog.

'Change is the only constant in life,' as the ancient Greek philosopher Heraclitus once said. In computer programming, something I work with every day, a constant is a value that cannot be changed. Heraclitus was being ironic, wasn't he? Change should be a variable, not a constant, but throughout my life, one of the few constants has been that every element in the data structures of my world changes, and continues to change. Maybe Heraclitus was right.

Growing up in New York City, I became numb to change. The Brooklyn I grew up in sold pizza slices for a dollar, spoke like Al Pacino in *The Godfather* and had subway turnstiles that only moved when I swiped my MetroCard at just the right angle and speed. Now, I don't know what it's like, because I moved away. But the last time I visited, the cost of a pizza slice had risen to three dollars, the people who spoke like Al Pacino had migrated to Florida or New Jersey and I no longer struggled with MetroCards to enter the subway. I don't miss the MetroCards, but I miss the memories of eating pizza after school with what little money I'd saved, and I miss the people who spoke like Al Pacino, because they were my friends.

Many factors contributed to my departure: rising living costs is one of them, and the easiest to explain. But I think, deep down, I always wanted to move out of New York City because it's brutal for an Autistic person. The roaring of the Brooklyn-Queens Expressway – my front yard for the first twenty-five years of my life – made it hard to leave the house. The pressure to succeed, which requires navigating confusing social hierarchies, was an invisible weight I had struggled to lift, and the weight in New York City was unbearably heavy.

Honking car horns, bright lights that made the night sky look like day and the pervasive stench of urine and garbage are not conditions one would expect an Autistic person to thrive in. But I did, like a weed growing through a crack in a sunbaked sidewalk. I often wonder why. People who understand me – therapists, and others on the spectrum – say I have a remarkable ability to cope. But I didn't know I was coping. I didn't even know I was Autistic.

One day, while I was still unaware of my Autism, I became online friends with a Liverpudlian who was obsessed with trains. I learned a lot through his frequent lectures about railway infrastructure – like British geography, which was not taught in my American education, and that Llanfairpwllgwyngyllgogerychwyrndrobwllllantysiliogogogoch is a train station in Wales that describes the name of the village, its local topography and some buildings nearby. That quirky fact alone was reason enough for me to visit his country, which I had not taken an interest in before. So I signed up for a study abroad programme in London.

The transition was not without difficulties. At my London university campus, cliquey flatmates scared me away from our shared kitchen, opaque computer science modules made me break out in shingles and someone in one of my lectures tried to persuade me to join a cult. Regardless of these challenges, I got to meet the man who talked about trains, and I fell in love with him and his country. Perhaps I liked it because it's quieter than America, with less pressure to be assertive and outspoken. But mostly, it had him: someone introverted and obsessively contemplative like me, who accepted me for who I was.

The United Kingdom was all I could talk about for the next few years of my life. When I returned home, I frequently brought it up in screenwriting workshops and wrote stories about British characters in my creative writing courses. I even designed and programmed a virtual reality world of a cottage inspired by one I'd visited in Wales. I drew up a plan to move, and at the age of twenty-five, I did.

Despite my meticulous planning and years of daydreaming about living in the country I had hyperfocused on for several years, I broke down at John F Kennedy Airport, where the reality of my decision slapped me in the face. I would be leaving my home, which I loved despite its loud streets and overpriced coffee. Most importantly, I would be leaving my family and every other person who helped me grow into who I am.

While every other traveller wore smiles, excited for their class trips to Europe or their honeymoons to Hawaii, I cried while checking in the massive suitcases that held all of my life's possessions: my clothes, documents, tech, art portfolios and the stuffed animals and *Archie* comics that had comforted me since I was young. I cried while hugging my mom before joining the security queue. I cried on the plane while talking to a woman from London about my reason for flying. I cried when the man I fell in love with picked me up from Gatwick airport and drove me four hours to our newly rented flat in Liverpool.

The experience made me develop a deep empathy for my parents, who immigrated to the United States from Malaysia before I was born. Prior to boarding the plane, I had a shallow understanding of the sacrifices they made. Now, I have a visceral understanding. They left behind more than just a country: they left behind a sense of belonging in the communities that nurtured them. And what they gained was more than just economic opportunity; they formed new identities they'd chosen for themselves.

I chose to move to the United Kingdom, but I didn't choose the pain that came with it, nor did I choose the financial circumstances that led to my departure. And it's the changes I *don't* choose that break me. I think that's why, throughout my life, I preferred to stay indoors and interact with computers, crafting virtual worlds with precise code dictating every rule and interaction. Because without those rules, I would crumble.

But every time I crumble, I piece myself together, like *kintsugi*, the Japanese art of repairing broken pottery. And that's one of the qualities I like about myself – the cracks I've fixed from all the changes I've endured. Cracks that my parents also wore when they raised me.

Maybe change isn't just a constant. Maybe it's an object containing attributes, properties and methods that guide the agile development of our lives. I think I encounter fatal errors more often than most people, but my brain won't rest unless I find a way to debug them so I can move on to the next problem and work out its solution.

I know homesickness is not something Autistic people uniquely struggle with, but it's something that's constantly on my mind. Ruminating. Fixating. Trying to debug. Every time I see a British person wear a hoodie or T-shirt with 'Brooklyn' emblazoned on it, I can't help but feel both pride and a bittersweet yearning to return to my roots, or have the roots planted near me. The New York-inspired coffee shops and restaurants I encounter don't help very much. They're not like the real ones at home – the bagels are never as good.

Home. Is that what I still call it? I no longer have a Brooklyn townhouse to return to. My entire family has moved out. But New York made me who I am, and the United Kingdom embraced me. I'm happy to call both places my home.

It's often said that Autistic people don't like change. I wish I had known that growing up, as it would have explained a lot of things. Like why I struggled to speak when I switched schools for the first time, or why I became upset when the old parquet floors in my living room were replaced with shiny new softwood ones. Or why I had a meltdown when my family sold my childhood house: a place I'd always thought would be my home.

When I received my Autism diagnosis at the age of twenty-eight, I discovered why I struggled so much with change, people and chaotic surroundings. It gave me a framework through which I could understand the patterns that stitch me together. I've always found comfort in patterns – whether in the knitted baby blanket that kept me warm as a child, or in the classes and methods I build when writing software. Identifying and understanding them has allowed me to accept myself and tell the child that grew into me that she wasn't broken, just different.

Maybe it will help me accept the changes that constantly come into my life too.

BREAD TIME, AND OTHER ANTIDOTES TO BURNOUT

Erin Riley

ERIN RILEY (they/them) is a volunteer surf lifesaver, social worker and writer from Warrane/Sydney. Erin likes reading, routine and swimming in the ocean. Their debut memoir, *A Real Piece of Work*, came out in 2023, published by Penguin Random House. Erin is interested in how individual and cultural stories impact bodies, behaviour, health and ideas. They're also fascinated by themes of work, productivity, time, bodies and curiosity as a form of resistance. Erin is currently working on a second essay collection and having fun trying to write a novel.

In the months when I am feeling overwhelmed by the demoralisation that is full-time work in a time of climate catastrophe – and will soon discover is also the cumulative cognitive, physical and psychological decline that is my newly diagnosed autism in the final stages of collapse – my partner and I go to visit our friends Rita and Tom in the Blue Mountains.

Their spare room has a big window that spans the entire length of the space, as high as it is wide. It opens onto the overgrown greenery of the garden next door, making it like a tree house. The spare room is filled with dappled light, even at dusk, and the burnt-brown bedspread is crisp and welcoming. Small wooden bedside tables sit on either side of the old wooden bed, each holding a soft-hued lamp. The bed sits low to the floor and by the door a squat bookcase is filled with books. The room is a soft embrace. I feel a shift in gears, a slowing down. I lower my bag to the floor, undo my wristwatch and place it inside.

Maybe it's because I am a visitor. I don't have things to do. I do not have to wash these sheets later, or tend to the big old beautiful Katoomba home, with its large double-glazed, stained-glass windows and its creaky wooden floorboards. I don't have to figure out a menu or shop for ingredients. I don't have to do the cooking or pick out the right wine. Tom picks the perfect wines, actually, from his natural wine subscription. We get drunk two nights in a row and each morning we wake up without a hint of hangover.

Along Rita and Tom's entry hallway are three large full bookcases. I stand in front of them, attentive and curious, as if squinting at the *Mona Lisa* – wishing this house and its library were my own. A haven to return to after the annihilation of a working week. The backyard, spacious and open to the sky. Beside the clothesline, a small brick shed for storing old beers and boxes of wine. In one corner of the shed is the washing machine and in another a solitary toilet, right there in the open, for people to have a quiet shit.

I marvel at the space in Rita and Tom's house, which, unlike ours, houses so much. So many more experiences and possibilities can fit inside it. There is space to read and write at a desk by a window or by the back door, for two people to cook a meal and safely get in and out of one another's way. A place to put all the cookbooks. Room for a table to sit down at, to serve a potluck on and even invite some friends to gather around. Space to play a complicated board game. I gasp at the size of the lounge room – which fits a couch and two reading chairs separated by a small glass-topped table, the perfect size for a coffee cup. I take a beautiful cookbook – also a work of art – from the shelf and sit quietly on the sofa, leafing through it slowly.

Inside are useful tips on flavour, on the combinations of ingredients. There is a step-by-step guide, complete with illustrations, on how to cook the perfect boiled egg. It says when you have the gist of salt and fat and acid and heat, you do not need to have specific amounts of ingredients or follow a recipe in minute detail. You will understand how things piece together when you understand the foundations of cooking, when you can use common sense to decide how much heat, for how long and what kind.

Tom shows me how to make bread. The quickest, easiest bread, he tells me. He makes it all the time. At the permanent, tiled kitchen island, he shows me how. In a glass bowl, he combines two cups of whole flour and one cup of double-zero flour. This will give the fast bread more lightness and bounce, Tom says. Into the mix, he heaps two teaspoons of instant yeast, a teaspoon of salt (or thereabouts) and one-and-a-half cups of hot (though not boiling) water. *You can just take this from the tap, real hot*, Tom says, as he leans over the kitchen sink with his measuring jug.

For this loaf, Tom adds rosemary and stirs the mixture together, just so. *We want the air to stay in there, so we don't hammer it too much*, he says. You can mix this bread however you like, add different herbs or olives, for example. The week after visiting Rita and Tom, I make one with whole garlic cloves and small pieces of potato that sink to the bottom of the loaf when I bake it. It's lopsided but tastes good. Tom covers the bowl in plastic wrap and places it on the kitchen bench under the window that looks over the Hills Hoist, on which cockatoos are making a racket.

Two hours later, the dough doubles in size and lets out a yeasty burp. Tom peels the dough out of the bowl, fashions it into a floury ball and bakes it. We have bread for breakfast. We eat it with fried onions and peppers, red and green. They are charred and flavourful. It goes together well with a simple salad of tomato and avocado, slick with olive oil and lemon juice.

Before going to Rita and Tom's, I had been thinking a lot about time. I'd been reading books about it and listening to podcasts about work-life balance and how to manage stress. How people plan their routines and fit in their hobbies. I've been thinking about how I use time: how I want to spend it differently, how I would like more of it. And about how, lately, finding any time has felt rare – and how, when I have it, I spend it with more anguish than I would like.

I am obsessed with schedules and routine and time-management hacks. I have bought overpriced time-block calendars in pursuit of mastering and partitioning life. Not because I want to be more productive – hell no – but because I have felt so completely crushed by the responsibilities of a day. My hope, always, was that this would soften my challenges of existing in the world with its unrelenting demands and the unyielding challenge of keeping up.

The years leading up to now have been ones in which I have felt burnt out – though from the outside, it would seem I live an easy-enough life. It is with an increasing sense of horror and heartbreak that I continue to sell my time, then scramble in an attempt to get it back so I can spend it on simple pleasures outside of waged labour.

If I think about it too much, I think *fuck, it's a sick game*, and then I remember it *is* a sick game. I spend more time at work than I wish, even though it is far less than those with less privilege do. The pace of life, in a frightening and sudden way, was just suddenly too much. Until one month ago, I did not quite understand why it felt so annihilating, but I had my suspicions. Capitalism sure – but it felt more disabling than that.

In her book *Saving Time*, Jenny Odell introduces readers to the ideas of horizontal and vertical time put forth in 1948 by Josef Pieper, a German Catholic philosopher, when differentiating work-life balance from the notion of leisure. Odell writes:

> In work… time is horizontal, a pattern of forward-leaning labor time punctuated by little gaps of rest that simply refresh us for more work. For Pieper, those little gaps are not leisure. True leisure, instead, exists on a 'vertical' axis of time, one whose totality cuts through or negates the entire dimension of workaday time, 'run[ning] at right angles to work'.[1]

Pieper's conceptualisation of leisure is that it is different from the weekend. It is separate from whether it helps someone work more efficiently. Even if it does revive someone for work, for Pieper, 'that is not the point' of leisure. Odell says Pieper's distinction between work, refreshment-for-work and leisure:

> strikes an intuitive chord for me, as it probably does for anyone else who suspects that productivity is not the ultimate measure of the meaning of the value of time. To imagine a different 'point' means also imagining a life, identity, and source of meaning outside the world of work and profit.[2]

Odell interrogates whether Pieper's vision of vertical time is even possible in the world as it is currently set up, with its vast inequities and injustices. She suggests Pieper's idea of leisure is a '*state of mind and not a place, product or service*'. This ideal psychological place cannot be divorced from the historical or political context that impacts people's ability to be free enough to even begin to contemplate leisure time. Odell wonders if we can see the 'vertical within the horizontal, the free within the unfree, and even peace of mind within a world marked by violence'.[3]

Odell, herself stuck inside the sick game, teaching college students in pandemic lockdown via Zoom from her apartment in Oakland to pay the rent – and desperately wanting more for herself – writes about paying attention differently. She encourages readers to notice time outside of the modern, narrow, extractive reality of time as money. How might we find meaning, joy and purpose outside of selling our time? How might we make the most of the gaps outside work?

Saving Time is inspired by the sense of demoralisation I feel working inside a culture that has internalised productivity on a personal level. A culture where narratives of efficiency and optimisation have invaded our hobbies – and our very selves. Odell points me in the direction of what philosopher Byung-Chul Han, in *The Burnout Society*, describes as the 'achievement subject':

> Today's society is no longer Foucault's disciplinary world of hospitals, madhouses, prisons, barracks, and factories. It has long been replaced by another regime, namely a society of fitness studios, office towers, banks, airports, shopping malls, and genetic laboratories. Twenty-first-century society is no longer a disciplinary society, but rather an achievement society. Also, its inhabitants are... entrepreneurs of themselves... Clearly, the drive to maximize production inhabits the *social unconscious*.[4]

To Odell, Han's achievement subjects are '*DIY bosses propelled from within*'. I think about my own internalised DIY boss. For a long time, I was a version of the achievement subject: over-extending myself, going on keto diets, thrashing myself at work. Saying yes too often.

In December, I was diagnosed with autism. I had been curious if my ADHD might be part of something larger. Amid the overwhelm of work, the pace of my life and the noise in my head, I had been feeling unmoored and irritable. I had also just been diagnosed with Graves' disease, an autoimmune condition, one of the leading causes of hyperthyroidism. The thyroid is responsible for a few things, but one of them is regulating metabolism and ensuring the body is in balance. Too much thyroid hormone being produced essentially speeds up all bodily systems, throwing everything from heart rate and digestion to body temperature into disarray. With Graves', your whole system is on fire. I felt so internally irritable, quite literally shitting myself most days, and so anxious all the time. For months, before I was diagnosed, I thought I was going mad. As with many autoimmune conditions, one of the biggest triggers for Graves' Disease is stress. And so, my insides were paralleling the unrelenting pace of my external world. The challenges of the everyday had once been things I could manage, but now they felt Sisyphean.

I wondered whether I might be experiencing autistic burnout. Was this why, for much of my life, being in the world was such a challenge? Why I was so anxious? Why I felt like such an outsider? Why at five years old I needed to know exactly what we would be doing each and every day of the school holidays or else I'd lose my shit? Why I was so obsessed with wrestling? Why I wore those white pedal pushers with the yellow trim and that Hawaiian shirt tied in a bow around my midriff in my attempts to be a girl? Was it the reason I was such a tangential storyteller, why I offered so much of myself so freely, and why, no matter how hard I try, I can never explain the rules of a board game? Why I can never give anyone the gist of a movie? Was it why structure and routine and rigidity were hallmarks of my life? Why I liked to eat the same food at the same time? Why change was so distressing? Was it why I had trouble regulating in moments of distress, even though I was always reading and having baths and yin-yoga-ing and self-improving and TRYING SO HARD? Why I was always so harsh on myself when I reacted abrasively to my partner, raising my voice in defensiveness, having a wally, then sliding into a spiral of shame because I just couldn't get it right? I was continually asking myself: *what the fuck is wrong with me?*

Autistic burnout has been mostly absent from the academic and clinical literature of autism – but it is something autistic people have long known about and experienced. One of the first solid papers exploring it, published in 2020 and phenomenally titled 'Having all of your internal resources exhausted beyond measure and being left with no clean-up crew: Defining autistic burnout', attempts to describe it:

> Autistic burnout is a syndrome conceptualised as resulting from chronic life stress and a mismatch of expectations and abilities without adequate supports. It is characterised by pervasive, long-term (typically 3+ months) exhaustion, loss of function and reduced tolerance to stimulus.5

Autistic burnout is a serious health condition, different from occupational burnout but with hints of similarity. It is characterised by pervasive fatigue. (Though in many cases this tiredness stems from a lifetime of camouflaging neurodivergent characteristics, ways of being in the world, desperately hiding the outsider in plain sight.) The fatigue from just *existing* this way adds a cumulative cognitive load that is, over time, exhausting to maintain. It can lead to a loss of skills – in the areas of work, in social skills and in the ability to communicate, to stay on top of everyday tasks.

V, the clinical psychologist who assessed me, told me the closer to burnout you are, the more your autistic traits emerge. I wondered why my usual structures and routines felt less nourishing, why I was leaning into more solitary time – unable to text my friends back or organise the simplest of tasks. Why finding words was harder and it was increasingly challenging to have a deep conversation. Holding on to other people's sentences was like free-solo-ing a rockface. Concentration was required just to keep up, to not fall. I read V's sobering assessment:

> Erin presents with the internalised or 'high-masking' presentation of the autistic neurotype. Over the years they capitalised on their intelligence and resourcefulness to 'mask' their social confusion. They are skilled at observing others, have learnt many behaviours commonly expected in neurotypical social situations, and developed various strategies to help them navigate neurotypical interactions. However, managing the daily expectations of neurotypical society, socially and at work, has been difficult and costly to their quality of life. They are at risk of autistic burnout.

The 2020 study on autistic burnout arrives at a simple equation. When the cumulative load of life stressors for an autistic person (like masking, ableism, stress) is in tandem with an inability to catch a break (like no ability to rest, poor boundaries, cultural gaslighting, lack of support), the expectations and demands of life outweigh the person's abilities to meet them – and they spin into burnout. They are, simply, running on fumes.

Byung-Chul Han reflects on Peter Handke's 'Essay on tiredness', which identifies two very different kinds of tiredness.[6] One connects people to the world and the other keeps people isolated. One tiredness has ego at its centre; the other is more curious and trusts in the world.

Odell notes that Handke's trusting tiredness is an 'inherently destabilising experience, a loss of individual power that helps us find a home in something larger'.[7]

I like this idea – that there is something to pay attention to in this tiredness, that it has something expansive to teach me, something less ego-driven. Han writes that Handke's concept of tiredness holds the potential to feel calm. To not do; to slow down and notice things outside your own edges:

> It is not a state in which the senses languish or grow dull. Rather, it rouses a special kind of visibility. Accordingly, Handke speaks of 'candid tiredness,' which grants access to long and slow forms that elude short and fast hyperattention… For Handke, deep tiredness rises to become a form of salvation, a form of rejuvenation. It brings back a sense of wonder into the world.[8]

The soft hospitality of my friends revives me, slows me down. I notice a deep curiosity while I am here, at Rita and Tom's. Things seem brighter somehow. Maybe it's the visibility emerging from tiredness that Handke speaks of – relinquishing my decades of camouflaging neurological difference. In trying to reach standards not built for brains and bodies like mine, in DIY-bossing myself, I have brought myself to the cusp of a health crisis. In doing less, I am obsessed with the simple wonder that is Tom's bread, the sounds of the birds. The silence I hear all around me in Katoomba.

Naomi Klein, in her book *Doppelganger*, reminds us there's a connection between the overinflated, individualised, partitioned self and the undercared-for planet. Klein, like Han and Handke, emphasises the need to separate from our egos. For her, healing both ourselves and the planet can only come with the de-centring of ourselves – and by connecting with the collective struggles that involve all of us, and the planet.

Klein tells the story of a coral scientist who has been studying the Great Barrier Reef for decades, who 'describes the journey of his life as one of de-centring himself so he has the headspace to truly see other life forms, human and non-humans alike'.[9] She likens this to Iris Murdoch's idea of 'unselfing' – where seeing something beautiful provides an opportunity to recognise the larger project of being alive in this world.

Unselfing is akin to Handke's 'more of less of me'. It seems like a great motto for resisting the pace of capitalism's demands to always be doing, optimising, better, busy, faster, more. It is permission to give up – to do something different, to step outside our ego-driven selves and notice the world. For Odell, 'maybe "the point" isn't to live more, in the literal sense of a longer or more productive life, but rather, to be more alive in any given moment'.[10]

Australian author and journalist Julia Baird finds a similar sweet spot in the ocean, during her gruelling cancer recovery:

> My illness has forced me to rest, and the ocean has taught me how, and now I understand that sometimes we need to sit for a little while to comprehend the immensity of the world we live in, and its beauty and fragility – as well as our own.[11]

It is in unselfing, Odell suggests, that we might bring about this state of mind Pieper alludes to, where we might find the vertical (true leisure time) within the horizontal (work-driven time). In unselfing, we can soften and look outside ourselves, whether prompted by burnout, by tiredness or – as is my new reality – reckoning with the limits of a disability. Its gift may be the opportunity to de-centre ourselves and to connect with the larger, collective world around us – to notice how sick it is too.

Burnout can spark light-bulb moments, like recognising that you live in a body that is unable to keep up in a world designed for able bodies – that the stress of that keeping up and the relentless busyness it requires is no longer something you want. Burnout can help us slow down enough to notice our reactivity, our inward-gazing, our fear of others, our deep tiredness, our obsession with optimising ourselves. Burnout is offering us, as Klein and Odell both suggest, a way out, a path to something better – for ourselves, each other and the planet.

I like reading cookbooks, but I remain a novice cook. My repertoire is slim: I stick to a few solid, reliable recipes. It is exciting to be in Rita and Tom's kitchen, to look attentively at all their cookbooks, to see their favourite recipes, easily identified by pages curled at the edges and dusted with hints of oily fingers. I find simple pleasure in rifling through their fridge and peeking into their cupboard, watching them make their favourite meals for us, their guests. I like drinking the coffee Tom grinds each morning in his enormous coffee grinder, kept under the sink. It is syrupy and warm, drunk from Rita's brown ceramic seventies mugs.

There are two big boxes of vegetables from Toddarello's, the fruit and vegetable market down the road from Rita and Tom's. One box sits on the kitchen bench, the other on the tiled kitchen island. They overflow with bunches of crisp spinach jutting from a cardboard corner, beetroots the size of a baby's head, radishes and carrots just wrestled from the earth. There are melons and boxes of berries, punnets of delicate, tiny multicoloured tomatoes, and enormous field mushrooms. There are bulging sweet potatoes, onions, peppers – green and yellow and red. A whole cauliflower hides insides its leaves. There's half a purple cabbage, avocadoes, apples and ziplocked bags jammed with rocket.

Crip time, described by disability activists, is an understanding that the clock time of modern-day industry assumes a normative way of operating in the world. Clock time does not allow for the ways disabled people may need or require more time to do something: to complete a task, to arrive somewhere, to achieve something. Crip time '*unsettles* what time means'[12]. It reimagines and resists economic productivity as a metric of human worth. Odell, quoting Alison Kafer, notes that crip time 'requires re-imagining our notions of what could and should happen in time'.[13]

The gift of crip time, of what disability activists bring to understandings of work and critiques of capitalism and normative ways of being, is its questioning of what 'the good life means… for every person with a body that is not a machine and a soul that is more than a worker'.[14] This applies, Odell points out, to both disabled and non-disabled people.

The way to avoid tunnelling into full autistic burnout is to rest, V tells me. Ideally, the solution is to not work full-time. But without work, I cannot pay the bills. The solution is to recognise I probably cannot work in the way I have been working. I need to grieve that old, unsustainable life. I need to fail better. My solution to burnout is *more of less of me*. More no. Less ego. It is noticing the small, the insignificant. It lies in gratitude and small pleasures. I tell myself I'll see it as a gift – one day, maybe soon – this chance to de-centre.

Rita gets annoyed because Tom slaves over the dinner for many hours and it is served at 9 o'clock, as if we were in Europe. Rita says, *Oh my god, Tom – it's so late.* We keep drinking the wine, so when the food comes we are jolly and stay up late laughing. It's a Saturday, and we have nowhere to be in the morning. We're in no rush for anything.

I watch Tom stir the tomato sauce he has simmering on the enormous stove – how beautifully he has tended to it throughout the night. He moves with ease and purpose. I notice the small things with more colour too. I walk the long entry hallway with my glass of wine. I get excited about its thin lip; at home, we do not have such delicate objects. Tom has put Steely Dan on the stereo – not too loudly, though. I am fine that the food is taking however long it takes.

I browse the titles of the books on the three large hallway shelves. I notice their shapes and sizes, their well-worn pages, the colours of their spines. There are books I have read and books I want to read, all here in someone else's home. There is Dorothy Porter, Kurt Vonnegut's *Slaughterhouse-Five.* James Baldwin next to Proust, Woolf and James Joyce. There's Annie Ernaux and Helen Garner and Emmanuel Carrère. I crane my neck to the side to read the spines of the books – slowly and carefully. I wander the hallway. It's a museum, everything so special, each book finely crafted and edited.

Many decisions, on design and typeface and words, went into every one of them. Each had its own long, drawn-out birth. I wonder how many people have created those books. I think about the letters sent back and forth between author and editor, back when track changes were still far into the future. Back in the many years before email. The slow, careful experience of writing and publishing a book.

If I could do anything at all, I'd freeze time and take books from the shelf and sit in the spare bedroom with the crisp burnt-brown bedspread. I would plump up the pillows and put on my most comfortable clothes: the warm, fleecy navy sweatshirt with the neckline that is ribbed and perfectly sized. I would pair this with the blue tracksuit pants and some fresh, warm socks. Beside the bed would be a cup of dandelion tea: it would never be empty and always be warm. I would read.

Tom sends me a text with the bread recipe, even though I have written in my notebook *Tom's fast bread*, along with a loose description of what I saw Tom doing at the kitchen island.

I buy the ingredients for Tom's bread soon after returning from the mountains. I toss the ingredients together in the green salad bowl. I cover it in plastic wrap and place it outside on the table in the sun. When the bread has risen, I pull back the plastic. The bread is alive; it breathes through hundreds of tiny holes. Pulling it from the bowl, the dough is sticky, like cooked mozzarella. Threads of it stretch and cling to the side of the bowl. I place the sticky lump on a cutting board dusted with flour. I roll it into a ball, dust the top and slice my sharpest knife across it, in the shape of a cross. It goes into the oven, in a pan lined with baking paper. It looks so tiny in the big pan. I place the heavy lid on top and bake it at 230 degrees for 30 minutes. I take off the lid, give it 12 more.

My first loaf is, of course, my favourite. It is no longer the size of a fist; its crisp edges burst towards the sky.

Thrilled, I take its photograph and send it to Tom.

Looking good! Turn out tasty?

Haven't even touched her yet, leaving her for lunch!

Just be careful – if it is too good, you'll have set a dangerous precedent for yourself.

I eat it with white beans and rosemary, made with vegetable stock in the cast-iron pan.

I make the bread regularly now. I find I do not need to look at the clock to know when time's up. The dough's rapid growth tells me change is happening – and I like experiencing time this way. I leave it out to cool. Later, I wrap it in a tea towel.

I make the bread for special occasions. I bake it for my friend Vicki's birthday. I wrap it in butcher's paper and tie a ribbon around it; it steams around the edges and on the drive the windscreen fogs up a little.

If, as Odell suggests, Pieper's leisure is less a destination and more an 'emotional posture – one that, like falling asleep, can be achieved only by letting go', perhaps I found a slice of the vertical plane, that leisure time removed from the concerns of work, at Rita and Tom's. I found it inside the interruption of burnout: in books, and in the tender ways Tom attended to his bread. I found it in marking time not in minutes or dollars, but in the swelling of warm dough. In the sound of fresh air, in the oily pages of a cookbook. In the thickening of a tomato sauce, lovingly cooked late into the night.

Sources

1. Odell, J 2023, *Saving Time: Discovering a life beyond the clock*, Bodley Head, London.

2. ibid.
3. ibid.
4. Han, B-H, quoted in, Odell, J, *Saving Time.*
5. Raymaker, DM, Teo, AR, Steckler, NA, Lentz, B, Scharer, M, Santos, AD, Kapp, SK, Hunter, M, Joyce, A & Nicolaidis, C 2020, '"Having All of Your Internal Resources Exhausted Beyond Measure and Being Left with No Clean-Up Crew": Defining autistic burnout', *Autism in Adulthood*, vol. 2, no. 2, pp. 132–143.
6. Han, B-C (trans. E Butler) 2015, *The Burnout Society*, Stanford University Press, Stanford.
7. Odell, J, *Saving Time.*
8. Han, B-C, *The Burnout Society.*
9. Klein, N 2023, *Doppleganger: A trip into the mirrorworld*, Allen Lane, UK.
10. Odell, J, *Saving Time.*
11. Baird, J 2023, *Bright Shining: How grace changes everything*, Fourth Estate, Gadigal Country.
12. Odell, J, *Saving Time.*
13. ibid.
14. ibid.

AUTISTIC TEMPORALITIES AND ADVENTURES IN CRIP TIME

Danni Stewart

DANNI STEWART (she/they) is an audio documentary artist living and working on Wangal land. Danni's practice spans journalism, sound art and live storytelling events. With each project they hope to create space for experimentation, community and deep listening. Danni previously explored their Autism in their 2023 audio artwork 'But I'm a Virgo', which weaves together memories, phone calls and VHS archives. For two years Danni worked at FBi Radio co-running *All The Best*. They've created work for ABC Radio National, UTS Impact Studios, Scitech and Transom. Danni also works as a casual academic at the University of Sydney, specialising in radio and podcasting.

Einstein's theory of special relativity says that time is relative to the perception of the person observing time. As I plunge into sensory overload, time seems to slow. I'm calculating the minutes until I can remove myself from the environment: how many train stops, how many songs left in the set, how long until she finishes her drink... How can these moments last an eternity but two hours scrolling Instagram feels like the blink of an eye. *Time is relative.*

The first of September 2005 was the day so-called Australia moved to a new standard of time based on the super-accurate atomic clock. It was also my eighth birthday. I was in Year 2 and what I remember about that time is the cushions at the back of the classroom, placed behind a bookshelf, out of view from the rest of the class. My teacher called this 'the quiet space'. Whenever possible, I situated myself there. It was also around this time that I started to have this feeling of not being able to keep up. I was always last to get the joke. I couldn't process the teacher's instructions and relied on copying those around me. When we did comprehension exercises the other kids would be writing out answers while I was still trying to read the first sentence of the passage, struggling to concentrate because of the whirring of a gas heater behind me.

Atomic clocks are more accurate than their predecessors, quartz clocks, which don't keep time precisely enough for today's high-tech world of internet, GPS and deep-space exploration. Aside from helping us navigate, atomic clocks are so precise that they've been used to prove Einstein's theory of special relativity. Physicists have put atomic clocks on planes flying at different heights to show that the passage of time varies depending on movement and gravity. The changes recorded by the atomic clocks are miniscule but prove that time is fluid.

Growing up, I had a purple Hi-5 clock on my wall. I spent long afternoons watching it tick. Transfixed by the arms circling around, around, around. I'd watch the clock in the classroom too. Not because I was counting down to three o'clock; I just enjoyed watching the arms go around, around, around. That was before I'd been told I was 'wasting time'. Now, clocks fuel a kind of anxiety inside me. A panic that I haven't done 'enough' in the seconds, minutes, hours that have gone by.

There's a difference between time and clock time. Clock time took hold during the industrial revolution as factory owners used clocks to manage factory workers. Before the temporality of capitalism, our perception of time was tied to the cycles of the natural world. Our ancestors kept time by the sun and the seasons.

I no longer keep a clock on my bedroom wall. Instead, I spend a lot of time staring at the ceiling. It's genetic. My dad does it, and I remember my grandpa spending a lot of time in bed in the middle of the afternoon. For most of my life I saw this as doing 'nothing'. But recently I've come to realise that doing 'nothing' is actually doing something. That time spent staring at the ceiling is time to rest, to recover from an overstimulating world.

Rest is a radical concept. I didn't know rest growing up. I constantly got the message that I was lazy. Sleeping in, watching TV, staring at the ceiling for hours – these are not things that 'productive' people do. I've tried to change my unproductive ways through various methods: pomodoro timers, calendar-blocking, extensions that block social media, alarms, white noise, brown noise… but there are still days, weeks, even months when I cannot get my work done. And for this I've so often felt like a failure, like the tick of my internal clock is broken.

The more I've learnt about time, the more I've realised that it's a socially constructed reality. Like gender, which I also felt like I was failing at for a long time. Don't get me wrong, I do find clock time useful in some ways. Being Autistic, I struggle with uncertainty. So, if I'm meeting someone, I do like agreeing on a time. I also need predictability and I rely on clock time to establish routines that are meaningful to me. But clock time isn't always useful, and my failure to sync with the clock everyone else lives by has been a source of shame for as long as I can remember.

When it comes to getting out the front door, the clock is not my friend. This is because I'm both a bad timekeeper and a stickler for time – a confusing contradiction. I'm always late, but being late causes me an enormous amount of stress. This is a common trigger for my meltdowns. Sometimes, unable to recover from the meltdown – make-up ruined by streaks of tears, anchored to the bed, the couch, the floor, wherever I've collapsed – I simply don't go to whatever it was I felt was so important to be on time for. Viewed through a deficit lens a psychologist might say that I have an 'impaired sense of time'. But how can we have an 'impaired' sense of something that isn't real?

Disability theorist Alison Kafer describes 'crip time' as a reimagining of what can and should happen within time: 'Rather than bend disabled bodies and minds to meet the clock, crip time bends the clock to meet disabled bodies and minds.'[1] Kafer advocates for a change in mindset, a recognition that expectations around 'how long things take' are determined by very particular minds and bodies. Crip time is not only a framework for understanding the need for flexibility, for extra time but also prompts us to consider how Disabled people perceive time differently.

Einstein imagined the three dimensions of space and the dimension of time together as a kind of fabric surrounding us called 'spacetime'. Within the fabric of spacetime, everything that has ever happened and everything that ever will all exist at once. When Einstein's closest friend and collaborator Michele Besso passed away, he wrote to Besso's wife: 'Now he has departed from this strange world a little ahead of me. That means nothing. People like us, who believe in physics, know that the distinction between past, present and future is only a stubbornly persistent illusion.'[2]

This makes sense when I consider my perception of time as an Autistic person. Multiple psychologists have told me I need to 'live in the present', that I spend too much time in the past and future. You see, I have trouble differentiating between my memories, my dreams and what's real. I find it hard to 'live in the present' when my past, present, future and dreams all exist at once. I feel like this insistence on focusing on the present rather than seeing ourselves as part of a spacetime continuum is a lonely way to live.

I find a lot of comfort in the idea of being one tiny speck in spacetime. I'm comforted by the thought of sharing a dimension with the Autistic people who came before me. Autism is heritage and I'm curious about my Autistic ancestors. Some survival strategies I turn to again and again I suspect live in genetic memory. Before anyone told me to, I knew to breathe deeply in order to regulate my nervous system. It's a comfort to think of my Autistic ancestors doing the same for many generations across spacetime.

In 'Six ways of looking at crip time', Ellen Samuels writes about crip time as a form of time travel with the power to extract us from expected linear milestones of life.[3] I spent childhood feeling constantly behind, but now I feel like I'm racing decades ahead. Needing ten hours of sleep, an inability to process speech in loud restaurants and persistent back problems are the expected reality for someone much older than me. This is hard to swallow when I'm in the 'prime of life', as they say. So, I pretend I'm not Autistic – inflated with pressure to not 'waste' my youth – I try to push through and pass as a 'normal' twenty-six-year-old. My sensory overload grows angrier, morphing into migraine, meltdowns and piercing pain that commands attention.

I've spent my life putting huge amounts of energy into trying to triumph over my uncooperative mind and body – to obey the clock by any means necessary. But I'm learning to pay attention to how my body communicates through pain. Through muscles tightening, hairs flicking up, a dull throb that gnarls into a twisting, churning sensation in my stomach. Now, when my body is speaking to me, I'm trying to listen. Samuels writes that crip time 'forces us to take breaks, even when we don't want to, even when we want to keep going, to move ahead. It insists that we listen to our bodyminds so closely, so attentively, in a culture that tells us to divide the two and push the body away from us while also pushing it beyond its limits. Crip time means listening to the broken languages of our bodies, translating them, honouring their words.'

Knowing that time can stretch and shrink – that, according to Einstein, the flow of time is an *illusion* – has helped me accept the intimate complexities of living in crip time. I hold grief for the ways in which I can't sustain the schedule of a 'normal' twenty-six-year-old. But within crip time I also find liberation. In *Feminist, Queer, Crip*, Alison Kafer urges us to imagine utopian crip futures that we create for ourselves. My utopia is community caring for each other in crip time and sharing space where we can be honest without fear of rejection or negative consequence. The more community I find with other Disabled people, the closer that utopia feels.

Sources

1. Kafer, A 2013, *Feminist, Queer, Crip*, Indiana University Press, Bloomington.
2. Dyson, FJ, 1979, *Disturbing the Universe*, Harper & Row, New York.
3. Samuels, E 2017, 'Six ways of looking at crip time', *Disabilities Studies Quarterly*, vol. 37, no. 3.

STARGAZING

Julie Farrell

JULIE FARRELL (she/her) is an award-winning writer and activist, living by the sea just outside of Edinburgh, Scotland. She is co-founder of The Inklusion Guide: a guide to making literature events accessible to disabled people. Her work on making the world a more inclusive place to all has seen her listed as one of *The Bookseller*'s Top 150 Most Influential People in Publishing. Julie's work explores the process of grief, loss and nostalgia in relation to family, identity and the planet. Julie serves as a trustee of *Mslexia Magazine* and on the Advisory Group for the new UK arts access scheme for D/deaf, disabled and neurodivergent people, All In.

'We are just an advanced breed of monkeys on a minor planet of a very average star. But we can understand the universe. That makes us something very special'

– Stephen Hawking

My first serious experience with space was one of abject terror, in my childhood. I was plagued with granular, recurring nightmares of my world being invaded by aliens, thanks to the eighties' obsession with trippy, weird films where extraterrestrials were portrayed with hideous, cheap props and costumes – like *Mac and Me*, *E.T.*, *Explorers* and *Flight of the Navigator.* I'd become consumed when I watched films: it felt like I was actually inhabiting these created worlds. I observed every minute detail, recalling them in reels in my dreams. When I could no longer muster the courage to go to bed, I eventually came clean to my parents in a fit of hysterical tears and spent a couple of months on my sister's bedroom floor before I was able (with much cajoling) to return to my own room to sleep.

A few years after the nightmares, when I was nine, a school project kicked off an obsessive interest in our solar system. I turned my rapturous attention and curiosity to my dad, who'd hung up his first mate's hat some thirteen years prior after a decade in the Merchant Navy. He had used the patterns of the sun, moon and stars to find his way when he was navigating a ship's course far out at sea, in the darkest nights the Earth affords, and on the largest vessels humans have built. For him, learning this language was a matter of the entire crew (and cargo)'s safety, with no GPS.

Patience is a freezing man, standing in his garden for hours at a time in the depth of a Scottish winter ('no' for weaklings'), teaching his young daughter how to recognise the patterns in the stars and sharing the ancient stories strung between them. He'd already taught me how to use a compass and the sun to navigate my way over land during the day, explaining the importance of paying attention to landmarks, and of knowing where you started.

I'd known for some time the coordinates of our home: 56° N, 4° W – a measurement of latitude (how far north or south of the equator a location is) and longitude (how far east or west of the Prime Meridian a location is) used by seafarers to chart their course at sea. He told me we can do the same with the stars and the moon, and that there are landmarks 'out there' too, if you know where to look. 'Latitude' becomes 'declination', indicating an object's position north or south of the celestial equator, and 'longitude' becomes 'right ascension', indicating its position in an easterly direction from the Vernal Equinox. (This point in time occurs exactly when the centre of the sun crosses the celestial equator moving north, at the start of spring in the northern hemisphere.)

My vivid imagination allowed me to easily project a gradually deepening 3D map of the celestial sphere out from my body and into the sky, any time I wanted. I learnt that Orion (the mighty but boastful hunter) rises in the east in winter (I'd wait with bated breath for him to peek over the top-right corner of our neighbour's house) and that he would cross over the southern sky in an arc, eventually setting in the west. He was easy to spot because of the three very close stars that make up his belt: Alnilam, Alnitak and Mintaka. Just below this hangs a faint, fuzzy cloud of giddy young stars, ionised hydrogen and helium, and some cosmic dust. The infamous Orion Nebula.

These quiet conversations under the stars with my dad made me feel seen and special. He got just as cold as I did, shivering in the dark but ignoring it and pointing out the International Space Station and various satellites anyway. I banked it all in my head: this was knowledge I would *never* relinquish, but build upon.

I took things a lot farther than the knowledge my dad shared with me. I made myself familiar with intimate facts about the solar system, like the core temperatures of the planets, what their chemical components were, eventually looking outside our own system and learning about binary systems, dwarf stars, neutron stars and supernovae. When I was thirteen, my dad gifted me Stephen Hawking's *The Universe in a Nutshell*, and theoretical physics became my jam. I lived in a world of theory, not absolution, where anything was possible, and much was still unknown.

A few years later, I was lucky to study astronomy and the cosmos in my first couple of years at university, and I revelled in calculating the rate of expansion of the universe, the parsec-leaps between stars, and in wrapping my head around Schrödinger's paradox.

It blew my mind to learn those same quantum particles that make our planet, our sun, our solar system, galaxy, universe and highly probable multiverse *also* make the very cells and atoms of us, of me – my consciousness! All of it, the universe and me, just quarks, gluons, mesons, electrons, protons, neutrons. Stuck together in infinitely chaotic and complex ways. Exquisite, perfect.

To know this, is to *W O N D E R.*

This all-encompassing, whole-body awe at the mysterious things that lie beyond our own world is *my most deeply joyous stim.*

It reverberates from my crown all the way to my toes, a pulsing celestial glow that fills up my cells and which stays with me for days, or even years. Banked in an internal library that I can revisit at any time, pulling a jar from the shelf and shaking up pink moondust from 2019's Super Blood Wolf Moon, when I hung out over the Juliet balcony of my living-room window in my pyjamas (in sub-zero temperatures, at five am) poking at my husband, who kept falling asleep, while I squealed with delight to see the rosy orb of the giant moon slowly turn blood-red. Opening another jar, I can climb back inside a velvet-blue evening on the Isle of Skye, the stars too numerous to make out the familiar patterns easily spotted under city lights. White-gold Perseid meteors streak gracefully across the whole sky, and I don't even flinch when the midges start biting.

I once stood at the edge of the Grand Canyon, knowing I wanted to pocket the moment forever, a wee grounding stone to pull out in tough times. I crouched down and gathered a handful of red dust from the ground, letting it slowly trickle through my fingers in the breeze as I mentally tiled the inside of my brain with the bronzed sunset unfolding in front of me, combining the power of my senses. Every time I stargaze I'm repeating that moment, deliberately reinforcing my connection to it, the Earth and myself, regulating my nervous system. I'm recording the sharpness of blue-white stars against the softness of the orange ones, all the constellations in contrast, and deep-space objects like the Pleiades Star Cluster, a literal treasure chest of glinting coins, trails of shining pearls, sparkling gemstones big and small and of varying hues and opacity – bursting at the seams.

My joy is intensified by watching clouds of my breath in the frosted winter air, tasting the sharp tang of ice on leaf mulch. Or, if it's early summer, smelling the fresh scent of ozone and the sweet perfume of blossoming lilac. Those memory jars hold the particular glow of the sodium-orange streetlights that lined the street outside my childhood home, and they retain the flooding warmth of the hot cups of tea that pinched my fingers when I dragged myself back inside, giving in to the temptation of a stack of dad's melty-cheddar-and-Branston's toast for supper.

It's a joy, too, because being autistic makes me a navigator. I know as well as *my own skin* how the sun charts her voyage across the sky through the year, and where the cardinal directions are. Just as I know where Pegasus and Andromeda rise and set in our northern hemisphere in midwinter, and that my own star sign, Gemini, and its two brightest stars, Castor and Pollux, hang up above Orion's left shoulder. I can spot the plough in a heartbeat, and I know to gaze straight up from where I'm standing in summer, where the tell-tale cross of Cygnus (the swan) is way up high at the zenith. I know Polaris can be found by simply extending an imaginary line up from the two stars at the front of the Plough (from Merak through Dubhe), so that I am never lost. I was shown by my seafaring, navigator dad how to lasso these celestial beings.

I am a voyager, without ever leaving the ground. With every single observation, a *whole new world* unfurls into being before my eyes, something almost too great and glittering to comprehend. I never feel so humbled, so small, as when I'm eye-to-universe.

It is who I am.

You might not know it, but you can tell which stars are hotter just by looking at them. Vega twinkles an intense blue-white, high in the northern hemisphere: mostly helium and some ionised hydrogen. Betelgeuse in Orion and Aldebaran in Taurus (the bull, just up diagonally right from Orion here in the northern hemisphere) are two rusted stars that are cooler, with some heavy metals present. Betelgeuse has used up all of its hydrogen, and when I peer through my binoculars at its richly oxidised glow, fifty-times magnified, I feel like I, too, am casting off my old skin – ready to explode in a supernova that will light up our night sky to the brightness of our half-moon for three whole months.

I've learned from my own experience of life, and from the people in it, that pain can become our whole entire world. Every time I set my eyes on some distant star cluster or nebulae, I'm doing the impossible: I'm climbing outside of myself and I'm flying, soaring way above the clouds, piercing little holes in the sky.

Ten-year-old me never knew just how literal an anchor Polaris would become for me. How many times I'd throw out my gaze, catch it, then steady myself in the storm.

Polaris, everything. Me, one tiny star in billions.

I'm a voyager out of inherent curiosity, but I'm saving myself every time I look up.

All of it teaches me resilience. I'm ending and beginning all the time, like the seasons, the waves, the days and nights. The fragility and rarity of the world is a beautiful thing, and it gives life meaning.

In knowing this, I hope I have some shot at comprehending my own fragile existence – my form, my impact and purpose. Human life, after all, is made from the elements that blew across lightyears of space in the very earliest, billions-of-years-old supernovae. I stare and stare at the flat red disc of Betelgeuse, and at Mars, more three-dimensional, relatively close in this winter's sky, and I feel simultaneously untethered and more whole. I look at them and I recognise them. We are made of the same thing.

My bones are my bones because some ancient star erupted calcium and carbon into the vastness of space. My lungs can breathe because the same thing happened with oxygen.

Is it any wonder that we are made up of tiny repeating solar systems? Our atoms are made of a nucleus, with electrons spinning around it like tiny planets. They interact and bond to form a molecule, the molecules bond and form cells – and cells combine to make proteins, DNA and complex structures like eyelashes, skin and muscles.

In the few hours it takes my old friends to make their glorious carousel above my planet, it feels like the ushering in of a new dawn: a dawn of time, of place, of me.

The air is full of vibrations.

I can offer only awe and gratitude, and the promise I'll never stop bearing witness.

Every moon gleaned, cluster devoured, every galaxy spied transports me, right back to my childhood garden, my dad's solid, soothing presence by my side.

I scoot myself around and pick up what diamonds I can in my feeble, human, Occam-obliterating hope that the molecules of him might be seeing them too, somewhere out there in the great, infinite multiverse, where our own story is now strung between the stars, just out of reach.

We are, all of us, the sum of parts. But we are so much more than that.

We are stardust.

RECENTLY I WAS DIAGNOSED AS AUTISTIC

Lauren Metzler

LAUREN METZLER is a designer by day, cozy artist by night. Originally from Oregon, she now lives in Sydney with her partner and their kitty, Luna. Lauren loves drawing comics, dabbles in writing and is currently working on her debut graphic novel *Side Quest*, which will be published by Allen & Unwin in 2026. As a late-diagnosed Autistic artist, she wants to shine a light on neurodiversity and help create a positive impact for Autistic children. Her aim to is portray strong lead characters who are neurodivergent and show how they learn to embrace what makes them unique, as well as help others who are struggling or being bullied for being 'different'. Lauren's hope is to share stories that will help diversify neurodivergent voices within the kidlit world and bring a message of inclusivity.

RECENTLY I WAS DIAGNOSED AS AUTISTIC.

you don't look...

FRIENDS & FAMILY TRIED TO BE KIND ...

WHILE I TRIED TO UNDERSTAND ...

TRUTH IS, I HAVE SPENT MY WHOLE LIFE STRUGGLING WITH SENSORY ISSUES AND MASKING BECAUSE I FELT ALL ALONE ...

BUT OVER THE YEARS ...

THE MASK STARTED CRACKING ...

AND I NO LONGER KNEW WHO I WAS.

I WOULD 'PUSH THROUGH'
BEING THE VERSION OF ME THAT I THOUGHT
OTHERS WANTED ME TO BE ...

FORGETTING WHO I WAS ...

NOT KNOWING THAT I WAS ACTUALLY AUTISTIC ...

I AM STILL LEARNING WHAT IT MEANS TO BE AUTISTIC, BUT I AM STILL ME. JUST WITH MORE KNOWLEDGE & UNDERSTANDING...
Art Therapy
AUTISTIC JOY
creativity
AUTISM 101
AUTISTIC BRAIN
AUTISM ♥
Stimming
Neurodivergent
OF MY SENSORY NEEDS.

BEING AUTISTIC

IN MY LIVED EXPERIENCE

I GET COMPLETELY ABSORBED

IN MUSIC & CREATIVITY ...

AND WHEN I START TO FEEL BAD ...
ART BRINGS ME JOY ...
BURNOUT
ANXIETY
DEPRESSION
CALM
AND CALM.

I LOVE CREATING COMICS

TO HELP RAISE AWARENESS

AND SHARE MY VOICE.

DANCE LIKE NOBODY (NEUROTYPICAL) IS WATCHING

Kay Kerr

KAY KERR (she/her) is an AuDHD journalist and author. She writes works of fiction and non-fiction exploring autistic experiences of adolescence, relationships, self-identity, community and parenthood. Her books include *Please Don't Hug Me*, *Social Queue* and *Love & Autism*. Kay lives with her family on the Sunshine Coast/Kabi Kabi Country.

One of my earliest memories – a fuzzy one with soft edges and dreamy lighting – is of living-room dance parties with my family. My parents' records spinning, me spinning, everyone and everything spinning. Plush carpet underfoot, piles of cushions to land on or spin or throw, freedom of movement until my small body was tired enough to rest. It was perhaps a Friday-night tradition, or perhaps not. Memory is a tricky thing; some things stick, while others dissolve, or warp, or merge. I had always clearly remembered us listening to a Beach Boys record – we were cycling through the catalogue of hits, from 'God Only Knows' to 'Wouldn't It Be Nice'. I have since learnt, as an adult, it was in fact the soundtrack to the 1988 Tom Cruise film *Cocktail*. And of course, track six is The Beach Boys' 'Kokomo'.

Research shows that autistic people, when recalling an event from memory, will report it with sensory details.[1] *The pillows, the carpet, the light.* That is certainly how I remember. Songs and smells are most evocative. Research also indicates that some autistic people can struggle with autobiographical memory – that is, long-term memories of the experiences of our lives – and this can impact our ability to form a sense of self.[2] We don't always understand the context in which those experiences happened and therefore struggle to perceive ourselves within them. This resonates. So many of my memories seem to exist without me in them, though I obviously know I was there. There is other research on autism and memory, but it's so skewed through the deficit lens that it doesn't consider the autistic perspective at all – so I treat it with similar disregard.

There is comfort in the memories of living-room dance parties, because they're not clouded by the perception of others. I felt unperceived in those moments, whether that was true or not. I felt free. But the moment I stepped into a dance class, dancing warped from something pure and expressive into something more fraught. The attraction was obvious: other girls (normal girls) loved dance class. My aspirations to be considered part of a collective, rather than distinctive in my differences, meant I loved dance class too. Did I, though?

I certainly loved movement and feeling as though I belonged. And dance class seemed about the only place where someone would spell out, through direct language and step-by-step demonstration, exactly the right way to be. There was a singular way to do things and getting it wrong was considered part of the process, rather than some kind of major transgression. In that way, dance was a lesson in masking: observe, mimic, practise, repeat.

I also remember the anxiety that came in the lead-up to a class. Fight or flight would kick in and I would struggle to eat or drink or talk. All effort went to swallowing my feelings, shutting down my instincts and trying to appear as relaxed about it all as every other girl waiting outside the community hall or school auditorium with her friends or mum. It felt like a punishment I had willingly signed up for, and I could never recall why I had.

The running joke is that I was very good at quitting dance. I quit Irish dancing, tap dancing, jazz dancing, ballet dancing, contemporary dancing and hip-hop dancing. The bottom of my wardrobe collected shoes designed to help my feet move in different ways. I shudder to think of the hours and dollars spent by my parents on costumes that itched every part of my body. The smell of hairspray still makes me retch.

As a teenager, I moved away from dance and towards entirely different uses of community halls, like Battles of the Bands and local live music. These worked best when paired with alcohol. The escalating agent allowed me to dial down the self-perception and social anxiety, and dial up the sensory enjoyment of noise that made my ears vibrate and hum. It felt, at its best, like the kind of freedom I had found with 'Kokomo' in the living room all those years earlier. But the flip side of binge-drinking, for me, was dangerous and dark. The crinkling of a thermal emergency blanket administered by a faceless paramedic can be found in more than one memory: me like a poisoned burrito wrapped in alfoil, doing my best to not exist within these moments.

Perhaps as a reaction to these experiences – in search of something – I made one brief foray back into dance. It did the trick of moving me on for good. The film *Bring It On* came out in 2000, when I was in Year 7. I was obsessed with it and rewatched it in that very neurodivergent kind of way, memorising lines and intonations and jokes I did not necessarily understand. Cheerleading, despite having no cultural significance in Australia at all, felt important to me, the way many American teen rites of passage have saturated our culture. What would be the Australian equivalent? Netball? I was shit at netball. So, perhaps – no, *of course* – this was a contributing factor when, towards the end of high school, I auditioned for a State of Origin halftime performance that required dancers who would be dressed as cheerleaders. (I make this distinction because the *actual* cheerleaders wore green Xbox uniforms and were required on the sideline for the entire game.) We waved pom-poms and did a few choreographed numbers, me going along with my more talented and far-more-suited-for-the-role friend. Perhaps because by this stage I was a skilled mimic, or perhaps because they needed participants, I made the cut and was given the maroon crop-top and hot pants, along with a schedule for rehearsals and instructions for making my own pom-poms. It all felt very abstract. Sure, I was doing the thing, but was I really?

Apparently, yes. The first sense that this had been a mistake occurred to me as we lined up in the stadium tunnel, waiting to run out onto the field. Emotional processing delays, much? The bitter, sweaty smell of beer turned my stomach, and the leering middle-aged men hanging over the rails to scream aggressive, sexual things at us teenagers (children) did too.

On the field of Suncorp Stadium, in front of a crowd of more than fifty thousand people, I had a moment of profound disassociation. When the other girls turned one way, I stood still, frozen, eyes glazed.

record scratch

freeze frame

Yep, that's me (in the maroon hot pants). You're probably wondering how I ended up in this situation. That's the autism, baby.

Honestly, I still can't perceive myself within the memory of this experience. If I think about it hard enough, I can smell the pyrotechnics, feel my ears ringing, but other than that, it's like watching a movie about someone else. Definitely not a *Bring It On* quality movie either – perhaps closer to one of the five sequels. (Did we know they were still releasing *Bring It On* movies as late as 2022?) Anyway, there were no more dance classes after that, though the intro to 'New Sensation' by INXS does still elicit a Pavlovian response all these years later.

Perhaps the life lesson could have been that I needed to get curious about my struggles with self-perception, dissociation, sensory sensitivities and social anxiety. That would have been swell! Instead, I punted these lessons down the road a good nine years, and instead went with: *dancing feels better when you're drunk*. Cool! And so, dance (the act of moving one's body, rather than the class environment itself) remained an important social masking tool, combined with alcohol, as I turned eighteen. I'm not sure I would have been able to set foot in a club without it. But, as so many of us know, drinking + dancing = an excellent time in the moment – a horrible time in your head the next day. *Hangxiety* is a silly portmanteau, but a seriously horrible state to exist in on the regular.

Since putting a cork in my binge-drinking habits, it has been hard to see memories involving alcohol clearly through the thick smog of shame. Some of that shame is warranted – for foolish actions, cutting words, lack of care for others and myself. But the further I move away from those times, the more clarity I gain. Alcohol was a destructive force in my life, but do I have to throw the baby out with the bathwater?

I love idioms, and this one particularly. Babies are wonderful; wouldn't it be ludicrous to get rid of something as precious as a baby when it is only the water you want gone? Absurd. And so, perhaps in the aforementioned scenario there is some joy worth preserving from nights spent on podiums with my best friend at our favourite club, where the playlist went from 'Livin' on a Prayer' by Bon Jovi to 'New Noise' by Refused, and everywhere in between. Intoxicated mistakes aside (send those down the drain) – we were the baby; *we* were wonderful. These memories are worth holding on to, I can now see. I struggled with binge-drinking *and* I had fun with incredible people. Maybe there is room for mistakes in my teens and early twenties – and maybe mine were relatively understandable, all things considered. Maybe I can treasure imperfection in these memories and make peace with them, rather than burying them completely.

Insert autism diagnosis story here

So, I learnt a thing about myself in my mid-twenties, and soon after I stopped drinking. Good life choices all round. The unfortunate thing was, for a while I found that *without* alcohol and *with* the understanding of myself as autistic, I no longer quite knew how to dance. There was too much perception, too much awareness. You couldn't pay me to enter the wedding dancefloor I previously was unable to leave. All that knowledge and body awareness: gone. What do I do with my arms? Perhaps this information had been encoded in the brain cells killed off by ten years of vodka sunrises and cheap white wine.

Fortunately, though, time has performed its strange, cyclical magic and brought me back to living-room dance parties. This time, I am the mother in the scene rather than the child. And I am doing my best to capture these memories in their entirety (with myself included in them). Ours is a home of musical statues, movie soundtrack performances, YouTube choreography lessons and special interest songs on a loop. Raising an autistic child as an autistic parent at this moment in time, with its growing understanding of neurodivergence, is... intense, man. It is not for the faint of heart. It is profound, all-encompassing, healing, triggering, terrifying, overwhelming, life-giving, beautiful. None of this is to do with the child. (Mine is 10/10, top-tier, no notes.)

It's about outside perception, namely that of a shifting world full of old structures and systems, built with outdated and destructive understandings of what being autistic means. About us parents whose autistic self-perception may have been forged in that fire – but who want greater things, for both the world and our children. This is the community I feel most at home within.

Things are moving too fast for some, but not fast enough for us. We have to actively choose to make generational changes and work hard at healing ourselves every day, while pushing back against those not ready to see things differently. And amid all that, we have to remember to dance with our kids (or swim, or bounce, or run, or play – whatever they are into). Because it is joyful – and we need to prioritise joy. They will remember the songs and the lights and how it feels to be loved as themselves. Their foundations will be stronger than ours ever could have been. While we fight for the big changes we need in schools, medical settings, employment, support spaces, government and our communities, we make our homes neuro-affirming spaces. Within these four walls, you will find acceptance, celebration, peace.

I still don't always have a solid perception of myself; it is too influenced by the extreme weather patterns of my mind. Anxiety hangs around, saying I am not doing enough. Body dysmorphia sometimes makes an appearance, fuelled by burnout and premenstrual dysphoric disorder (PMDD), which disproportionately impacts autistic people, as well as those with ADHD.[3] But I do consider myself a good mum, partner, daughter, sister, friend. Or at least one who is learning and doing their best and cares a lot about the people they love.

And when we are dancing in our 'big room' (which is objectively quite small), I can take a break from perceiving myself. I just need movement and music and mellow lighting – and people I love.

Sources

1. Zamoscik, V, Mier, D, Schmidt, SNL & Kirsch, P 2016, 'Early memories of individuals on the autism spectrum assessed using online self-reports', *Frontiers in Psychiatry*, vol. 7.
2. Crane, L & Goddard, L 2008, 'Episodic and semantic autobiographical memory in adults with autism spectrum disorders', *Journal of Autism and Developmental Disorders*, vol. 38, pp. 498–506.
3. Obaydi, H & Puri, B, 2008, 'Prevalence of premenstrual syndrome in autism: A prospective observer-rated study', *Journal of International Medical Research*, vol. 36, no. 2, pp. 268–72.

autismDARK

Sara Kian-Judge

SARA KIAN-JUDGE (she/her) is an autistically artistic Walbanja-Yuin woman inhabiting a confounding sensory-social world where animals, elements and places speak more familiar languages than other humans. Her art and storytelling draw on shared experiences of dehumanisation between marginalised humans and non-humans, challenging romanticised narratives in favour of the raw, honest personhood of all beings. Currently, Sara is producing a graphic PhD thesis comic alongside multisensory works using everything from soundscapes and shadows to Bat urine and human hair.

'What makes you *sparkle*?'

SPARKLE.

The word makes me feel like I've been punched in the eye with a fistful of grit every time I see or hear it. It cuts and scratches uncomfortably behind my eyelids like glass sandpaper. I feel it on my tongue, up my nose, abrasively irritating. SPARKLE is a new buzzword to describe autistic joy, obsession, and aptitude… yet it makes me feel reduced to a child. One in sensory distress, no less.

I can't think of a more inappropriate word for people who often struggle with bright, dazzling sensory stimuli and with being taken seriously as adults. While SPARKLE might work for some autistic women (and power to them for owning and rocking it), I find it violent. SPARKLE makes me feel as though autism is being used to shove me back into the 'helpless little princess' box that I have kicked and screamed my way out of. The word is too sharp for my eyes to read, my tongue to say, my ears to hear. It physically hurts because of sensory processing difficulties. It psychologically hurts because after years of sensory overload awareness… people still don't get it.

Social media is saturated with autism awareness material like this. Infographics with bright, pastel colour schemes, hyper-patterns side-by-side with hyper-rainbows and suspiciously child-like illustrations of autistic adults make me cringe. Inspirational quotes with palatable depictions of neat, young autistic women running about carefree in manicured, G-rated forests make me straight-up angry. All the messy complexity of my autistic identity gets lost to these watered-down narratives of innocence, fragility and passiveness. I can't find myself (or most of my autistic community) amongst it all.

Autistic-Me is not child-like, colourful, neat, passive or palatable – not by a long shot. The forests I run in aren't tame places styled after placid Disney woodlands. I'm cranky, scruffy-looking, wild, morbid, cynical, outspoken and rough – a multi-layered, deliciously flawed being shaped by pleasures that can be abrasive, disturbing, even downright disgusting to others. My autism is autism**DARK**.

What brings me true joy and a sense of identity is often intense, controversial and weirder than a Bat's spindly wing. Autism**DARK** has impatient teeth that bite hungrily into the alternative and fierce, lurking in the shadows of the strange and primal. My passions are big, bold and rarely gentle. Euphoria can hurtle at turbulent speeds, bursting into uncontrollable flames that burn red-hot for a long time. Autistic-Me is unapologetically a **FEROCIOUS, FERAL FREAK**. I know many other autistic people who comfortably occupy similar spaces, described in different ways.

Yet autism**DARK** doesn't get represented much – presumably because it is neither palatable nor passive. Some of what I describe as autism**DARK** is, in the neurotypical world, sexually fetishised, which is not the case for me. Other things – particularly around smell and behaviour, and their links to perceptions of personal hygiene, mental stability and morality – are socially unacceptable. Being **DARK**ly autistic can come with enormous risk of shame, judgement and persecution.

Frankly, I no longer care.

I adore who I am and I'm excited to write about this part of my autistic identity. I want to be described and understood in complicated, messy, intense ways that reject outdated narratives of the fragile, special, perpetual little girl whose disabling innocence renders her incapable of being an active, outspokenly dissatisfied, sometimes **DARK** force in the world. After all, without **DARK**ness there is no light. In sharing the **FEROCIOUS**, **FERAL** and **FREAK**y aspects of my autism**DARK** identity, I hope to remind you that not all **DARK**ness is evil – and not all that SPARKLEs is good for everyone.

FEROCIOUS

People are often shocked to learn that I – autistic *and* female – love heavy rock and metal music. After all, don't autistic people have sensitive senses needing slow and quiet – the very opposite of what defines these male-dominated genres? For every sensory sensitivity I experience, there is a sensory pleasure that I seek out the way some seek out drug-induced highs. Metal is my favourite poison, indulged in alongside and with equal abandon as men since my teens. Metal makes me **FEROCIOUS**ly strong.

The pounding bass rhythms, the satisfying ripping and engulfing chunks of guitar, the powerfully raw screams… Heavy music speaks a sensory language that I recognise. It rumbles, quakes and strikes like the voices of thunder, crashing oceans and grinding tectonic plates. It is deep and cavernous like the caves that resonate with wind-rush and echo from the guts of the Earth. Metal looms strength, landing heavily with the weight of mountains, the solidity of cliffs, the engulfing gravity of our planet's **FEROCIOUS** core. I love the guttural growls and roars of metal vocals that summon the screeching, shrieking, blood-curdling likeness of nocturnal animal voices.

My autism**DARK** includes intense sensory disturbances and synaesthesia – so it is not to be taken lightly that I willingly choose to pay the social and sensory cost of partaking in live heavy music. The unsurpassed euphoria outweighs the unavoidable difficulties of navigating the crowds and sensory chaos on either side of the music experience itself. I pay for it later, but it's totally worth it.

Mosh pits are among my ultimate sensory-social highs. In the pit, there's no such thing as an excruciating feather-light touch that makes my teeth hurt, only the firm compression of thousands of hot bodies packed together like cells in a surging, heaving, writhing, pulsating beast that moves collectively in a haze of exhilarating conviction and heady sweat-scent. The rhythmic head-banging, flailing arms and running together in circles are like group stimming – and no-one thinks you're weird for doing it there. Mosh pits are communities of people who *know* each other without having to *get to know* each other, united by a common experience of being drawn to music that horrifies – and, for many, heals.

Quiet, invisible individuals become part of an obnoxiously loud, swelling horde releasing frustrations together in a very visible way. Mosh pits are one of the very few times I enjoy being surrounded by humans. Something social is gained from these experiences without ever having to talk to a single person. Just being there, connected in mass physical contact and shared experience, is enough.

People who don't get metal negatively describe it as angry and aggressive. Metal is positively angry – it is **FEROCIOUS**. In solidarity, it expresses anger, frustration and the determination to overcome its source. Metal is powerful music that invites you to take your own stolen power back. I feel especially drawn to bands who wear extreme make-up and masks. It feels like an outward expression of the monstrosity and invisibility many have been made to feel about themselves while turning it into an intimidating, graphic shield of self-empowerment.

Metal has protected me from real monsters. My socioeconomic circumstances once forced me to live for several months next door to a man who had attempted to sexually assault me. Metal played at disgusting volumes from my car created a 'wall of sound' around me every time I had to return to this nightmare, giving me an inner power during a time of powerlessness. Metal reminds me that I am **FEROCIOUS** enough to withstand and stand up to injustice.

With heavy music comes tattoos, another surprising revelation that unsteadies assumptions about autism. I salivate hungrily from the burning pain of needle-delivered ink under my skin, the vibrating buzz of the gun, the intoxicating smell of antiseptic. My numerous self-drawn tattoos are battle scars, stories of survival against the odds. They are warning marks that I am no damsel in distress awaiting rescue. I wear them with **FEROCIOUS** pride.

As a multi-marginalised person, tattoos and heavy music shield me with my own ferocity often – sometimes protectively, sometimes rapturously. Being **FEROCIOUS** is loving and trusting the iron-scaled dragon within my seemingly small, weak exterior. The beast stirs, rising slowly from all fours to hind legs, ready. Its massive heart pounds, shaking the world. Surging forward, it roars unapologetically: *'I am **FEROCIOUS**ly here.'*

FERAL

Ever get that feeling that you're in the wrong skin, where not trying to claw your way out of it to freedom is considered a good day? I've always felt like an animal thrashing around inside a human body-cage. Humans are animals that pretend not to be. They make disgusted faces at the humans who don't play along, calling them names meant to shame. My hunted behaviour, scruffy appearance, disturbing sensory pleasures and strange hygiene habits have led to many descriptive terms: grot, grub, high-strung, volatile, intense, savage, gross, unladylike and – my favourite – **FERAL**.

FERAL means wild, undomesticated, uncivilised. Unlike the word 'wild', it hasn't yet been tamed into a romanticised paradise full of clean, carefree beings recklessly diving into danger and seeking out adventure. When I call myself **FERAL**, it is with the animal definition of wild. Nature isn't clean – there are bugs, smells, parasites, blood, dirt. Nature is very often brutal, where freedom walks in the same tracks as predation, competition and hardship. Wild, **FERAL** beings are governed by survival instincts and connection to the laws of their territories and species. Nothing is done recklessly; survival depends on extreme caution, calculated risks, experience and familiarity.

The **FERAL** of my autism**DARK** is a wild animal living within human nature, full of heightened survival instincts and lowered adaptability to human expectations. **FERAL**-Me is quiet and slow-moving, yet flighty and constantly alert. **FERAL**-Me doesn't care how I look or smell. I'm just another animal, existing and keeping herself alive.

Leaving the safety of my den is always risky. Like many autistics, when cornered or forced into something unfamiliar or unpleasant I become reactive. Escape is a strong instinct. Flighty, high-alert behaviour in non-home situations is an animal experience I relate to like no other. Each sensation is a potential threat. Flinching at every touch, jumping at every sound, the slightest too-fast movement makes me crouch for cover, ready to take off.

If I can't run, I fight. Being trapped or restrained has provoked biting, scratching, hitting, kicking, spitting and shrieking more than once. Fighting is **FERAL** taking over. Survival mode awakens. It's life or death now; I'll hurt anyone preventing me from escaping the danger or die trying.

My **FERAL** is territorial and competitive. I don't like uninvited people in my space. My home is a carefully negotiated alliance between the humans and animals living there together; disruptions to that balance are threatening. Choosing a mate was a fussy process; now he is proudly defended. He and the many animals who rely on our leadership and protection in our home motivate me towards the pursuit of meeting our collective life needs. Competition is never healthy. I compete as though losing means death and arrogantly, antagonistically boast my triumphs in symbolic displays of behavioural and sensory territory-marking. I talk big, I advertise my awesome presence, I put my stuff in other people's spots and use their things.

There's **FERAL** elation too. It's easy to forget that I occupy a poorly equipped human body until perched on cliff-edges resisting the urge to leap into flight without wings. Full moons and thunderstorms provoke an insatiable desire to be outside, running around wide-eyed and manic, leaping up at the sky, and howling loudly to the ever-present forces of planetary creation.

My favourite game is hiding in the bush, drunk on the sensation of hunting and being hunted by others.

FERAL is uncivilised by human standards, a complete sensory disregard for what is considered 'nice'. Following birds and interesting smells I bush-wander barefoot, dragging bits of crunchy leaf and scraping stick in my torn skirt. Dirt lodges under my toenails and in the creases of my foot-soles for days. Reaching into murky waters, my hands caress the languid, slimy bodies of gliding Eels in motion. A cooling lie-down in sandy Wallaby digs gives time to think about their beating hearts and hungry bellies just like mine – even if it means risking a tick. Parasites aren't so bad – I enjoy the suction-like stretch and popping release of pulling Leeches from my flesh, feeling bloody teardrops dribble from their kisses. With an itchy twitch of fascination, I watch Mosquitos suck my blood.

Being **FERAL** is disgusting to others – especially when you're female. It's somewhat expected and acceptable for men to be a bit gross, but not women. **FERAL** women with all their shameful extra curves, crevices and wetness are *especially* offensive because they don't fit the neat, ladylike narrative. Autistic women get a double dose of stereotypes, with media portrayals as fastidiously clean germaphobes committed to rigid orderliness. **FERAL** autistic women are part of the unsexy disability trope of failing, unclean people who cannot care for themselves.

Well, I love being **FERAL**. **FERAL** is the human-animal autism**DARK** remembers how to be, unapologetically enjoying the scents of the body and world I inhabit.

Smell is identity; without it I feel uncomfortably bare. The scentlessness of clean disturbs, like fading out of existence. If I can't smell myself, I panic. Days can pass between showers, comfortable in my own scent. River or seawater bathing is always preferrable to stripped, chemically deodorised water. After washing, olfactory identity is immediately restored by wearing used clothing. Artificial fragrances used to cover up the bodily smells that humans have taught ourselves to be disgusted by sting my nose and ring in my ears like sharp noise.

The scent and taste of many bodily flavours are guilty pleasures not well received in a civilised human world. No-one wants to hear, see or feel relentless licking and sucking on salty skin, bleeding wounds or hair. The scent of thick menstrual blood and cervical fluids – unless sexualised – are not to be enjoyed. To observers, a nose buried deep in a plastic bag full of raw meat is more nauseating than 'quirky'.

As a smell-driven **FERAL**, oral sensations are never far away. Intense bodily odours – my own and others – rain salivation into my mouth. My teeth quiver under my licking tongue, suddenly more sensitive to their sharpness. Barely cooked meat is savoured with deep, heavy bites and the primal satisfaction of slowly tearing threads of flesh apart. I love animals more than humans, and I also love eating animals. I am okay with the idea that an animal might eat me too. I have killed animals for food and to end their suffering. None of this is ethically complicated for me.

It's sensory, it's social and it's perfectly **FERAL**.

FREAK

Historically used to ridicule and ostracise people with physical, neurological, and psychological differences, **FREAK** is a word that many autistic people continue to have painful experiences with. Hurled with targeted hatred and ridicule at my very existence, **FREAK** dehumanised and damaged my confidence in everything I knew and loved about myself. It convincingly turned my differences into wrongness. **FREAK** is the most violent, ugly reason for an exhausting, self-defeating adulthood of relentless autism masking.

Yet no amount of masking can fully hide a **FREAK**. **FREAK** doesn't just mean someone who is weird, strange or obsessed with unusual, peculiar interests and activities. **FREAK** means too different to fully hide, too different to be safely ignored. I will always be considered a **FREAK** in a world unwilling to accept extreme difference. I will never be able to entirely hide it or be happy doing so. What is called **FREAK** is who I am, so it should serve me – not the hateful people shouting it.

Today, **FREAK** means openly living my differences, an unmasking and healing of autism**DARK**. Once used to shame, **FREAK** now celebrates my strange, eccentric ways of being and my obsessive love for the peculiar, macabre and obscure.

FREAK is off with the fairies, seeing, hearing and feeling imagined things like real. Inside my head exists a whole world and life behind unblinking eyes. In this mind-place, I can time travel, shapeshift and world-build freely. It's a place where I know all the social rules. The people and events of this world are as real to me as this world, sometimes they get confusingly tangled together. Talking about this other world is dangerous – at best you're a **FREAK** who lies. At worst, your imagination linked with sensory synaesthesia and social difference is misdiagnosed as psychoses that don't fit well enough to hold true but enough to be dangerously mis-medicated.

FREAK is feeling creaturely. When describing the anatomy of Bat wings, I physically feel my arm and hand transformed into a spindly, membranous limb. Sometimes being animal isn't creaturely enough. Werewolves, dragons, vampires, *aos sí*, witches and ghosts lure my senses into their extreme otherness. I can't feel or imagine wearing my own face or body, but can easily see myself with scales, horns, fangs and claws. I'm not just obsessed with creatures, I become a creature. Sadness and nostalgia feel spectral, like becoming a see-through apparition. When remembering those who have passed, I feel their faces instead of my own as though my body is haunted by their ghosts.

I haunt places, too. **FREAK** revisits places where dead animals have been found. Watching decay is reading stories of life threading back into the Earth. Touching old bones is remembering the beauty of death turning one life into another, the continuous chain of all existence. Forgotten cemeteries, still and quiet, bring so much peace. I lie on old graves to think and dream, run my fingers over the stone-etched names, existing nonverbally with humans who no longer speak head-splitting words. Old, abandoned buildings and places leave echoes of long-gone humans whose less-intense presence wraps around me like a story, another experience of being with people without being *with people*.

FREAK dwells in weird, **DARK** histories. Opening a cabinet of curiosities or performing candle-lit rituals is sure to get my full attention. Though fascination with ritualistic practices made me vulnerable to childhood indoctrination, it also opened a fantastically **FREAK**-worthy journey into strange occultic histories. From a young age I was tempted into taboo forms of 'black' witchcraft, paganism and bizarre cults that indulged my love of formulas, principles and philosophies about how and why things are.

The weirder and more unknowable the history, the more I'm drawn like a moth to a flame. Subcultures live on in the unexplained oddities, secret folklore, occult objects, mysterious encounters and cautionary tales of the past. Their voices are preserved in the exaggerated misunderstandings of the single-storied, narrow-minded societies who tried to erase them. In these histories are clues to the past lives of people like me. Though they are often heartbreakingly tainted by atrocities, they also speak of the tenacity, wisdom, creativity and resistance of extreme others. They are histories of the different, stories from the social underground – the stolen, silenced and persecuted lives of those who absolutely could not hide.

No-one should need to hide who they are or what brings them joy just because it's different. That's all **FREAK** really means – unhidden, unhide-able difference. **FREAK** only exists because fear and intolerance of difference still dominates – especially when difference is **DARK**. So what if I'd like to be a shadow-lurking werewolf or thundering dragon. So what if I'm not afraid to rattle old bones. So what if my mind thrives when off with bad fairies, drifting somewhere between here and fantastic. Why does it matter so much to others what happens in my own world?

Like most **FREAK**s, I'm quite happy being left alone there.

THE BLACK, BROWN & GREY PARTS OF THE SPECTRUM

Autism**DARK** doesn't *SPARKLE.* I'm not childlike. I'm not helpless. I'm not an inspirational quote emerging from tragedy. I am a **FEROCIOUS, FERAL FREAK** – and I love it. These are the strongest, most empowering, most enduring parts of my autistic identity. Autism**DARK**, in all its forms and ways, is about celebrating otherness, invisibility made visible and raw sensory-social difference openly indulged despite judgement.

Austism**DARK** doesn't *SPARKLE. SPARKLE* launches an attack on my autism. Too many bright, shiny colours disrupt my senses, plunging them into vertigo, dizziness, nausea. *SPARKLE* makes me feel belittled, degraded and humiliated as an autistic woman.

Autism**DARK** doesn't *SPARKLE.* It burns, growls, surges, smells, bites, haunts and howls. It swears too much to create verbal rhythms and time to think. It gets angry about social injustices and the state of the Planet. It thinks humans are ridiculous, infuriating animals.

Autism**DARK** doesn't *SPARKLE.* It drapes itself in a lot of black. Black feels soft like velvet or fur. Black smells like smoke and herbs. Black sings in voices that grow from silent shadows, moving from slow tones into thunderous rhythms. Black tastes like metallic cherries.

If some want to *SPARKLE*, great. I don't want to *SPARKLE.* And I don't want *SPARKL*ing or any other form of infantilising narratives or stereotyping to dominate how autism is thought about and represented. I want there to be room for the **FEROCIOUS**, the **FERAL** and the **FREAK**ish, too – because autistic people deserve the same right to darkness, complexity and non-mainstream paths of self-determination as everyone else.

Autism**DARK** isn't for everyone; neither is autism *SPARKLES* and all the colourful, bright infographics. Autistm**DARK** is for me; it is who I am and who I love being… So, I'm here, representing the tattooed folks in black band shirts, dirty bare feet, imagined dragon scales and so much more. It's been liberating writing this stuff out loud for once – maybe I'll draw an autism**DARK** infographic next.

SARA KIAN-JUDGE

A SHAMELESSLY AUTISTIC GUIDE TO ROMANTIC LONGING

Jerico Mandybur

JERICO MANDYBUR (she/they) is an author, arts therapist, creativity coach and tarot reader. They have published five books and tarot decks, including the award-winning *Neo Tarot: A fresh approach to self-care, healing and empowerment*, and their books have been published in seven languages. Jerico's work has been featured in *New York Magazine*, *LA Times*, *The New York Times*, *Vogue*, *The Guardian*, *Refinery29* and many more – and they've been a guest on programs including ABC's *RN Drive* and Triple J's *The Hook Up*. In 2022 they gave a TEDx talk on the power of authentic, autistic self-expression, called 'The world needs weirdos'.

You are a rockstar. The lead singer in a band. Not only can you shred on guitar, but your voice is transcendent. Just the right amount of pain and poetry. You're wearing a babydoll dress that looks great on you. Your posture is perfect. You move with fierce, distinctive grace. You seem a little drunk, but it's only because you're so cool. Your set list is full of songs that already exist. But in this place and time, they're originals. And at just the most lyrically apt moment, you make eye contact. Looking up at you, with appropriate horniness, is The One. The person who hurt you. This is the moment when they realise that, wait, they're actually in love with you…

If you're obsessed with love, you're no stranger to this form of maladaptive daydreaming centred on romantic longing. We see this pining dynamic everywhere in our culture. It's very *Beauty and the Beast*. It's *Labyrinth*, it's *Pretty in Pink* and *Clueless*, it's *Reality Bites* and *Wuthering Heights*. And rereading *Wuthering Heights*. It's Hollywood and Bollywood. It's endless journal scribbling and mixtapes on mixtapes on playlists. It's the state of being exceedingly interested in a frenemies-to-lovers brand of lovesick yearning. And it's bootcamp for twenty- to thirty-something manic pixie autistic girls.

What's redemptive about a special interest-cum-perspective on romance conveniently informed by patriarchal power dynamics? One, not much. But, two, it whittles you into a shape so resilient, so singular in passion and sentimentality that you have no choice but to dedicate your life to art. There is no room for the bored or boring here. Only those who burn.

So, here it is, a shamelessly autistic guide to romantic longing. (The author will not be held personally liable in the case of toxic partners or results. Generalisations incoming.)

A fearless moral inventory

The first step to admitting you're hyperfixated on romance, as you might have guessed, is auditing your mind. Where does your mental energy go, really? Be honest. If you spend more than a few hours per day in an imaginal state similar to the one described above, then congratulations! You're likely a fellow chronically misunderstood bullying survivor with early developmental trauma :)

Of course, this isn't always the case. But, let's be honest, someone did hurt you. I'm yet to meet an autistic woman or femme of any gender who hasn't been looked over, laughed at, mocked, lied to or outright tricked by a love interest. Perhaps it's because we're 'gullible' and trust easily. We hear that a lot. Or perhaps it's because we can relate to someone else's experience and position exceedingly well, making it easier to justify our occasional ethical relativism, if not our mistreatment. But universally, it seems, we have a deep longing for connection. For being fully seen in our complexity, by any means necessary. Enter a love interest elated by our unique perspective, quirky dress sense and naive promiscuity.

Magical thinking

How do you find a love interest to obsess over to begin with? My advice is manifestation. (Hear me out.) You need to live and breathe romance. In all its pleasures and sorrows. You need to wake up every day and decide, again, to put yourself in front of love. You need to walk down the street like it's a significant moment in a musical and seek out beauty like a dowsing rod seeks water. That way, even if you *don't* find it, you'll find someone or something willing to resemble it, if only for a while. It's as simple as walking up to someone who's single and saying something confidently weird enough for them to think, *I bet she's good in bed.*

While that might sound nice, if foreboding, it's a hard life. Not for everyone. You'll be required to think and act as if there's an arthouse-film camera following you around. This is called masking. Living as if the voyeur is in your own head. As if, to quote Margaret Atwood in *The Robber Bride*, 'you are a woman with a man inside watching a woman'. Now that you're suitably exhausted, you're ready to embody the sad boy or masc's fantasy of broken and beautiful. An easy confidante. Albeit one who cries a lot.

The co-conspirator

Who is this boy or masc? (If you're dealing with a femme-for-femme dynamic, you'll need a whole separate tome.) Likely they share your autistic subtype or are tap dancing on the edge of it, although they probably don't care to be told that. Either way, they'll feel you're distinctly easy to talk to and enjoy the following aspects of your relationship:

You communicate 'at' each other, relishing a captive audience and taking turns to share various interests and niche expertise in the style of a lecture, rather than a back-and-forth conversation.

You trade emotional truths via indirect means, letting films or music or literature go some way to make up for what you can't verbalise, or even acknowledge, directly.

You spend all your time together one on one, preferring to give the other your full attention away from the mundane, distracting or just stressful outside world. This will often include digital, rather than face-to-face, communication, which has the added bonus of giving you time to process what was said and respond cutely.

Unfortunately, if you want to be about that shameless romantic longing life, you'll have to deal with the downsides of this dynamic as well.

Because both of you have low self-esteem, neither of you will volunteer (or, again, even acknowledge) your true feelings.

Instead, you'll prefer to stay in the early, vague-pursuit phase. Forever sensing a strong affinity and yet forever feeling each other out. Unrequited romance is what's known and therefore safe. Good for you, for sticking to a routine!

Whether you like it or not, this person's – or multiple people's – presence in your life is going to take every ounce of your attention. You'll think about them when working, you'll imagine various scenarios involving them before bed, and you'll neglect the actually healthy interests you have in favour of fantasising about all the ways you could transform them into a demonstrably adoring lover – as opposed to a hyper-verbal, autistic-friendly conversationalist and sex partner.

Get ready to doubt your entire reality. What did they mean when they said *that*? What are they thinking when they're *not* saying anything? That's for Goddess to know, and you – gifted detective that you are – to find out. Naturally, the more you try, the more they'll distance themselves. The arc of romance is long and it bends towards unfulfilled yearning.

Make sex weird

Listen, autistic people have a hyper- or hypo-sexual sex drive; either way it will be seen to be weird. So, why not lean into it and make it even weirder? If things between you and the object of your romantic longing are feeling a little too intimate, rather than your brand of unrequited, add back in some hesitancy or mistrust by: saying someone else's name in bed, acting a little too 'performative', refusing to kiss them due to an undisclosed sensory trigger or immediately launching into a niche-interest lecture as you wrap up, instead of cuddling. If all those fail, just tell them about all the other people you're sleeping with. Hell, tell *them* to sleep with more people. Assume a shared philosophical stance on polyamory, despite your emotional devotion to them and the fact that you're a Scorpio. What could go wrong? Granted, these aren't always things ~~I've done~~ you'll do with the conscious intention to create distance, but the impact will be the same.

Grist for the mill, baby. The machine of romantic longing won't fuel itself! It needs fresh sacrifices and you are the visionary Joan of Arc of yearning: sooner dying a misjudged martyr than changing your learnt, habitual approach to romance. What you lose in real love, you gain in a more acute depth of feeling and creative inspiration. Heroic.

Be inconsistent

Romantic longing is nothing without grudges. Thankfully, autistics know how to burn a bridge. So, here's what you do: build a whole imagined relationship with, and world around, a person. Create the canon. Develop the origin stories, antagonists and quests. Then, when they do (or don't do) something – real or imagined – to show you they don't care about you, smite them with the heat of a thousand suns. Hell hath no fury like an autistic person, pretending not to be in love, predictably scorned.

In other words, burning a bridge is easy. You just harness all your fixed, black-and-white thinking, and recall one by one every hurtful, flippant or stupid thing a lover has ever said or done. If you've spent any length of time purposefully obscuring someone's flaws and icks, this will be easy to do. Play these over and over in your mind as you block the person from all means of contact. Remove their number. Delete their emails. Rip out the pages that mention them in your diary. Write a list of all the ways they screwed you over and the ways that every kind thing they ever said to you (Were there even that many to begin with?) was a lie. Once you've done that, stew in your anger for anywhere from six months to two years before lovelorn cravings get the better of you and you unblock them again. When communication resumes, for Goddess's sake, act casual.

Let love in

While you might be tempted to be mortified by your own capacity for love-related self-harm, please remember that this is a *shamelessly* autistic guide to romantic longing. Like all aspects of being autistic and a woman or femme, an intense interest in the hide-and-seek, push-pull nature of romance can be both a burden and a gift.

Where's the gift in longing? Longing reveals a depth of emotion – a love so grand – that reality alone can't contain it. When your heart has the capacity to hold all the love it can ever possibly imagine, when it can direct it to one person or to multiple people, you know that it's strong. That you are alive to feel everything. To forge real connections. To cultivate a passion so big that just being in your body feels like being on fire.

If you've been blessed-cursed with a longing heart and a confusing mind, you're the kind of sensitive, blazing autistic person with an artist's destiny. You're a poet. Don't try to change the way you're wired. Don't engage with anyone who doesn't treasure you for it. You know, better than anyone, how to let love possess and hurt and utterly consume you. And you've been bestowed the opportunity to understand and express something key to the human experience because of it. Something not everyone has the words or imagination for. Something beautiful.

And guess what else? You deserve to be – you can be and maybe even will be – profusely, fervently, unashamedly longed for in return.

THE WORD MADE FLESH

Alison Sampson

ALISON SAMPSON is an ordained Baptist minister, a writer and a dreamer who has had a lifelong love affair with Jonah. She spent seven years pastoring Sanctuary, an emerging faith community in Warrnambool, where queer, neurodivergent and questioning folk found a home and assumptions about church were exploded. She is passionate about creating safe spaces for people to explore faith, share their stories and encounter a loving God. Alison's writing has been published in *The Age*, *Eureka Street*, *Zadok Perspectives* and elsewhere; she has won multiple Australian Religious Press Association awards. Find more of her work at <alisonandthewhale.com>.

In the beginning was the word: for the word is the womb of the world. Before words, the world is dark, shadowy, formless. It makes no sense; it tells no story. But with the word, everything is made light: so at dawn I rose and slipped outside and collected the word. *The Age* newspaper, wet with dew, lying on a star-dappled lawn. I brought it in and copied it out and taught myself to read; and, at half-past six, took printed word and hand-lettered straggle to my parents' bed for them to read aloud and speak the world into being.

The word, the words, the rollicking words became my joy and my delight. *In the word was life*: with fullness and savoury mouthfeel. *Rambunctious. Mephistophelian. Rapscallion. Flibbertigibbet.* Words like these rolled like raspberries in my mouth-mind, sharp and sweet and juicy.

But ah! Sunday school. Now, that was sawdust to my mind. Drab and dry and shallow words, *told by an idiot, full of sound and* blurry, *signifying nothing.* Thank God for songs and stories and fistfuls of fresh bread.

And for my mother's words, spun from the pulpit from time to time. No dull doctrine for her, but *word made flesh* in women's sewing circles seen through gospel eyes; vulnerable folk and refugee friends were given an honoured place in the story. My mother was a pastor, you see, one of the first Baptist women in formal ministry. She was deeply empathic, spoke passionately, transformed lives and was adored by all. But at home, she had daily meltdowns. She was the volcano I turned to books to avoid; stories were my safe harbour. *When all about you // Are losing theirs and blaming it on you*: tune out, shut down, turn the page and read another story.

Like Jonah. The first time I read Jonah, I was hooked. Jonah was a man sent on a mission against his will. I was a child dragged around churches against my will, and the experience nearly swallowed me up. I became rageful and resentful. We moved every two years or so, spreading the word, speaking the words, living the word, and meanwhile I was wondering what it was all about. I rarely made friends, never fit in, hated school and felt like an alien everywhere.

Even worse for a minister's kid, I was an atheist child. Words were my good news, my gospel, my delicious drug of choice, but the words I mumbled in my night-time prayers mashed flat against the ceiling. *God bless Mummy and God bless Daddy* and why is Mummy so angry? *God bless Grandpa*, unbending as iron and anxious as the day is long. *God bless my sister and God bless me*, but why do I never fit in? *God make me a good little girl*, but I don't know what it is to feel like a girl, or to feel like a boy, either – what's that all about? *Guard my lips from evil*, but when I speak they say I'm brutal. Why does truth make people mad? What am I supposed to say? If my prayers didn't fall so flat I might have asked, *God, what the hell is wrong with me?*

Instead, I encountered an angry man who ran away from God. *Do this*, said God, and Jonah said, *No, thanks*, and fled in the opposite direction. It led, of course, to high seas and chaos and that fateful encounter with the whale that swallowed him up. And words. Among *billows and waves* and *the deep* and *weeds wrapped around [his] head at the roots of the mountains*, Jonah prayed and made his vows. *Deliverance belongs to God*, he said. *I will sacrifice to you.*

Words and whales and vows: they planted a seed which lay dormant for years while I hung around churches and slammed out of churches and came back *like a dog returns to its own vomit*. But *even the dogs eat the crumbs*, vomit-encrusted or not, and some of those crumbs were good.

So I began questioning words: theological words, sermon words, words like *faith* and *love*. I wondered if *truth* had to mean science, or whether truth could also be found in stories. I pondered the psalms, I played with parabolic puzzle-boxes, I attended to daily prayers. And gradually, tentatively, on high alert, I slowly returned to church. But when they asked me to take on formal roles, I'd think of my angry mother and shudder. I'd yell, *What, are you crazy?* and, like Jonah, find a boat headed in the other direction.

It seems I'm more stubborn than him: this happened more than once. But God sent high seas and storms, and sailors to throw me overboard and whales to swallow me and hold me fast in the sub-sea belly-womb, where I could swim in murk and words and gloom, and where one day I prayer-dreamed a typewriter.

Gradually, tentatively, on high alert, I began to write. Words to make meaning of my life and faith, blogging words, parenting words, words to swim and wallow in. Words that made me laugh or cry, or riffed on an older story. And gradually, tentatively, on high alert, some of those words became sermon words or printed words: and those words became gifts to others who hadn't found the words to say and were grateful when they heard them.

I searched out rippling, rolling, robust words, loving words, life-giving words, words that shone truth *bright like a diamond* into dank, dark, dimly lit places. I found words that sheltered little birds, and gave them rest and nourishment. I used old words, well-manured words, emerging from the rotted shit and compost of our lives. I found words to evoke the mystery and wonder of language that speaks us into being, and I showed other people how to use their words and share their stories, too. Indeed, that which came into being through *the word was life*, as the words we prayed and the words we found brought more love and light into the world.

But my words spoke from the margins to the margins, emerging as they did from a quirky woman at a suspect church where nothing looked 'normal' to the powers that be. So despite the call of the church and the affirmation of the people, it was hard to get ordained. The denomination didn't know what to do with me; I didn't fit at all. I was female where they expected male, spiky where they expected feminine, truthful where they expected nice. When they sought certainty, I asked questions; when they wanted answers, I told a rambling story. When they longed for a pat on the head and a biscuit, I gave a sermon that turned their world upside down. And my empathy scores were off the charts: a problem, said the testing psychologist; how do you establish good boundaries with empathy levels like these?

I didn't know what to say except, *When you feel pain because someone else is hurting, you sit alongside them very gently* and *I am fascinated by mirror neurons and commune with people that way.* She didn't know what to think, so she told me about her trauma. I didn't know I was autistic then. Nor, I think, did she. I just wondered at her own boundaries as I gently held her story and helped her on her way.

Eventually we got through, and at my ordination I painted a word picture of a future church that made our trans friends cheer and the atheists laugh and the bishop curl up like a snail. The truth-telling tendency is most often appreciated by those who are outside the church, I find, or dancing at the edges. On the edges I was, and am, and always will be, especially now I'm telling this story.

What next? I moved from inner-city Melbourne to do something new in southwest Victoria. I was an inner-city feminist sent to the bastion of country conservatism; a kid who grew up in a bilingual church moving to the whitest place in Australia; an introvert going about the extroverted business of meeting strangers and planting a church. It was one of God's little jokes: the belly laugh that spit me up, weedy and gasping, on the shore of a city with whales.

My work was among folk who had left church or been kicked out of church and were trying to make sense of their world. Gay folk. Trans folk. Questers and questioners, agnostics and seekers, and a surprising number of autistic kids. I knew nothing about autism, but quickly learned a thing or two. We set up in an old hall and I was given carte blanche. For once, I could make church as I imagined it to be: intergenerational, colourful, gentle and fierce. No crashing cymbals, no corporate blandness, no theatre-style seating. Instead, we had muted colours, lots of them, and a cappella singing, with soft furnishings, op-shop chairs, playful paintings and crocheted rugs. I found ways to pray with words that ripple and roll off the tongue and ways to pray with no words at all, but through movement and sensory practice. In a region brutalised by clergy abuse, I made a safe place for vulnerable people, traumatised people, queer people, autistic people, guarded by angels with flaming swords – or, at least, a strong and determined woman wielding a robust Safe Church Policy. In sermons and services and pastoral conversations, I spoke strengthening, truthful, playful words that drew in diverse people and honoured their lives. Stories were told and tears were shed and rooms would fill with the rich, heavy presence that lies beyond words, beyond silence.

Many of the people turned out to have sensory needs and all-encompassing passions, and many of those passions looked like *tikkun olam* – that is, work for the healing of the world. They were sustainability officers and market gardeners and growers of Indigenous plants; they were therapists and artists and teachers and lawyers. Some of them worked in overseas development, while others sought justice and healing at home. One of the people who joined the gathering was autistic psychologist Dr Wenn Lawson, who writes, speaks and teaches about neurodivergence.

Soon after we met, Wenn began giving me books. At first, I read them to be polite. I like stories, not theories, but I'm interested in what makes other people tick. So I turned the pages and gradually learned a whole host of new words: Autism. ADHD. Neurodivergent. Alexithymic.[1] Interoception.[2] Echolalia.[3] Executive functioning. Time distortion.[4] And monotropism, developed by Wenn with Dinah Murray.[5]

I learned that monotropic minds tend to be deeply engaged with a small number of interests at any given time, leaving fewer resources for other neurological processes. So, for example, they become hyperfocused on an interesting task and don't notice they're hungry until their world implodes. Reading about this, I heard echoes of my mother's exasperation at my father's one-track mind, and how I'd be so completely lost in a story I'd not notice the calls then the shouting as I failed to turn up to dinner. Wenn and Dinah argue that monotropism can explain nearly all the features commonly associated with autism, which was all very interesting – but it was also sounding uncomfortably familiar.

While serving the congregation, I had been surprised by how often people reminded me of my grandfather or my mother, but now I kept being surprised by something in this book or that which reminded me of myself. I began thinking about myself in new ways, with these new words, trying them on for size. I was reluctant at first, because who wants more labels? But I gradually came to realise they fit like a glove, or a lens that brings the world into focus. I took a bunch of online autism-screening tests and came out A+++, no grey areas at all, and quietly pondered and wondered about these new words, a whole new world being revealed.

And not just my world, but my family's too. Gradually, I realised my fundamentalist grandfather hadn't meant to be rigid and harsh; he only knew how to do things by the Book. My mother hadn't screamed at me because I was a failure; she was a perfectionist racked with anxiety and was melting down daily. And as I began to see these things in sharp relief, I came to realise that I'm okay.

I've always known I'm a bit weird, a bit quirky, and for some reason can't seem to perform normal. For this, I have often struggled to fully accept and inhabit myself. I never feel hungry, only suddenly, blindly enraged. I can never really answer when you ask how I feel, because I can only tell you tomorrow. I can never perform femininity, because no gender cloak seems to fit. Sometimes when I speak, people say I'm being brutal; yet when I'm overwhelmed in a group setting and stay quiet, I'm told I fail to contribute. I can't think clearly with many background sounds or fluorescent lights, which makes most shopping and professional gatherings a nightmare. I can easily do interesting, complex tasks, but to call a plumber takes months. And to the disdain of every medical receptionist, I might be able to talk my children through a body scan of emotions and help them decompress, but I can never ever remember their birth dates.

But as I read, I realised that my eccentricities and failings – my strange aversion to synthetic fibres, busy patterns, cosmetics and fragrance, my need to walk, my verbal tics, and all the other things I have tried to hide or change about myself – aren't problems to be fixed but simply me through and through. And I realised that without the brain that has these quirks I wouldn't have my way of seeing and speaking the world into being, or the passion to create safe, life-giving spaces for others. In a powerful and healing way, I came to understand that *I am fearfully and wonderfully made*, and now accept and celebrate it all. As this new understanding washed through me, I began to know the clean scent of forgiveness: for myself, for my angry mother, and for the systems and institutions that do not know how to hold a person like me. But for a while, I kept things to myself.

Then, one day, while Wenn and I were chatting, I suddenly blurted out a waterfall of words. *Wenn, I need to take off my pastoral hat for a moment. You keep lending me books. I'm reading them to understand the congregation and how to pastor them better, but I keep on seeing me. Is it possible, I mean, I'm kind of wondering, I think I might be, you know, autistic. You're the psychologist. What do you think?* And his face broke open with a smile like God's. *I've been waiting for you to ask*, he said.

So: Alison. Jonah. Quirky. Christian. Pastor. Preacher. Autistic. Alexithymic. Not quite non-binary, but not far off it. My memories of the past are all crumpled together; the future is a blur, unplannable. Deeply empathic, I'll know my own feelings tomorrow; I'm a paradox postponed. I create fierce and gentle spaces for queer and neurodivergent and questioning folk; we dance at the margins of the church. And I'm filled with passion for words for the healing of myself, and for the life and healing of the world. Indeed, *the word* – so many words – *became flesh and lived among us and we have seen the glory... full of grace and truth*. And for these words, this flesh, this grace, this truth, this overflowing fountain of good and glorious language, for this boundless joy in a world of tears, and for my place and role within it: thanks be to God, and thanks be to God, and *Yes*, I say, *yes*, and *Amen*.

As we all know, autistic people have no sense of self, no theory of mind, no empathy, no sense of rhythm, no sense of humour, subnormal language skills and nothing to contribute to this world. At least, that's what I've been told.

Sources

1. Alexithymic people find it hard to identify or respond to emotions in themselves or others.
2. Related to alexithymia, low interoception makes it difficult to identify or respond to internal signals, whether physical (e.g. hunger, fatigue, pain) or emotional (e.g. anger, fear, delight). Happily, this is a skill which can be learned through the use of body scanning and other techniques.
3. Echolalia is a conversational habit where a person repeats what another person has said. Sometimes this is to buy time to sort out what was said and frame an acceptable response. Sometimes it's to practise conversational skills such as language acquisition and turn-taking. Sometimes it's for the sheer joy of riffing, such as the way I use other people's phrases in this essay or quote and play on lines from books, TV and movies in conversational banter.
4. Many autistic people experience time distortion. That is, they have an impaired sense of the passage of time which affects not only day-to-day experience but also memory and planning.
5. A theory developed by, for and about autistic people – see <monotropism.org>.

MONOTROPIC SUPERDRIVE AT HOME

Fergus Murray

FERGUS MURRAY (they/them) is a writer, science tutor and autistic community organiser based in Edinburgh, Scotland. They have been involved in several autism research projects and co-authored a number of papers, as well as contributing chapters to several academic books, but deny being a real autism researcher. Fergus was a co-founder of AMASE (Autistic Mutual Aid Society Edinburgh) in 2017, and was its Chair from 2021–2025; they also served on the board of Autscape, an autistic conference/retreat, for a few years. Their writing has been published in the *Psychologist* and *Thinking Person's Guide to Autism*, among other places. They run <monotropism.org> and <weirdpride.day>.

Growing up 'weird'

I realised I was weird when I was pretty young. Other kids kept telling me so – I expressed myself weirdly, I reacted weirdly, I occupied myself doing weird things. I had no interest in team sports and often struggled to join in with other games. If I was raised in a different family, this might have been a real blow to my self-esteem, but my mum (Dinah Murray) had long since come to terms with her own weirdness, and neither of my brothers seemed particularly concerned with being seen as 'normal'. When I thought about it, all of my favourite characters from stories – fictional or historical – also seemed to be pretty weird. Very often, they were bullied for it too. So I learned to take 'weird' as a compliment, or at worst, a neutral observation. If someone thought it was an insult, they had obviously misunderstood something fairly basic about the world: all the most interesting people are weirdos.

Like many unidentified autistic kids who don't grow up hating themselves, I took pride in what I *could* do and decided that caring about the things I struggled with was silly. Who wants to be seen as *normal*? Football is rubbish anyway. Lying is bad and causes unnecessary confusion, even if it's to spare someone's feelings. Correct spelling and grammar are very important.

While it helped get me through many difficult years of school, it is important to recognise the dangers in this sort of attitude. Taking pride in the things that make you stand out is generally healthy and should be encouraged. Looking down on people who lack those characteristics is the path to Aspie supremacy, which ultimately leads to people like Elon Musk. Pinning your self-esteem on talents is always a risky strategy anyway: sooner or later your talents will fail, you'll meet people who are much better at your Thing than you are, or – horror of horrors – you will get bored of it. It is vital that people understand, from an early age, that they are valued as human beings, not just for what they can do.

There is another train of thought that risks leading people in the same sort of direction, and that I recognise in my own upbringing, to a point. This is the idea of families whose eccentricities and distinctive contributions should be celebrated. As my mother, Dinah, wrote in her chapter 'One that got away', in the book that she edited about coming out as autistic:

> I suspect most 'autistic cousins' as well as those more clearly on the spectrum, will have a similar sense of having grown up as members of an interesting and unusual family. With luck and care that can give them a sense of being special in a good way and also a sense of belonging.

I think this is true, and again, it is not the celebration that is the problem, but the idea that what makes you distinctive makes you *better*. It is possible to cultivate pride in your family and roots without developing a sense of superiority about it, but as Dinah says, it takes luck and care. In our case, I think it helped that fighting for equality was a recurring feature of our family history. As she wrote in 'One That Got Away':

> The environment I grew up in welcomed and respected my intellectual turn of mind and universalising egalitarianism, and accepted such oddities as I revealed: this certainly minimised disaster and strengthened confidence.

I *like* that I come from a line of thinkers known for their focus on injustice, and for taking unusual perspectives on problems and attacking them with passion. I also know that this legacy is not something I did anything to earn; that plenty of people don't have anything like this; and that like any family, we have our share of problems and struggles. Still, it is true that an awareness of our eccentric family history helped me, and my mother before me, to feel confident and accepted, growing up weird (and, as it turns out, autistic) in a world where the idea of neurodiversity had not yet been formulated. I hope that it is a comfort to my brothers' children too. I feel particularly lucky that, thanks to my mother's work, we avoided the incredulity and resistance that many people meet when they first suggest to family members that they are neurodivergent. I know that in some families I might have met comments along the lines of 'surely that's normal, we're all like that – you're just being a Thistlethorpe!'

The birth of Monotropism

Fifteen years before publishing that chapter, Dinah had read a book about autism, and – relating it to her recently completed PhD on the relationship between language and thinking – started formulating the theory of autism she would call Monotropism. For her, this was always a natural extension of her more general theory of the mind as a system of interests, competing for our limited attention. A monotropic mind is, in short, one in which a relatively small number of interests are aroused at any time, strongly pulling in whatever attention is available.

I am aware that the theory sounds a bit abstract when expressed like that, which might be part of the reason it took a long time for it to gain wide acceptance. I don't have space to get into it deeply here – I refer you to <monotropism.org> for fuller explanations and applications – but I had better give you a bit more to work with.

Monotropic people concentrate attention and other processing resources on relatively few things at a time – interests, concerns or filters. We have a tendency to become deeply absorbed: we enter *attention tunnels*, and often miss things outside of them, or else experience them as deeply uncomfortable intrusions. It usually takes time to enter and exit attention tunnels comfortably, but it is possible to build up complex interests, which allow us to bounce around rapidly within a single attention tunnel. This process of *chunking*, where we learn to see many things as part of an integrated whole, is a normal part of learning, but the way it looks in monotropic people can be disorienting to people who don't share the same frameworks for understanding.

Attention tunnels are closely associated with flow states and can be a source of great joy, serene satisfaction and deep learning. Being wrenched out of them can be painful and discombobulating, and it tends to happen *a lot*, especially at school. Intense interests are often reliable sources of flow for autistic people.

Neurotypical communication usually assumes *polytropic* processing, where many interests can be aroused at a time, making it easier to integrate information from multiple sources. A polytropic communicator will use words along with tone of voice, facial expressions, body language and eye contact – and expect you to keep track of them all simultaneously, while keeping in mind the specifics of your relationship and correctly guessing how to resolve any ambiguity. They will also expect you to manage all of these channels in *your* communication, and often hold it against you when you don't – for example, reading things into tone of voice or facial expressions that you never intended.

Again, over time a monotropic processor might learn to see communication as an integrated whole and become very good at it, if we have the time and motivation. Still, this basic difference in processing style, which is inherently neither positive nor negative, explains many of the social difficulties encountered by autistic people, especially when we are young. Getting good at anything, for us, usually depends on it capturing our interest and becoming a target of our 'monotropic superdrive', leading to the spiky profile of skills so common in autistic people.

After working out the bones of the theory, Dinah set out to meet and work with other autistic people, to get a sense of how well it holds up. She ended up being a support worker for decades, with autistic people and those with learning disabilities, and she got to know early autistic self-advocates like Larry Arnold, Damian Milton and Wenn Lawson. It was a non-speaking autistic friend, Ferenc Virag, who first pointed out that she was clearly not neurotypical herself (he said this with a very eloquent look, in case you are wondering).

Wenn Lawson, an Australian writer and speaker, turned out to have formulated a very similar theory independently of Dinah. After meeting at a conference in the 1990s and discussing the huge overlap between their ideas, Wenn and Dinah worked together for many years. In 2005 (the same year as 'One That Got Away'), they published a paper in the journal *Autism* together with fellow autistic scholar Mike Lesser: 'Attention, Monotropism and the Diagnostic Criteria for Autism'. This paper showed clearly how Monotropism explained nearly everything that was known about autism.

The point

As important as I think the theory is, I suspect Dinah would have agreed with Marx when he wrote, 'The philosophers have only interpreted the world, in various ways; the point, however, is to change it.'

This would help explain why she never finished the book she had been commissioned to write based on her PhD thesis. What had started out as a chapter for that, titled 'Holy Fools and Bullshit Artists', became her main professional focus for life. In the early days of the internet she started a small organisation with Mike Lesser, called Autism and Computing. They promoted and enabled autistic people's access to information technology, explaining why computers suited people who processed the world monotropically.

Dinah made friends with many autistic people, as well as parents and professionals, and made a habit of connecting them with each other. She worked to ensure that autistic people were taken seriously and listened to by professionals and policy makers, at a time when this *very* rarely happened.

At one point in the late 90s, she realised – thanks to her experiences as a support worker – that antipsychotics (neuroleptics, also known as 'major tranquillisers') were being dangerously overprescribed to people with learning disabilities, largely to make them more passive, and she devoted several years to fighting this practice. She quit her day job, started an organisation called Autistic People Against Neuroleptic Abuse (APANA) together with Wenn, taught herself enough neuroscience to write authoritatively about why these drugs are so dangerous, wrote a report called 'Potions, Pills and Human Rights' for the first issue of the journal *Good Autism Practice*, and more…

It was a classic example of the power of monotropism in action: her persistent hyperfocus allowed her to attain an expert level of knowledge in a subject she had no prior training in, while pursuing every avenue available to make sure that the right people were getting the message. As she wrote in 'Liberating Potential' in 2017, 'There is potential for extraordinary – atypical – levels of productiveness, resourcefulness and creativity in many autistic people when they are pursuing concerns close to their heart.'

For the next generation

I want all autistic people to have what I had growing up. Firstly, Weird Pride – the knowledge that being different doesn't make you inferior, and that weirdness is very often a net positive for society. I have to credit my mum for the term, as well as my own pride in the things that make me weird; she made herself a *WEIRD PRIDE* badge to wear to official functions and other autism-related events, as well as in day-to-day life. I declared the 4th of March to be Weird Pride Day in 2021, partly in her honour, when she had advanced pancreatic cancer, and it has been celebrated ever since.

Secondly, opportunities to pursue their passions, and do whatever else they need to, to gain some sense of peace and purpose in this disorienting world. I see it as a sign of something wrong with society that having 'special interests' – intense focuses, passions – is regularly interpreted as a 'symptom'.

Thirdly, chances to connect with other people who experience the world differently from most. It can be intensely meaningful to connect with other people who share your passions, or people who have always felt like outsiders, for whatever reason, but I am thinking here particularly of other autistic people. Autistic community has been an established thing since the early 1990s, often making such connections far easier to access – and creating opportunities for people to share vital insights about what it means to be different in this way, and how to make the most of it. It is a crime that so many autistic people still don't get the chance to be a part of that.

GIANT ROBOTS AND THE REVOLUTION OF SELF-DISCOVERY

CB Mako

CB MAKO (cubbie/they/them) is both a violist and a writer. Based in Naarm, cubbie is one of the violists of the newly formed Inner West Symphony Orchestra. As a writer, cubbie is a contributor to anthologies *Raging Grace: Australian writers speak out on disability*, *Growing Up Disabled in Australia*, *Collisions: Fictions of the future* and Mascara Literary Review's *Resilience*. They have won the Grace Marion Wilson Emerging Writers Competition, and have been shortlisted in *Overland*'s Fair Australia Prize and the Lord Mayor's Creative Writing Awards and longlisted in the *Liminal* Fiction Prize. Writing by cubbie appears in *The Suburban Review*, *Peril Magazine* and *Kill Your Darlings*, among other publications.

The military tank in front of me is bigger than a bus. This unmoving tank is blocking the superhighway devoid of traffic and flowing vehicles. I have never seen a tank in real life before. Until today. Its gun turret slowly whirls in my direction, capable of blasting me into pieces. I resist the impulse to climb up and ask if the main gun is loaded with ammunition.

The imposing dark-green tank does not move. I do not move, my feet no longer fidgeting. My only sneakers are glued to the bitumen. I look around. I am a tiny drop amid a sea of people in the middle of a superhighway that has six lanes – one of the widest and longest roads in the city. As I look around, there are other kids my age walking and strolling about, like we're all friends in one giant park.

In a few months, I will be thirteen years old. I can't wait to be a high school student. However, at this very moment, I feel older than I am. I feel brave, standing in the middle of the superhighway with tanks, with thousands and thousands of Filipinos, in what the country and the world would call 'People Power'. These Filipinos are about to overthrow a dictator, in such a peaceful manner.

I want to touch the tank, to run my palms over the metal behemoth. Would it be warm? Smooth? It's not moving now. There is no rumbling of its engines. The barrel of its gun, pointing at me, is still.

The tank's hatch opens and a couple of soldiers emerge. They stare in awe at the giant crowd surrounding their tank. Perhaps at their height, at their point of view, they can see how many people have come to join in the People Power.

Some people climb up on the tank to offer food, drinks and even flowers to the soldiers. I want to climb up and offer the freshly baked pastries my aunt made, which I am helping to carry, but I don't. I remain still, staring as people climb the tank.

Throughout my life, I will often question myself, question the people around me. I want to do things outside the norm, but I'm supposed to follow the rules of the grown-ups.

I wonder how our small group – a parent, my aunt, one of my older cousins, me – should distribute the pastries. I want to eat one. We are all far from our own suburb. Yesterday, at my aunt's house, amid the wafting scent of *mamon* and *enseymada*, the grown-ups gathered and spoke in hushed tones, a community radio station blaring in the background.

The grown-ups told me the world as I knew it was about to change. An uncle and his family have already left for Australia, and soon others will leave for other countries. But right now, my mind is still in a bubble, overwhelmed. I stare at the military tank in front of me – with the other tanks and military trucks scattered around, cramped with armed troops.

But my mind is consumed by one question: could all these military vehicles transform or combine into one giant robot?

Blunt fingertips dig into an arm of the plush dark-blue two-seater sofa. Alone in a big room, I wait in trepidation for my assessment results. I desist from chewing my nails, from pacing around the room. Letting go of the sofa, I place my palms on my lap. I take a deep breath and calm myself. This step – a formal diagnosis – is a conscious, informed effort.

The assessment, at almost $1500 (loose change for the rich and the privileged), is not cheap. I am not rich, nor privileged, but I crave a formal diagnosis – solid proof, written down by a person of authority and expertise.

The assessment costs so much, I even took out a loan for it through a No Interest Loan Scheme (NILS). Applying was exhausting. It took more than two weeks to gather a dozen required legal documents, then to wait for the loan to be approved.

A few of my friends want to get formally diagnosed but can't afford the assessment fee. They opt to self-diagnose. Other friends discourage me from taking this test. They tell me I already have a lot on my plate. They say I tick almost all the 'diversity boxes': being a person of colour, non-binary, hard-of-hearing and living with mental health issues. I'm also a full-time carer to my disabled child. Oh, and I live in a rented home, in a low-income household.

And now, I'm in debt. Centrelink will automatically deduct a portion of my meagre carer's allowance to pay for the NILS loan every fortnight for the next twelve months.

All this at the start of a pandemic, two weeks before the first of Melbourne's lockdowns.

But here I am: seated in a spacious, high-ceilinged room with pastel colours and minimalist décor, awaiting my one-on-one feedback session with the assessor-clinician.

A couple of months before the assessment, my psychologist at a local community clinic suggested I take an initial screening test: the same one a friend and I clicked on online just for fun, a few years ago. My psychologist confirmed it's a real diagnostic tool. This time, I didn't laugh at the results. Especially when my psychologist told me to go to a specialist clinic for a formal diagnosis.

Curling and uncurling my sweaty fingers, I rub my palms on the black fabric of my pants. With a deep sigh, I sink into the sofa. The plush furniture is so soft I feel I will disappear into a rabbit hole of uncertainty. The specialist clinic, exclusive to women and girls, is located on the opposite side of the city – the leafy, privileged side – to where I live.

Since I do not drive, I booked a rideshare. The cost was more than my meagre discretionary budget would allow.

The test took three hours: a combination of face-to-face interview and answering psychometric tests, both in print and online forms.

When the clinician enters the room and takes the seat in front of me, she tells me the test results show that I fall within the autism spectrum. I meet the criteria for autism spectrum disorder, or ASD – assessing me as level one (the level requiring the lowest support) of three, based on the DSM-5. What does this mean? What does level one entail? The clinician adds, 'Don't even bother to apply for the NDIS.' (While levels two and three attract automatic NDIS funding at the time, with a level-one diagnosis you need to provide evidence of significant reduced functional capacity.) I would later go home confused and start extensive research about autism, especially about level one. She then hands me a two-page summary, which is all I could afford. If I'd wanted a lengthier analysis, the assessment cost would have been higher. My loan does not cover this cost.

After a brief explanation, I am summarily dismissed. Leaving the clinician's office, I find myself to be the only person of colour in a waiting room packed with white people.

Later – much later – I call my parents, who live overseas. I tell them bluntly that I am autistic. They laugh. Hard. How do I even deal with this kind of reaction?

While still reeling from the two-page result summary, I wonder about how to move forward, how to find a psychologist specialising in adults with late-diagnosed ASD. How do I explain the diagnosis to my ableist partner, who will lack empathy?

I want to look back at how I thought about my world, my society, my clan, my family overseas, who are all non-disabled people. Why is there no specific translation for my diagnosis? Do they simply call it '*otistik*' – in a Tagalog pronunciation, with a harsher accent? Was it like how 'diabetes' sounds more like '*diyabetis*'? Do I look back to my childhood? Do I reimagine and see my past through a different lens now I know I'm autistic?

In the meantime, I escape reality. I decide to reread fanfiction I've written. In this universe, I'm with sentient, magical robot lions, who arrive just in time to protect me. When they fly in unison, up into the stratosphere, they form a mighty giant robot with a blazing sword. Here, in this headspace, my diagnosis is forgotten.

The thick lenses of my new eyeglasses sit atop my flat nose. I am barely five years old, a brown-skinned child – definitely not white-passing like my younger sibling.

Masking tape winds around the middle of the frame; the skin beneath is scraped, itchy and uncomfortable. I do not like my new eyeglasses. These heavy brown plastic frames not only weigh on my barely-there nose bridge but also bite the narrow space on top of my tiny ears. I've already broken them, much to the anger and dismay of my parents. Did I sit on them by accident? Did I deliberately break them after the Year 7 students in my big school started teasing me, calling me '*lola*' every recess and lunch break? I wonder why they shout the word 'grandma' in Tagalog, when I love my grandma (who we all call '*Nanay*') so dearly. Don't they love their own grandmas?

Throughout my life, I will break many, many pairs of glasses. But right now, I'm more focused on something else. Something that will define the course of my life. For the very first time, I am part of a fandom – a word that will later become part of my vocabulary. But now, all I know is that giant robots are my favourite, particularly *Voltes V*. (We all pronounce it as 'Voltes Five', the way it is dubbed in American English.)

Our household has just become the first in our condominium to have a colour television. This makes me the coolest kid on my floor. It has push-buttons and a remote control, which I have never seen before.

My best friend Marie and her younger brother Mikey, who live on my floor, join me and my younger sibling for *merienda*. We all live in a newly built social housing complex, with maze-like walkways high above the ground connecting six to seven buildings. Many of my schoolmates live here, and many of my classmates live here too, on the fifth floor of Building Two.

Marie and I are still in our school uniforms, icky and sweaty from school, sharing hot *pan de sal* lathered in Kraft Cheez Whiz – my favourite afternoon snack. We all scramble to catch the afternoon cartoons in full colour.

I love *Voltes V* so much that I want everything *Voltes V*: T-shirts, lunchboxes, schoolbags, colouring books – the whole fan experience. But for now, I settle for a coloured television, a soundtrack on vinyl record, and the odd, rare trip to the cinema showing *Voltes V* on a giant screen. When I grow up, I will find out *Voltes V* was dubbed by Manila's local talents. I will meet the voice actor – a well-known classical singer for a performing arts company – of one of the characters, Prince Zardoz, by sheer accident.

We all watch and shout along with the five pilots in the show the mighty words 'Let's volt in!' to form Voltes V. We sing and dance to the catchy music while the five flying vehicles transform into their signature giant robot. I even memorise the English lyrics and sing the Japanese ones, too. My kindergarten brain doesn't know the lyrics are Japanese. All I know is this is another way of singing the theme song. I constantly listen to the single-playing vinyl album, regularly spinning on my parents' turntable.

Other robot cartoons attract my imagination. There's *Mazinger Z* and *Daimos*, too. Each weekday features a different robot cartoon. I tell my parents I need a *Voltes V* T-shirt, but I end up getting a *Mazinger Z* one. Apparently, the grown-ups couldn't tell one robot from the other. But I can. 'It's so easy,' I say with authority.

I explain *Voltes V*'s bad guys are royalty who have horns on their heads. *Daimos* is a single robot with only one pilot, who falls in love with a princess with angel wings from another planet. ('That's Richard and Erica,' I add.) *Mazinger Z* – here I point at my brand-new T-shirt – is a giant robot with a sidekick giant girl robot with missiles firing from her chest. The grown-ups all laugh at my serious explanation, especially about the chest missiles.

I never think chest missiles are funny. For one thing (I later find out), I was never breastfed. I have no association with breasts, despite being assigned female at birth.

According to my parents, I kicked my way into this world after rendering my poor mother bed-ridden for a month in the hospital and waiting until at least the eighth month. The nurses then placed me inside a different kind of incubator, separated from other newborns in the hospital nursery for a full month.

In a developing country under a dictatorship, what were the chances of me surviving at barely eight months without private healthcare? How did my parents pay for such expensive private hospitalisation anyway? Didn't my father hold a job as a messenger at a small company in the shipping industry with a British expat for a boss?

When I was three years old, my mother and I would visit my father at work on a Saturday (considered a half-day working day). I remember seeing miniature ships in glass cases and noisy telex machines, spitting out unending strips of punch-holed paper resembling carnival ride or air-conditioned bus tickets. And I heard my father's boss speaking English in an accent different from the American English on *Sesame Street*, which I watched then in black and white.

Later, when I watched *Sesame Street* on our new colour television, I realised one of the monsters with sharp teeth was blue. I hid every time he showed up on screen. Some of the Muppets frightened me – enough to give me nightmares. I didn't know why.

All I wanted was more of the giant robots. For my entire life, I had craved my very own toy robot. But, because I was assigned female at birth, the grown-ups insisted I play with dolls, while handing me one gifted by my father's British boss. My mother gloated that I owned the first Barbie ever, even before the doll was popular in Manila. What did Mum mean? Then they told me robot toys were only for boys. *Why? Why can't I have my own toy robot? And why do I feel so confused?*

One day, a regular school day, without any warning, all the giant robot cartoons disappear from the television channels. I had turned six less than a month ago.

I wail. Hard. Crouched in front of the colour television, I cry brokenheartedly. My parents slowly explain to me in the simplest terms that the country I live in – I can't even spell 'Philippines' properly yet – is still under martial law. I hear the name President Ferdinand Marcos for the first time. Life under the Marcos regime and this thing the grown-ups call 'martial law' has become difficult even for me, a kid who simply loves giant robots. There is no free speech under martial law. And, as a dictator, Marcos controls the media – whether newspapers or television. Anyone who opposes his rule simply… disappears: never to be heard of again.

My favourite robot cartoons *Voltes V*, *Mazinger Z* and *Daimos* are gone. Instead, cutesy, sparkly cartoons appear. *Ron-Ron the Flower Angel*, *Candy Candy*, *Paul in Fantasy Island*. They are all horribly, sickeningly sweet. Did the dictatorial regime sanitise what's on television? Is its sweetness meant to prevent anyone thinking of rebellion or revolution?

I must wait a bit for the robots to return. Though the dictator Ferdinand Marcos is still in power, there will come a time when he *will* no longer be president and his regime *will* end – just before I start high school. But I must survive kindergarten, then elementary school, which goes up to Year 6 or 7, depending on the school and how my grades turn out in the future.

I will come to realise that my grades and ranking in the big school's annual honours awards will matter a lot: I will need them to gain the love and affection of my parents. I will need to show I can get high grades too! Like my *mestiza* younger sister – who's so *maputi*, so very white, who later graduates from a prestigious university, summa cum laude.

Meanwhile, my schoolmates, my uncles and aunties, and my cousins relentlessly taunt me: I'm so *maitim*. I, the bespectacled child, my skin as dark as chocolate and coffee combined, won't go very far in life. This thinking is deeply embedded in the Philippines, a country colonised multiple times. I later learn words to describe it: the intersectionality of ableism and colourism.

Eventually, the day in the future arrives when Marcos is replaced by a woman president. Her name is Cory Aquino. I come to love the colour yellow, Aquino's symbolic colour during her campaign to oust the dictator. And she continues to wear yellow as the president of the Philippines.

During the Aquino administration, the strict media censorship of the Marcos regime is lifted. New channels and shows appear. There are even new broadsheet newspapers.

Finally, the first giant robot appears on television! This time, it's in the form of *Voltron: Defender of the Universe* – a different cartoon. My inner fangirl rises again.

Let the fangirling begin.

DISCOVERING NATURE AND A POSITIVE AUTISTIC IDENTITY

Shadia Hancock

SHADIA HANCOCK (they/them/theirs) is the proud owner and founder of Autism Actually and enjoys presenting and consultancy. They are also an ambassador of the Autistic-led organisation Yellow Ladybugs. Shadia has completed a Bachelor of Speech Pathology (Honours) and a Certificate IV in Animal Behaviour and Training. Shadia was formally identified with Autism at the age of three and ADHD combined type at twenty-three. Being non-binary, they enjoy discussing the intersectionality of Autism and the LGBTQIA+ community. As an Autistic person with experience accessing therapeutic supports, Shadia is passionate about sharing how to view Autism from a neurodiversity-affirming perspective.

I remember being fascinated by leaves, bark and trees as a toddler, spending hours climbing trees, carrying bark and observing with fascination the venation patterns in leaves. Nature was my stim palace. When my kindergarten visited a children's farm, while other children were interested in checking out the various animals on the property I took great delight in sitting in the long grass, pulling the stems and flicking them through my fingers. I would sit in the sandpit and let the sand run through my fingers, seeing how the light hit it. Nature didn't judge me. To this day, I will cry if I see a tree felled – like I have lost a good friend. My love for the natural world grew when I watched documentaries narrated by David Attenborough and marvelled at its diversity and complexity. There was also sadness in learning that not everyone appreciated nature and about the damage humanity has caused to our ecosystem. I feel that my connection to the natural world has influenced my interests in eco-friendly living and environmental activism.

During my high school years, I would regularly engage in discussions (sometimes heated) about climate change and renewable energy. I helped set up the school's Environmental Action Plan and a student-led committee. One of my proudest moments was facilitating a festival that brought together community members interested in the environment, such as representatives of renewable energy companies, farmers and owners of sustainable businesses. I also attended a three-day environmental conference, the first time I had been to such a massive event. It was wonderful connecting with like-minded people who valued environmental awareness and sustainability. Incidentally, it was the first time I trialled using they/them pronouns; I felt it was a safe and welcoming space in which to be myself. My passion for protecting the environment gave me the confidence to advocate at my school and try new things in a safe space. I am eternally grateful for the opportunities provided and for being at a school that encouraged student-led initiatives.

Today, nature remains my solace in a world I often find chaotic and overwhelming. I take joy in the calm and quiet, the rustling of the trees in the wind and the native flora I encounter on my daily walks. I love seeing my dog engaging in 'sniffaris' and imagining what smelly wonders she has found. We co-regulate and take time to process the scenery at our own pace. It is important for both of us to slow down and appreciate our environment. While traditional mindfulness practices don't work for me, I find engaging in my environment like this is a great way to destress and redirect my anxiety and thoughts. I feel lucky to live in a house that looks out to bushland. It is so restful being able to gaze out of the windows and look at trees. We also get a lot of king parrots, kookaburras and eastern spinebills right outside our windows. Nature has been my main subject in drawing, with a lot of my high school artworks starring landscapes and incorporating leaves and bark. Fellow art aficionados will not be surprised to learn that such approaches were inspired by landscape artist John Wolseley, whose admiration for the Australian landscape was captured via watercolour, nature printing, collage and frottage.

Funnily enough, I wasn't like other animal lovers – in that I wasn't instantly obsessed with animals. Plants were my fascination for most of my toddler years. This all changed when I came across a pony up close for the first time. I still remember it; it was my friend's sixth birthday party and they had a pony for short rides up and down the driveway. I felt immediately drawn to the creature. When I got on the pony's back, it was an electric experience. I felt strong warmth and connection to the pony and then immense sadness at having to get off and say goodbye. Ever since this experience, I have been thoroughly obsessed with horses, sketching them, begging my parents for riding lessons and a horse of my own, learning about all the breeds and coat types, and acquiring an impressive collection of horse-related books. When my mother told me, aged ten, that I would be having my first lesson at Riding for the Disabled, I squealed with excitement.

My childhood dog Charlie introduced a new special interest (SpIn) to do with all things dogs. He came into my life when I was eight years old. He was quite a goofball but fiercely protective of his family. He wasn't the most affectionate dog but then I wasn't the most affectionate child, so it worked well for us. I used to enjoy playing with and reading to him. The great thing about Charlie was that he enjoyed being around us but didn't necessarily need to join in; I had to learn to respect his space and his sensory needs, which helped with my own self-awareness and self-acceptance. His empathy shone when he saw me in distress. One day I was crying, and he went and got a giant palm frond and ran around the yard ripping it to shreds. I couldn't help but laugh at his silly antics. He would also lick the tears off my face. I always felt safe with and very loved by Charlie. No matter what kind of day I'd had at school or how I was feeling, he would always greet me excitedly at the gate, ready to shower me with kisses and cuddles.

Sadly, dogs don't live as long as us, which meant, inevitably, I had to say goodbye to Charlie. Like many other Autistic people, I find death a difficult thing to deal with. From a young age, I used to worry about losing my loved ones and panic at the idea that they may not be around forever. As an adult, having had some of these losses come to pass I feel their absence intensely.

During late primary school and high school, I experienced bullying and exclusion from so-called 'friends'. I felt incredibly isolated and alone. But at least when I came home I was enveloped by unconditional love and acceptance. Charlie didn't care that I needed to stim, or had meltdowns, or communicated differently. We didn't need to talk to each other to communicate. When Charlie passed away, I felt his loss acutely. Dogs become a part of your daily routine, and in my case a social outlet. Small things like remembering it was his dinner time, going to greet him at the front door in the mornings and noticing it was the time of our daily walk triggered a waterfall of emotions.

It has been difficult losing loved ones over the years, but I have learnt that grief is an ever-evolving process. There is not one 'right' way to grieve. I have reframed grief as a cherished state in the sense that I have had the pleasure of knowing someone so special and loving them so deeply as to feel profound sadness from their passing. This helped me prepare for the loss of my grandfather, as I knew there were ways of honouring his memory that would not erase his presence from my life, such as writing a dedicated poem, drawing pictures of him or doing activities that reminded me of him. These activities by no means take away the pain, but they are healthy ways for me to channel and process my feelings.

In primary school, I was surrounded by fellow Neurodivergent and disabled students so, while some children didn't understand me, I certainly did not feel like the only different child. This started to shift in my later primary years, an experience many Autistic people can relate to. My 'friends' started to change. They talked about me behind my back. I was suddenly dropped and shunned for no apparent reason. I was teased for hanging out with the boys. It began to hit me that I was different, and I felt incredibly lonely at that time.

As luck would have it, my high school had a large Working With Animals program, and I immediately dived in to help with the caretaking. I began reading more about Autistic people and their resonance with animals, and I drew parallels between their interactional styles and mine. People would remark that I related well to animals and that animals responded well to me, and say they didn't know how I did it. To be honest, it came naturally to me: I didn't understand why other people found it so difficult! There were many reasons I found it easier to communicate with animals than with people. For one, there was no talking or lying, so I didn't have to second-guess whether they were being truthful. For me, animal body language is on a much larger and more obvious scale than human body language. We also have a lot in common, with our fight, flight and freeze responses both physiologically and behaviourally, as Autistic animal expert Summer Farrelly wisely pointed out in one of their presentations on animal-assisted learning. I also noticed similarities in how people treat and label animals and Autistic people: 'naughty', 'non-compliant' and 'doing it deliberately'. Whereas my interpretations were that the animal was stressed and overwhelmed and was exhibiting similar signs to myself when I am experiencing overload or shutdown. I question who the behaviour is inconveniencing and why we focus on them so much; is it a concern for the animal's welfare or is it because it is inconveniencing us?

Indeed, a lot of traditional animal training methods rely on intimidation and punishment to reduce behaviours deemed by humans as 'undesirable'. This reminds me of how Applied Behaviour Analysis has been used to decrease the 'inappropriate' behaviours of Autistic people, including stimming and communication differences, in order to make them 'fit in'. As with Autistic people, animals were once thought to not possess a wide array of emotions or thoughts, but emerging research has now brought this into question. I would argue any animal lover who has spent enough time with an animal knows that they are more than an unfeeling machine.

As I learnt more about myself and animal communication, I became more uncomfortable with the compliance-based methods often used when training animals. My traditional riding school was a clear example. Their motto was to show the horse who's boss and take control of them. I started to question the instructors; surely there was a better, kinder way than this? I decided to stop riding after falling off a distressed horse and then being encouraged to get back on. I was lucky to find a trainer who did not rely on intimidation and fear tactics to interact with horses but who instead educated me on equine body language, consent-based methods and groundwork. I now no longer ride and prefer to interact with horses at liberty. I believe you learn and notice so much more about the animal in front of you when you are not on their back. Not to mention that it should be seen as an absolute privilege and symbol of your bond to get on a horse in the first place! It is exciting to see more relationship-based methods arise in the animal-training world as well as in neurodiversity-affirming therapy models.

As I connected with more Autistic people, I noticed that many of us resonate deeply with animals. I wanted to find a way of merging my love of animals with my Autism advocacy work. After many deep-dive sessions and hyperfocusing, I came across animal-assisted services. When I first started researching in 2014, there was not as much information out there as there is now on including animals in therapy, education or assistance work. A wonderful careers counsellor who took an interest in disability work suggested that I pursue an allied health degree and incorporate animal-assisted services as part of this. Having completed my Bachelor of Speech Pathology (Honours) and Certificate IV in Animal Behaviour and Training, I am so glad I chose this path. It is great to see more support for animal-assisted services professionally as well as discussions on animal welfare and training methods. I hope to contribute to the field by promoting kind, force-free and relationship-based methods when interacting with animals and clients, and to support the Neurodivergent community with assistance and therapy animals. We still have a lot of work to do, but with the increased recognition of Autistic animal trainers and allied health therapists, I am hopeful that change will happen!

FISH GIRL

Lucy Rose

LUCY ROSE's (she/they) fiction and non-fiction have been published by *Dread Central*, *Mslexia*, the *Observer*, the *Nerd Daily* and more, and her films have visited BAFTA- and Oscar-qualifying film festivals internationally. She is also a *Forbes* 30 Under 30 Europe class of 2025. Lucy's *Sunday Times* bestselling debut novel, *The Lamb*, is published by Weidenfeld & Nicolson in the UK and HarperCollins in the US. Lucy lives on the north-east coast of England with her black cat, Figgy, and is currently working on her next story.

There was no word in my vocabulary to describe the way I was, the way I felt inside my body and the way I acted. I had no diagnosis or pathology. Nothing. As a child, I was only given the words *weird*, *angry* and, later, *obsessive*.

That's what it was like being undiagnosed.

(Oh, and I really wanted to be a fish.)

I'm nine years old, and I haven't stopped watching *The Little Mermaid*. The moment the VHS crawls to a stop, I painstakingly rewind it back to the beginning and hit play. I do this over and over. It is compulsive.

But it's not just the Disney version of the story I love. It's anything that involves a person being half-human, half-fish. *Hook*, for the few seconds that Peter Pan encounters mermaids; *Peter Pan* itself, for Mermaid Cove; and the film *Mermaids*, despite the absence of any actual mermaids – just for the title. I have a collection of made-for-TV movies, each reimagining the story of the girl who is secretly half-fish. A few years from now, I will discover *Aquamarine* and *H20: Just Add Water* (which will be an awakening for me because I'll realise I have a big bisexual crush on Rikki). And of course, the crème de la crème of modern mermaid classics, Daryl Hannah's *Splash*. I watch this on repeat and fill my baths with salt so I can be just like her. The fish girl.

I love mermaids, but I'm a nine-year-old girl. What nine-year-old girl doesn't love mermaids? What nine-year-old girl doesn't resist her school uniform at all costs because she hates that the zipless jumper traps her in while she yearns only to wear her mermaid outfit instead? What nine-year-old girl doesn't go to the nearest body of water, hoping her skin will sprout scales? And what nine-year-old girl doesn't build dams so that she can lie in the beck with the bullheads and the brook lamprey eels?

I take over the family computer to look at pictures of mermaids every weekend. It's 2005, so it takes about seven minutes for the pictures to load in full. But it isn't enough just to look at pictures of mermaids.

I need to know everything about them.

On a Monday in the summer, while the other kids scrape their kneecaps on the playground, I use the school library printer to collect photos of a so-called mermaid corpse. Wikipedia claims it washed up somewhere on a beach after a storm. I don't care that she is ugly and that she doesn't look like the mermaids from the storybooks, because to me she is a *real* mermaid. Here is the proof I've been searching for that the thing I think about every waking moment is not just real, but legitimate, acknowledged by an online web page.

(Oh, sweet summer child.)

I take absolute delight in leaving the picture of said mermaid corpse on the desk of a teacher who told my parents that I needed to *grow up* last parents' evening. He described me as *imaginative*, but he used the word like it was dirty and said I was *distracting*. That I needed to *focus more*.

In hindsight, maybe this is why I don't get a diagnosis for another nineteen years. God forbid an Autistic person is: 1) a girl, 2) imaginative and 3) obsessed with something other than trains.

I'm twelve, and I've been sitting at the kitchen table for two hours. All I know is that I'd rather drink bleach than eat a single bite of fish pie. It's not just the way it flakes apart in my mouth, I hate the taste too. The wash of saltwater that lingers at the back of my throat. That horrid algae aftertaste I dread. I've always hated fish.

(This is deeply ironic for someone who dreams of becoming one.)

The pie goes untouched for two hours more. It cools steadily as the breadcrumb topping hardens and the creamy sauce forms a skin. A family friend saunters into the kitchen, red wine marking the inner flesh of her lips, and tries to encourage me to eat it. Her scent makes me want to vomit. It's that rich mix of cheap perfume and pinot noir.

There are too many smells in this room.

And all I want to eat is pasta. (Delicious.)

The family friend piles a helping of pie onto my fork and pushes it inside my mouth, because *you have to eat*, but I spit the mouthful back out and onto the plate. I don't just dislike her for this, I *hate* her. A familiar feeling runs through my nerves – an alchemy of blind rage and fear that makes me want to crawl out of my fleshy, sinewed body and hide under my bed.

Hours later, I am still in my chair. I wait for the food to congeal. I wait until it is dark. I wait for the bad smell to stop as night frost fills the kitchen with the shadows.

And I don't care that my family hates me. All I care about is that I don't have to eat that f*cking fish pie.

They all think I'm such an ungrateful little girl. I know they do, and I can't explain how, but there is a distance between my family and me now. Like we exist on different sides of the veil.

That night, I cry myself to sleep at the dinner table. No one understands why.

I'm fourteen years old, and it's Pink and Blue Day at school.

No one suspects I'm Autistic (not even me). I'm just *difficult* and *strange*.

I hear that a lot: *she's an old soul, that one. So different.* People mistake loneliness for otherworldliness, a neurodevelopmental disorder for quirkiness. That's what happens to undiagnosed girls. They become muses. *Unlike any girl you've ever met.* The sort of girl people love to romanticise but find *difficult to put up with* in real life.

I've been looking forward to Pink and Blue Day for weeks. It's a non-uniform day to raise awareness for charity, and I spend a whole week getting my outfit together. I visit charity shops after school and borrow bits and pieces from Mam's wardrobe. Blue trainers, pink leg warmers, blue leggings, a pink tutu, a cute blue top with pink writing and a pink wig topped with a blue beret. The top is something I wear repeatedly, because it has sequins that remind me of fish scales.

It isn't until I get on the school bus that I realise I've done it again. I've taken the *pink and blue* instructions of the non-uniform day too literally.

Most people wear a pair of blue jeans. In class, I listen to an endless cacophony of whispers about how weird I am. About how my clothing choices make me some kind of freak. And later in the morning, some girls in my French class use scissors to chop at the back of my wig, only I don't realise until it's too late. And when the teacher makes me stand at the front of the assembly hall, to show me off like a prize pony, I understand (not for the first time) that I'm not like anyone else in the room.

After lunch, I escape to the school bathroom and throw my choppy wig in the bin. I realise the girls cut off some of my real hair too. I swallow all my feelings as I tear my leg warmers from my calves and the tutu from my waist. And, so I don't feel like a fish anymore, I pluck the sequins away from my top one by one.

I will be normal, I promise myself. *Even if it kills me.*

I'm eighteen years old, and for the first time I've found something I'm good at *and* enjoy. A rare combination.

I leave school straight after my GCSEs and, after a couple of failed attempts to launch into life, and some seasonal work at a tourist trap, I decide to do a full-time vocational course instead of A-levels.

I pick something I can really throw myself into. Something I can become infatuated by.

There are no words to describe how I feel when I look through the viewfinder of the camera. I prep and shoot pictures every day. I spend every waking second looking for models who need portfolio work, sewing old curtains found at car boot sales, making crowns from chicken wire and searching the charity shops for rare fashion finds.

For the first time in my life, I am good at something. My pictures are great, and, of course, my love of fish and mermaids provides ample inspiration. (Cue models in shimmery dresses and scale-like make up. Cue shoots in seawater and rivers, and by waterfalls and streams. And cue doing something that makes me feel happy.)

Taking pictures is like a drug. I'm compelled to spend every spare penny I earn on my new hobby. And I do. Because my impulse control is nil and my bank says I can have a low-interest overdraft – which later morphs into a tight hand squeezing around my windpipe. (Cue realising that debt isn't fun.)

I tell myself all of this is okay, because at least I'm not doing cocaine or alcohol. I'm just shooting pictures... And that is harmless.

But my obsession with photography eats me alive. Inside my body, there are feelings I can't control. Anger and confusion and frustration simmering just below the surface, and there's nowhere for it to go. But I put it into my pictures. From the negative emotions in my body, I create the most beautiful pictures possible. I experiment. I graft. All because I want to make people shimmer like water.

Time passes and I find that photography isn't swallowing my feelings the way it used to. The anger no longer underlying. It breaches the surface. It is everywhere. I feel it when my food isn't right. When I hear unwelcome noises from the flat upstairs. When my jumper scratches me in the wrong way. When my hair tickles the back of my neck. When I'm at the supermarket checkout with the beeping and the screaming children. When my socks shuffle down my ankle. When there is a stone in my shoe. When my flatmates don't engage with my fish facts. When someone is speaking but they aren't talking about the deep ocean, so I simply do not care what they have to say.

A doctor and I begin to flirt with potential diagnoses (because I know there is something deeply wrong with me).

Manic depression. Severe anxiety. Bipolar disorder. Obsessive compulsive disorder. Borderline personality disorder. We look at everything in the DSM-5.

But not Autism.

It couldn't possibly be Autism.

I'm twenty-three, and I think I have Autism.

It's 2019. I've scrolled countless hours on TikTok, and I think this truly could be *the thing* that is wrong with me.

My dreams of becoming a fish.

Intrusive thoughts of scales hatching from my skin so I can move through the water, where it is heavy and quiet and dark – where my sensory icks can't reach me.

The years spent taking things so literally I became a social outcast.

The intense anger at everything that rubs me the wrong way.

The friction and distance I feel in every relationship I've struggled to hold down.

But I'm discovering people don't like girls who self-diagnose via TikTok. The comment sections are brutal, so I keep this label – *Autistic* – at arm's length.

It doesn't belong to me.

I spend a lot of time wondering if it would belong to me if I were a boy who likes trains.

A client I'm photographing comes to my flat for a consultation. We give each other a quick hug, because we've known each other a while from the creative scene in the north – but he lingers longer than he should. His hands stay at my waist, and they don't move until I heave myself away. We sit on opposite sides of the kitchen table and talk shop for a while. Endless conversations about his music and the source of his inspiration. The sort of pictures he wants. How he wants to be framed. But he is gazing at me, and he won't stop.

I wish he'd stop looking at me like that.

After a few coffees, he tells me I'm *not like other girls* and that

I *have a special way of seeing the world*. He tells me I'm *the sort of girl he wants to write a song about*. (Cringe.)

This has happened before. People don't realise they're meeting an undiagnosed Autistic person, and it blows their mind. I don't like maths or trains, and so it's easy to slot me into the category of *the sort of girl you want to write songs about*. (I don't even know if I am a girl: the concept of gender doesn't make sense to me.)

To him, I'm not disabled. He doesn't see my angry outbursts or my dreams of becoming a fish. He doesn't see the days I spend rotting in bed because one social interaction has eroded me to nothing. He doesn't see the bruises forming as I hit myself to disappear the meltdowns. He doesn't know that one time I came home from school and cut off all my hair because I was overwhelmed. This artist sees someone who is fiercely ambitious and curious about the world in a way other people simply aren't. Someone who has accepted that they're a quirky, unforgettable character. And so he gets to meet the manic pixie dream girl. She's funny. Otherworldly. Not like other girls. (Not into trains.)

You have no idea how much he likes that about her.

But she thinks he's a creep, and an idiot, and never speaks to him again.

I stop taking photos after that. I lose my love for it.

I'm twenty-eight now. I'm in the bathroom at London Book Fair when I get *the* call – the one I've been waiting years for. A very tired nurse from NHS South Tyneside lets me know that one of those rare and shiny assessment slots has opened up due to a cancellation, but I'm on the wrong side of the f*cking country.

The nurse lists information about how the process will work, but I feel like I'm underwater. Her words aren't sticking. I start to panic in the bathroom as editors and agents I recognise from online spaces filter in and out of the stalls (and I hope to hell they don't remember me *like this*). The nurse tells me we can do the assessment online via video call instead.

Thank f*ck.

I grieve the hours I've spent obsessively researching the clinic. How I would get there. Exactly what bus I would take. What time I would catch it. What the clinic would look like inside. If the seats would feel plasticky beneath my skin. If it would have that overbearing pine disinfectant scent that all clinics possess.

I hate going to unfamiliar places, and every time I have to go somewhere new (including this very bathroom at London Book Fair, where I'm having a full-on meltdown), I heavily research it in advance – in excessive detail. I need all the places I go to feel like I've inhabited them before.

A few days later, I have my online appointment. I tell the nurse about my childhood dream of becoming a fish and my love of mermaids. To my delight, she smiles and actually engages. She asks me questions about mermaids and seems genuinely interested in my fascination with the deep ocean and rivers and streams. She asks me about the reams and reams of forms I filled out while I lived in the purgatory of the five-year waiting list, and I get to tell her I don't care about trains *at all*.

That makes us both laugh.

But this still feels like a test. I wonder if I am *one of those terrible girls* from TikTok who is appropriating the label (even after years and years stewing on that waiting list).

I tell the nurse about my writing, something I've only been doing for a few years after I rediscovered oral stories from the coves of my past. I tell her how I feel when I get lost in writing things down opposed to speaking them aloud. How it feels to form the perfect sentence, rhythm and clause. How the act wakes up a part of my brain that makes me feel both creative and logical at the same time.

And after one hour and thirty minutes of vomiting up a lifetime's worth of strained social experiences, meltdowns and traumas, she tells me she will call me in two weeks and let me know what they decide.

Over the next two weeks, I convince myself I am a fraud. I erase the years I spent hoping I could disappear somewhere at the bottom of the sea, my history of picking up hobbies like drug addictions and my inability to *really* connect with others. I tell myself this is all a lie.

It's easier to believe I'm a strange and terrible person.

I get the call.

It is a normal morning, and the sky is smudged grey on the north-east coast. I'm working from home and when the phone rings, my lungs seize up. A heavy weight sinks through my chest.

When I can bring myself to pick up the phone, the nurse tells me she understands I've waited a long time for this and she knows exactly how I feel.

She tells me *everything is okay.*

She tells me that I'm Autistic and that she can only imagine how many questions this must answer for me.

When I start to cry, she tells me that Autism isn't something you can develop and that my brain has always been this way – even when I was *one of those attention-seeking girls* scrolling on TikTok. Even when I was wearing a ridiculous amount of pink and blue at school. Even when I imagined gills breaking out on my neck and a dorsal fin sprouting from my spine.

When the nurse hangs up the phone, I sit in the quiet for what feels like a month. A migraine churns at the centre of my head. My eyes sting as I soak up the saltwater dribbling down my face, and my cheeks aren't just hot, they are burning. I wonder if I am finally changing. If the inside will make its way out so I can live at the bottom of the ocean, where the world is heavy and compressed. Where no sunlight can reach me. Beneath the weight of my duvet, the closest thing I have to an ocean, I daydream my sheets are made of silt and mud.

I imagine growing scales and fins.

I stim, playing with my hair, folding it into knots and brushing my lips.

I breathe in the air and pretend it is water.

All I know is that I'm going to be okay.

DOG YEARS

Tash Agafonoff

TASH AGAFONOFF (she/her) lives and works on Gunaikurnai Country (Gippsland, Victoria) with her partner and two feline co-authors. She writes personal essays, memoir and poetry – and many, many lists. In 2020 she won the Grace Marion Wilson Emerging Writers Competition and was published in *The Victorian Writer*. Tash was also longlisted for the Richell Prize in 2021. She is currently completing a Master of Arts (Writing and Literature) at Deakin University. Tash begins far too many sentences with conjunctions and owns more (blank) notebooks than one person should ever be permitted.

I jingle the latch on the gate at the end of the patio. The German shepherd comes running from down the back of the yard. He likes to lie under the tree with the possum nest so he can supervise their comings and goings and bark orders when they become unruly.

'Good boy,' I say, holding out his halter as he trots towards me. 'Nose!'

He pushes his face into it and I clip it around his neck onto his collar. He's only learnt this command since he's been here; who says you can't teach an old dog new tricks?

'Good boy,' I sing-song as I rub his shoulder. 'Are you ready for a walk?'

He looks up at me and tilts his head. His dark brown eyes are bright. One smaller, uneven bottom tooth gives him a wonky smile. The growing patches of silver-grey around his mouth are the only signs that betray his age. He sits on my foot, leaning on my leg, waiting for me to open the gate.

The dog isn't mine. He's lodging while his owner travels around South America for a year. But he feels like mine. I pretend he's mine. He was just a puppy when I met him: six months old. His owner added me on Facebook after noticing we had a mutual friend. Technically, she was someone about to *not* be my friend – due to a lack of communication and empathy on my part, she said. I find you abhorrent, her email had read.

A couple of months before I met the dog – and his owner – the mutual friend had been at my apartment, a block back from Newcastle Beach. We'd sat on my balcony, where you could usually see straight down a lane to the surf. But that night it was too late, too dark; we could only hear the waves. On the corner of the lane and the ocean promenade was a high-rise hotel. I stared across the dimly lit gravel car park at the back of it, and wondered what the price difference was between the rooms that faced the ocean and those with a view of the dumpster, chain-link barbed-wire fence and my pale-blue boxy apartment building. The sticky salt air combined with the stench from the weed my then-friend was smoking stung my nose.

'I haven't seen him for years, not since he moved,' she said. 'He makes guitars by hand, in Buenos Aires. The most beautiful guitars. I have my ticket to visit next month. And today, he asked me not to come.'

She stubbed out her spliff in the black plastic ashtray and sat silent for a moment. I took another sip of my merlot and counted the number of hotel rooms that had lights switched on.

'Did you hear me?' she asked. 'Do you have anything to say?' She turned to look at me.

I licked the paper edge of the cigarette I'd been rolling, sealed it, and said, 'Isn't the pattern of the lights on the hotel interesting?'

She grabbed her Tally Hos and pouch of tobacco, stuffed them into her bag, and pushed back from the flimsy outdoor table.

'I'm off,' she said and let herself out. I watched more lights flick on as people checked in for the night, lit my cigarette and inhaled. Nicotine and wine buzzed through my body.

The next day, the email arrived.

I was pouring out my heart to you, devastated that he'd rejected me. Your response was to talk about patterns. Lights on buildings. Were you even listening to me? You have no empathy.

I stared at the screen for a long time before beginning to type.

I'm sorry. I'm unable to read social dynamics the way you can. It's something I've known for a long time, but awareness doesn't help me read the cues any better. I didn't know you were sad. I just don't have those sorts of feelings. I'm sorry, I couldn't relate. If you want to talk about it, you know how to reach me.

The next time I heard how she was doing, it was from the dog's owner. It was late when I sat with him on the small verandah of his ground-floor flat. We leant back with our feet up on the brick wall, each with a glass of wine in one hand, cigarette in the other. They'd been at the dog park together and he said she'd revelled as she told him *all* about me. The dog curled up beneath my legs on the green, painted concrete. I said he should make up his own mind about me. And my not-friend.

He said, 'The dog cries when you leave.'

The dog's name is Bud, the same name an ex-boyfriend uses for friends and strangers instead of 'mate'. But it means the same thing, doesn't it? Bud. Mate. Friend.

A month after we met, I pulled up across the street from where he was waiting outside his apartment block with Bud.

'Hey, you!' I called as I clomped across the road in my steel-cap boots and hi-vis workwear. We'd established a routine of walking Bud around the nearby racecourse when I finished work and he wasn't on the closing shift at the bottle shop.

'Why don't you ever use my name?' he said. 'It's always you, or matey, or some other generic thing.'

I leant down and scratched Bud's shoulder, avoiding his owner's gaze and the question. There was an answer, but not one I could articulate. Names were intimate. Names implied familiarity. Friendship. And I was never sure when people were my friends. I'd been wrong too many times. Connections that seemed promising evaporated without warning – I didn't usually get an email. But animals? All animals were friends. Animals didn't judge me the way people did.

I stood up and forced a tight smile. 'Hi, Matt,' I said.

The words felt weird in my mouth. I imagined saying it again, and again, repeating it quietly under my breath. Hi, Matt. Hi, Matt. Hi, Matt.

Bud's name tag strikes a familiar rhythmic clink against the metal clasp of his lead as we walk. In ten months, we've only missed four days. Halfway around our usual loop, we spot Hillsy on the other side of the road. He's bent over, weeding in his front garden with Cougar, his German shepherd, lying nearby.

When he sees us, he stands up and waves.

'How are you ever going to give him back? You're not going to want to give him back. I reckon we'll see you with a puppy soon.'

'Yeah,' I say, smiling. 'You're probably right.'

He says the same thing every time we walk past and so do I. It's an easy interaction, but not one I would have had without the dog. Bud provides a type of social scaffolding, a focus point, a conversation with clear boundaries.

The first time I walked past Hillsy with Bud, he crossed the road to introduce himself – 'John, but you can call me Hillsy' – and let Bud have a good, long sniff of his hands and legs.

'He's not a young dog,' he said, eyeing the grey whiskers. 'How old is he?'

'He just turned eleven, a month ago,' I said. 'He's not mine. I'm just looking after him for a friend while he's travelling.'

'He's a beautiful dog. How are you ever going to give him back? You're not going to want to give him back.'

'Yeah, I know,' I said. 'He's my goodest boy.' Bud pushed his nose into a patch of clover, flopped and rolled over. 'I love him. I don't know how I'll do it.'

Things I've learnt about Hillsy since: he barracks for Collingwood, he's a retired police officer. Cougar is the same age as Bud but has a lot of health problems. Hillsy mows the nature strip of the council green space opposite his house so his wife, who plays golf, can practise teeing off. These are small details about someone's life, collected through fleeting exchanges facilitated by Bud.

The dog and I keep walking.

'What's going on for you right now?' my psychologist asked as I teared up. 'What emotions are behind that?'

I shook my head. 'I don't know.'

Whatever the feeling is that's supposed to accompany tears was missing. Absent. I'd been in treatment for an eating disorder for almost two years and I'd raised my lack of emotional response to my now-not-friend with my psychologist.

'If the heart is a muscle,' I said, 'and you don't use it – the emotion thing – for a long time, does it atrophy? Do you lose the ability to feel? I don't remember being able to. Can you learn how?'

She leant forward a little. 'Do you want to?'

'I don't know. No? Not really.'

It would be more than ten years before I'd learn that my inability to identify and articulate my emotions is called alexithymia and it occurs in anywhere from 33.3 to 63 per cent of autistic people.[1] Although I'd raised many of the social, relational and sensory challenges I'd experienced with my psychologist, the research had not yet caught up for women. My struggles weren't recognised as autistic traits or differences. At the time, my psychologist attributed my reduced emotional capacity to the eating disorder, which, as it turns out, also has a strong overlap with autism.

I left Newcastle for Central Queensland just after Bud turned one. Before I went, Matt and I met at Redhead Beach and walked the length of it while Bud chased seagulls. It was winter, and although the sky was blue and the sun was out it still had teeth, as my grandfather had often said. Bud didn't notice the cold; he bounded in and out of the surf, snapping at seaweed being thrown onto the shore. Back at our cars, Matt handed me two smooth rocks about the size of duck eggs: one a dark golden colour, the other creamy beige.

'These are the egg rocks of destiny,' he said. 'Whoever possesses them will be rewarded with the Earth and all its understanding.'

I laughed, took the rocks from him and ran my fingers over their cool surfaces.

'Nah,' he said. 'Just kidding. They don't mean anything. They're just neat rocks.'

In Queensland, I unpacked them and put them on top of my bookshelf.

When I go back to Newcastle, I text Matt. Can I come and see the dog? Meaning, can I come and see you?

He's moved out of the flat and Bud – now two – has a yard. We sit outside on the step because we haven't quit smoking yet. I throw a squeaky hippo toy I've brought for Bud. He fetches it relentlessly, dropping it at my feet every time.

'Watch this,' Matt says, taking the toy from me. 'I've taught him something new.'

'Bud, look.' He holds the hippo up and waits for Bud to look at him instead of the toy before he hurls it down the driveway. Bud spins as it flies over his head and he speeds off after it.

'I've been playing the piano again,' Matt says, 'Ludovico Einaudi.' He plays me 'Nuvole Bianche' on Spotify and I order the sheet music for myself when I get back to Queensland.

After two lonely years in Central Queensland, I move again, with my cat, into a Sydney share house. A couple of months later, Matt wants to go to Thailand for a few weeks and I volunteer to look after Bud because my housemates will also be out of the country. I walk Bud every day, and at night he sleeps on the back deck right beneath my window. In the mornings, I wake up to him standing on his back legs, front paws up on the windowsill, wet nose pressed against the glass.

One of my housemates is scared of cats and, although she's tried to accommodate mine, when she returns from overseas she asks if I can house him elsewhere. He moves in with Matt. It goes well for several months, before Bud chews through a dividing door in the laundry to get to him. Matt arrives home from work to find his door destroyed and the cat pressed against the wall beneath a piece of furniture Bud is too big to squeeze under. I take the cat back and ask my new partner, who lives in Victoria, if he will take him. He does. Three months later, I move to Victoria as well.

When Ludovico Einaudi announces he's coming to Melbourne in January 2020, I send Matt a message: If you can get a flight, I'll get the concert tickets and accommodation. Bushfire smoke hangs over the Sidney Myer Music Bowl as we take our seats a few rows back from the stage. That night, as Einaudi's fingers fly while he performs his final flourishes to our applause, we don't know that COVID-19 lockdowns loom behind the last wisps of smoke, or that it will be the last time I see Matt for a long time. It will be two-and-a-half years before I see him again, when he brings Bud to Victoria.

At the end of May 2022, I receive a message: Hey Tash, got a question for you. Only a hypothetical one. What's the chance you'd be equipped to take care of an eleven-year-old German shepherd? I'm planning to go travelling around South America for a while in a couple of months.

A few hours later, after talking to my partner about the logistics of dog fences, I message back. We will have him!

Really!? You're sure? I can start making plans?

Yep! And we can have him for as long as you need. I've already adopted him in my head for a year haha.

There's no-one I would trust more to take good care of him.

Bud and I walk down the gravel track alongside the local racecourse and I wonder if he remembers when we used to walk the one in Newcastle eleven years earlier – do all racecourses smell the same?

'Look!' I say to Bud as I hold out my phone to take a picture. He looks at me and I snap a photo of him gazing right into the camera and send it to Matt. 'Look' works for taking pictures, too, I message. We turn for home so I can get ready for work; I'm about to start my round and tonight is a night shift.

*

'I don't understand why you are so rude to people on the phone,' my partner said after I hung up from a call with our bank. I burst into tears. He'd criticised me for the same thing two weeks earlier and this time I'd tried so hard to be friendly, light, breezy. I thought I'd succeeded.

Within days of the second reprimand, I scroll past a picture of my nephew online and note it's tagged with autism awareness. My cousins and extended family all have neurodivergent kids but I always thought it had skipped our family. I can't ask; we're not a close or social family, and I haven't spoken to my brother for years. That same week, a list of 'non-diagnostic autistic traits in women' pops into my social feed. I check twelve of the sixteen boxes. I begin to do some intensive research.

I start to suspect I've gone undiagnosed, like so many women my age, and I send Matt a message. He's been a support worker in the disability community for a few years since he left hospitality and I'm interested in his opinion.

I think I might be autistic, I message.

Well, he replies, as someone who knows you and has worked with the autistic community, there could be something in this.

It's the first glimmer of validation. When I tell him several months later that I've been formally diagnosed, he responds to my message: That's fantastic!

And it is.

So much of my life makes sense, now, I reply.

I leave for work one night and Bud doesn't come to the gate for his usual pat, instead staying on his outdoor bed. I ask my partner to check on him later and when he does, Bud's put himself away in his room on his mattress. He is flat out asleep, like always.

It's dark when I get home in the morning. Bud is still sleeping and I don't wake him. I put myself to bed too and set an alarm so we can squeeze in a quick walk before my next shift. In the afternoon, I go outside to get him ready. He's lying on his outdoor bed again and doesn't come when I call him.

'What's up, Bud?' I say, moving to squat down beside him. 'Are you okay?'

He licks my arm.

'Are you tired from our walk yesterday? Want to play instead?' I pick up his favourite yellow crackle stick but he doesn't move. *That's weird.* I go inside and call the vet.

'Yeah, hi, my dog doesn't seem to want to stand up. He was fine yesterday but now he seems… off,' I tell the receptionist as I walk back outside.

'Oh, wait. Sorry, might be a false alarm. He's standing up having a drink now.'

Bud has walked several metres to his bucket and is drinking with his back to me. I'm about to hang up the phone when he tries to turn around. He tilts his head, wobbles, and falls down into a sitting position.

'Nope,' I say to the receptionist. 'I'm going to need to bring him in.'

The vet thinks it's something called vestibular disease – sort of like vertigo – that can impact older dogs; it comes on suddenly and within 24 to 72 hours they recover, I message Matt. He's about to board a bus to Bolivia. But the next morning Bud is not showing signs of improvement; he is worse. He can no longer stand on his own and struggles to lift his head. The vet says they now suspect a tumour or a stroke and ask me to begin thinking about euthanasia in case the steroid treatment I've authorised doesn't help.

'He's not my dog,' I say, gulping for breath, my voice thin.

Bud wasn't mine. But he felt like mine. I pretended he was mine.

I got our boy back today, I message Matt a few weeks later. He's very heavy. I don't know what I expected.

Does he smell, like, smoky?

No – but the ashes are paler than I expected. A light grey. I've never seen ashes before.

Me either! he replies.

I pull the snap-lock bag of ashes out of the navy velvet bag, take a picture, and send it to him. Then, I put them back inside the oak box, close the lid, and place the box on my bookshelf. Alongside it are the egg rocks of destiny.

Sources

1. Kinnaird, E, Stewart, C & Tchanturia, K 2019, 'Investigating alexithymia in autism: A systematic review and meta-analysis', *European Psychiatry*, vol. 55, pp. 80–9.

WHITE NOISE

Marlee Jane Ward

MARLEE JANE WARD (she/her) is a neurodivergent writer living on Wurundjeri land in Melbourne, Australia. She studied creative writing on Tharawal lands at the University of Wollongong and is an alumnus of the Clarion West Writers Workshop. She is the author of the award-winning *Orphancorp* series. Her short fiction is published in *Aurealis*, *Apex*, *Interzone*, *Terraform* and others. She writes memoir under the name Mia Walsch, and her book *Money for Something* was released in 2020. You can find her non-fiction in *Overland*, *Meanjin*, *Kill Your Darlings* and more. She is currently living her dream of being someone's weird goth aunt.

His sweet smell was white noise roaring all around me. His fingers burnt where they gripped my upper thigh, my ass: so hot, I almost couldn't bear it. Almost. White sparks zinged through my blood, my muscles. When I pulled his shirt off and ran my fingers down his back, it was covered in light, coarse hairs I'd never noticed on the long summer holiday afternoons we'd spent together, jumping off the footbridge at the lake. I felt those transparent hairs bristle, his skin going goosebumpy under my fingertips. When he asked if he could take my dress off, I nodded in reply, too overwhelmed to say a single word, or even remember which shape to make with my lips and tongue to indicate the affirmative. My lips and my tongue, they were for other things.

I was braless, so when he slipped my rumpled sundress up and over my head, I was almost naked. Then he pressed back into me, and I felt his smooth, bare chest against my smooth, bare chest, and I'd always wondered what that would feel like, and now I knew. It was better than I'd imagined. I could. Not. Breathe. I almost couldn't bear it. Almost.

This was twenty-five years ago. I was sixteen. It was my first sexual experience and I can recall the details with a razor-sharp focus. I can almost *feel* it still: the hot, soupy air of his disgusting teenage bedroom; sweat in the press between our skin; his lips tracing trails across my breast. I can locate the way he smelt in my memory, pull it up from the little box I keep it in. Relive it.

I told my friend Mel when I stayed at hers two nights later. I explained the mechanics of what we had done, the proper names and known euphemisms, but I just couldn't find the words to describe the other stuff. Those sparks in my blood and the hot-flame fingers on my thighs, the way his touch and smell were so *loud*, the way the feel of his goosebumps tugged a nerve that ran from the pads of my fingers down between my thighs, previously unknown to me.

'What was it like when you did it with Sam?' I asked. Mel was more experienced than me, in that she had made out with several guys and had sex *once* already.

'It was okay,' she said. 'I dunno, I thought it would be… better?'

Okay? I could not imagine anything better than what I'd felt in that messy room as my body almost vibrated off his dirty sheets – levitating, shooting sparks and fireballs. I didn't say that. I didn't say anything, because this was just another way I was different, and I didn't want to stack it on top of all the other ways I knew I wasn't like everyone else.

I didn't know what sensory processing disorder was until I was in my late thirties. I'd heard of the term before, but never connected it to how loud I find lights, smells, tastes and sensations, why I bump into everything and how I have a hard time trying to find my body in space. I thought there was something wrong with me.

I was sure it wasn't normal to be driven to self-harm because the fluorescent lights in my office were so *loud* and they got into my *spine* and *teeth* and *eyes*. How it was so unbearable that I'd always quit, or I'd get so distressed that I'd lose my shit and get fired. And when I'd try to explain it, I never got it right. I'd get that *look*, the 'Marlee, you are so fucking crazy' look I have received at least once a day throughout my life. So, when I read the definition of sensory processing disorder for the first time on some Insta infographic, my vision tunnelled, my head filled with the *warg-warg-warg* feeling I always get when something big happens, and suddenly my entire life made sense.

I am not insane. I'm just not neurotypical.

Sensory processing disorder is a kind of disorganisation of sensate experience. Touch, taste, smell, sound and sight are processed atypically, as are body awareness (proprioception), internal bodily sense (interoception) and balance (vestibular perception). People with sensory processing disorder can experience under- or over-responsivity (sometimes a combination of both), either avoiding or seeking out certain sensations. We can experience extreme discomfort from certain stimuli – fluorescent lights, for example – but seek out other kinds of input for the positive feelings they inspire.

I always knew that specific things made me feel 'crazy', agitating me to the point of distress. Smells and tactile sensations feeling 'loud' isn't exactly usual for most people. It is weird to whack my boob on the same jut of the banister every day, even though I know it's there. And I've never had a phone I didn't drop at least every few hours. I just never knew it was all related. I didn't have that knowledge, and I didn't have the language to express it.

When I found out what my sensory issues were, I did not connect it to my sex life until someone mentioned offhandedly, 'They say autistic people either really hate or really love sex.' I'm not sure where they got their information from. I cannot quote their sources. I'm not sure exactly who said it. But suddenly, my entire sex life made sense.

I've had two reasonably consistent special interests in my life: words and sex. I am using both precious interests here, right now – informing one with the other. I think these are my main two special interests because I'm good at both. They come easily to me. I have only won awards for the writing, though.

Once, I was on a panel at a writing centre and the conversation turned to sex. 'We've all had heaps of awkward sex,' someone said, laughing. Without thinking, I said, 'I haven't,' and the mic three centimetres from my mouth sent my words to the audience. The conversation on stage paused a little – just a quick quiet, like a skipped heartbeat – and it bounced off the back of the room. I know that silence far too well. It often happens when

I say things to other humans. Sometimes I think I shouldn't say words in public. It rarely goes well.

But it's true! I have had funny sex and slapstick sex. Casual, serious, drugged-up, fucked-up and fucking hot sex. I've had hate sex and loving sex and utterly desolate sex. Misguided sex. But I've never felt awkward. I've always been too lost in the sensations of my body to feel awkward.

Anyway, I don't think the writing centre asked me to do more panels after that. It could be unrelated, but also it seems like my experience is not universally relatable. Maybe only autist sluts with sensory processing disorder can identify? I might have made them feel bad with my lack of fumbly sex. Sorry, not sorry.

Many of the papers and posts I've read about sensory processing disorder and sex mention being 'frightened' and 'disgusted', or experiencing 'frustration' and 'distress'. I wanted to write about the way my sensory processing disorder and autism has enhanced my sexuality from a positive perspective, because I've been lucky enough to mostly experience it that way. Still, I know it's not all positive. When someone can set my body on fire with a touch, or send me mute as I reach sensory critical mass, it means they can hurt me. And they have. Accidentally and on purpose. It means they can take advantage, and they have. Mostly on purpose.

There *are* many elements of sex that can be unbearable when you live like a raw nerve. I'm particularly sensitive to the texture, taste, and quantity of saliva in a given mouth, and am only rarely keen on hectic kissing. Thankfully, my autistic bluntness means I can say, 'No tongue kissing, please,' if the situation calls for it. If scent becomes overwhelming, I'm just like, 'Hey, let's have a shower.' I make it worth their while by being filthy in other ways. I've had some lovers take offence, like I think the saliva content of their mouth is a personal failing on their part, as if I'm disgusted by the smell of their body. To all my future lovers: spit and sweat are not your fault. Look, if your mouth is too wet for my comfort, I can think of ten other things we can do instead of making out. Want me to show you?

At first, I wasn't sure I really had sensory issues. My first impression of them was the 'hyper' kind (too much). I have a lot of those, but I also experience many of the 'hypo' variety (not enough). Sometimes the brush of the hairs on my arm against the hairs on someone else's arm feels like a bullhorn blasting next to my head. Other times, I can barely feel my body and need to be touched hard so I can feel it. I have used sex to locate my body and to lose it, to feel and to numb. Contradictions like this have always made me doubt myself, but I have learnt to trust that my reality, however contradictory, is real. Being able to name it helps. Knowing other people experience the same ambiguity makes it real. To all the other greedy, needy, thirsty, sensory-seeking sluts: I see you. There is nothing more assuring than being seen.

My body sings and hums and strums. It is music reaching a crescendo, my synaesthesia. The feeling is like a wall of sound. I'm in the bathroom of a club, muffled metal riffs grinding outside, bass thrumming a wall my cheek is pressed to, body thrumming under the hand of some guy I'd spent twenty minutes eyeing from the other side of the dancefloor. I'm in the bathroom of a restaurant, lo-fi beats piped in, and she bites my nipple hard like a high, sharp note – held so long, you almost stop hearing it. I'm in a pub bathroom with two of the guys I work with, their rhythms harmonising as the band starts up in the front room. I'm in someone's mum's ensuite bathroom with one of my high-school lovers, her smell echoing around my brain and through the window comes the sound of drunk teenagers singing along to Nine Inch Nails.

I *do* want to fuck you, like the song says. Come to the bathroom with me. You can make my body wail.

‘LOOK HOW BIG THIS ENGINE IS’

Jess Ho

JESS HO (they/them) is a freelance writer, journalist and critic based in Naarm/Melbourne. *Raised By Wolves*, their memoir, was published in 2022 by Affirm Press. They host and produce *Bad Taste*, a podcast that explores who we are through the foods we eat. They were previously the food and drink editor of *Time Out Melbourne*, and their work has appeared in outlets such as *Gourmet Traveller*, *Eater*, *The Guardian*, *The Age Spectrum* and *Good Weekend*. While Jess is primarily known for being a food writer, their work is skewed towards decolonising how we consume food.

I'm standing at seat 11A after throwing my carry-on luggage, with the exception of my backpack, in the compartment over my head. I take out two gallon-sized Ziploc bags, my book, my glasses, a ballpoint pen and my passport and arrange them in the locker by the window. There is a sign that tells me I should not fill it with more than two kilograms, and I am grateful that no-one is walking through business class with a digital scale. I tear open one of the bags and take out my family-sized packet of Dettol antibacterial wipes and furiously scrub the seatbelt, the remote, the television screen, the food tray and every button or hinge I might touch. I realise that I popped open the locker before wiping the button, so I pull out another wipe to give my fingers and the handle a once over. I look at the wipes after using them and they're both black. I gag. I don't care what they say about cleaning and disinfecting on planes. Trust no-one.

I unzip the cover that goes over the seat to provide the illusion of a bed and wrap my chair in it before I sit down. I take off my shoes and swap them for slippers, placing them in the cubby by the aisle.

'Wow, you're still so vigilant,' says 12A behind me. All I can think to myself is, *It's the 'tism*, but I smile at her in response instead. She doesn't see it; I've been masked the whole time.

'Want one?' I hold up the wipes.

'Oh no, I'm good. I just had COVID, so I'm fine.'

My ritual is seen as acceptable these days, but I've been doing it ever since I started flying. Before the pandemic, a host told me my ritual was 'ahhhhh-mazing'. When I asked him why, he said it's what Naomi Campbell does and instructed me to google it. Before we left the tarmac, I watched a clip of her flying to Doha doing the exact same thing, only she brought her own blanket to place over the seat. *Genius*, I thought. *Except, how would I wash it at the other end?* Naomi has assistants and a team of people organising her.

In my other Ziploc there are facial wipes, a toner, a serum, a facial oil, eye cream, hand cream, steroid cream, lip balm, a change of underwear, a pair of compression socks, a toothbrush, toothpaste, floss, ear plugs, sunscreen and hydrating face masks. Even though every business class seat receives a toiletry bag with most of these items, I still bring my own. I don't know what is in the products provided or how my skin will react. I also doubt that any of their products are a match for my clinically dry skin. (My friend who is a tattoo artist once grabbed my moisturised arm, inspected it and said, 'In my professional opinion, you have the driest skin I have ever seen.' This comment comes second only to a Korean aunty I had never met before, pressed up against me during peak hour at Gangnam station, who suggested I use a better moisturiser. Bless her, because she was right.) I must have full control. This is no time for gambling, even if the bag is free. My Asian ancestors would be rolling in their graves if they knew how much I spent on the contents of that plastic baggy.

Let's break it down.

Wotnot natural face wipes for sensitive skin, $11.50 for twenty-five wipes. In an ideal world, I would be cleansing my face properly before applying skin care, but beggars can't be choosers. I read on a Reddit thread once that non-drinking water on planes is just filled up in giant tanks that are never cleaned and I imagined mould growing in my pores and my face turning into a giant mushroom. No thanks. Even though I shower before every long-haul flight, I still cleanse my face on a plane. The trip to the airport and the hours of recycled air while waiting to board always make me feel like I've walked through a dustbowl.

COSRX Full Fit Propolis Synergy Toner, $37. Admittedly, I had to siphon this off into a travel bottle so I could take it onto the plane, but I can't live without it. The propolis extract and honey are like a drink of water for my face and it feels like an impenetrable barrier is being formed between my skin and the air circulation system. It's also antifungal, anti-inflammatory and antibacterial, which suits my temperamental, eczema-ridden skin.

The Dream Skin Clinic Advanced Treatment Serum, $421. I go to this clinic as they specialise in ethnic skin, and they are the reason why I am poor and have the face of a cherub. I have no idea what is in this bottle despite owning the product and googling the hell out of it, because it has been specially formulated by the clinic's parent company in Korea and I can't read Korean. Well, no, that's a lie, I can sound out all the words because I know the Korean alphabet, but I have no idea what the words are in English. All they mention is six multi-growth factors at 95 per cent purity, but I have no idea what the six factors are or what they grow. As for the purity, it means nothing to me as I don't know what it is pure in. All I know is, my dry-ass face has never been this hydrated.

Paula's Choice Resist Anti-Ageing Eye Gel, $55. Do eye creams actually do anything? As someone in their mid-thirties who has just started using eye creams, I call bullshit. If anything, this is just something to put between my skin and the stale, sky air. I dab some on anyways despite my cynicism. After all, the aim of the game is hydration.

The Dream Skin Clinic Dream Peptide Complex Mask, $75 for five. Again, I have no idea what is in this, but every time I use one, my face looks like a newborn's butt for the following week. I mean this in the poreless, supple way, not the poopy, rashy way. You might be asking yourself if I really sit in my seat for twenty minutes with an opaque sheet mask on my face while in the air. Yes, yes, I do. I am completely shameless. I also refuse to do this in the bathroom of the plane for two reasons: 1. I don't want to be the jerk who takes up a toilet cubicle for twenty minutes; and 2. think of the poo spores.

Cosmedix Remedy Oil, $79. I don't bother messing around with moisturisers when I fly. In the air it's a complete waste of product, because as soon as it hits my skin it is sucked up like a drop of rain in the desert and I crumble like old cake. In its place, I use this facial oil comprising extracts from plants like bergamot, tangerine, coriander and avocado. A person who isn't as dry as me might use it to supplement their routine in winter, but I whip it out at high altitudes, when there is low humidity or when it's windy. In other words: all the damn time.

O'Keeffe's Working Hands hand cream, $13.95. After working in hospitality for most of my life, I am left with a compulsion to wash my hands every time I touch something. While this was great at the beginning of the pandemic because I was smug as hell about my hygiene practices, it also has a downside. Having dry, cracked and bleeding hands is normal for me, and this is the only product that has made any difference. If I could lather my hands in this and seal in the moisture with gloves, I would. Sadly, this is not conducive to reading on planes.

Laneige Lip Sleeping Mask, $31. Am I sleeping? No. Are my lips dry and cracked after a long-haul flight? Also no.

Mesoestetic Mesoprotech Light Water Antiageing Veil sunscreen, $96. I, as an Asian person, have had it drummed into me that I have to wear sunscreen and shield myself from the sun at all times. As an Australian millennial, I have been taught to fear the lack of ozone and its potential cancerous effects with the incredibly effective Slip, Slop, Slap campaign that has left my generation with a severe vitamin-D deficiency. Even though I know that a little bit of sun won't kill me, I can't expose myself to it at any cost. Between the fear of melanoma and the terror instilled in me over hyperpigmentation, melasma, premature ageing and irreversible sun damage, being in the air means that I am around thirty to forty thousand feet closer to the ball of fire in the sky. Logic dictates that the UV rays are even more damaging because I am so much closer to the sun. I slip, slop, slap my light-weight, hybrid sunscreen on and set an alarm to reapply every hour while in transit for maximum protection – even if I immediately push my shade down as soon as we have safely taken off.

For those of you mathing along, it's $819.45 and I haven't even added my prescriptions, underpants or dental hygiene products. Travel has to be this way. After a lifetime of severe eczema, learning that I am Autistic and feeling overwhelmed, trapped and anxious every time my skin barrier is compromised or uncomfortable, prevention is superior to repair. Money and embarrassment aren't considerations for me compared to the meltdowns I experience every time the largest organ of my body is damaged. The prolonged sensory discomfort can leave me debilitated and non-verbal for weeks.

At $819.45, not only have my ancestors rolled over in their graves, but they've died again in the afterlife. To add insult to injury, I don't imbibe any of the free-flowing alcohol or eat on planes. I stick to water and I choose to fast. After all, what's the point of the N95 mask if I take it off to shove food in my face over an extended period while sucking in mouthfuls of everyone's sneezes, coughs and farts? Also, it doesn't matter what class you sit in, airplane food dehydrates you further due to the salt content and it always inevitably backs you up. I know this for a fact. I have asked around. And I don't know about you, but there is nothing more disruptive to my life than an interruption in my poop schedule. Not eating for the duration of my flight isn't going to kill me. Turning down food I've paid for? If my ancestors could, they'd revoke my Asian card.

Travel is expensive, but for me, I spare no expense. It's not that I am rich, it's that it is the only way I can leave the country. I take fewer holidays and make them count because I can't deal with the sensory overload of being in economy. It is no accident that I am seated in row A or K, because these are solitary pods. There is no risk of a stranger wanting to make conversation with me over the middle divider. In the past, I have pretended that I don't speak English, but recently I've found international travel through Cathay Pacific to be the most reliable. The problem with that is, most flights from Melbourne go direct to Hong Kong first, and, linguistically, there is no escape.

*

Before the doors to the plane are cross-checked and sealed, I cleanse my face and meticulously layer on my skin care, waiting for each layer to sink in before applying the next. I cover my face in a sheet mask, a face mask and sunglasses and put in my ear plugs. I'm in my own world. A bubble. A muted, darkened, moist, protective bubble. I don't exist. You cannot perceive me.

Now, and only now, it is okay for me to fly.

'That's so fierce,' mouths the statuesque host as she hands me an extra bottle of water. It's not the first time a host has validated my routine, and it won't be the last. I marinate in the word *fierce*. Fierce is a word that's synonymous with Naomi Campbell. I'll take it. But I am no Naomi Campbell. She is also fabulous, pragmatic, poised and incomparable. I am none of those things. I am merely an Autistic person.

TWELVE HAIRCUTS

Caitlin McGregor

CAITLIN McGREGOR (they/them) is a writer, editor and illustrator. Their writing has been published in a range of magazines and literary journals, including *Meanjin*, *Kill Your Darlings*, *Sydney Review of Books*, *Going Down Swinging* and *The Big Issue*. Caitlin was the winner of the inaugural KYD Creative Nonfiction Essay Prize in 2022, and in 2023 they were the illustrator for the debut issue of *Sunder* poetry journal. They are currently a PhD candidate at the University of Melbourne.

Marie is a speech pathologist and works out of a converted garage at the bottom of her garden in Naarm's inner north. I sit in her waiting room, a strip of garage sectioned off from the office part with drywall and a pair of doors, currently closed, with stained-glass windows. In the waiting section there is a bookcase, a basket of children's toys and some seats. I take note of some of the titles on the bookshelf: *Engaging Autism*, *Asperger's and Girls*, *The Complete Guide to Asperger's Syndrome*, *A Colour Atlas of Human Anatomy*. A dog barks from somewhere inside.

When I was in kindergarten, my best friend Michelle and I had the same length hair – long enough for us to sit on the ends if we tilted up our chins. We would sit on the heater vents and then hold the warm ends of our hair up to the skin on our faces.

The hairstyle I had at this age was the best I have ever had. It was copper, with lighter streaks at the temples, and it was healthy and shiny, and my fringe was like Jane Birkin's.

Once inside Marie's office, I can glimpse her house through the two windows at the back of the garage. I see it in full whenever Marie opens the back door to let her cavoodle Henrietta in or out. The house is large and white, and you would have to climb a flight of stone steps to reach it from here.

Henrietta is small and reddish. I tell Marie I like dogs. In a way that will become familiar to me over the course of this two-hour appointment, Marie seizes on this comment and plumbs it for hidden meaning.

'Are you telling me that you would like Henrietta to stay in here while we talk?'

I have no designs or wishes related to the behaviour of Henrietta. I simply like dogs and thought Marie might like to know.

When I was about seven, I read Charlie and the Chocolate Factory *and then stuck a wad of chewed gum behind my right ear for safekeeping. Mum, furious, had to cut it out of my hair with scissors.*

Wanting to fact-check that it had been Violet Beauregarde from Charlie and the Chocolate Factory *who had given me this idea, I come across a Reddit thread: 'Did anyone else stick gum behind their ear as a kid because of Violet Beauregarde and have to have an emergency haircut?' 22 upvotes. I'm simultaneously elated and disappointed to discover that the experience wasn't mine alone.*

It is Marie's job to assess my 'pragmatic language' (social communication) skills. She explains that she's going to identify 'glitches' in our conversation, and am I okay if she stops the conversation when these happen so she can explain them to me? Yes, I confirm, I am okay with this.

Here is the first glitch (of many) Marie identifies.

Marie: Tell me about where you are living.

Caitlin: I live in [redacted].

Marie: That's in the country, isn't it?

Caitlin: Yes.

Marie: Do you live with family, or by yourself?

Caitlin: I live with my partner and my son.

Marie: Do you have property there?

Caitlin: Yes, we built a house a few months ago.

Marie flags my answer here, because I have taken 'property' to mean any kind of land or house of which I am the owner. But by 'property', Marie had meant, specifically, acres of land, perhaps farmland. A neurotypical person, she explains, would have been able to infer this was what she meant.

In their 2022 book *On the Inconvenience of Other People*, Lauren Berlant writes: 'A glitch is an interruption within a transition, a troubled transmission.'[1]

The town I live in does not have much farmland and is mostly small residential blocks – this is knowledge I have, but Marie does not. It strikes me there are any number of differences between us that could have led to this misunderstanding, but Marie writes, in the report that results from this appointment, *CAITLIN DOES HAVE CHALLENGES WITH THE MECHANICS OF CONVERSATION.*

Berlant goes on: 'A glitch is also a claim about the revelation of an infrastructural failure.'

When I was in Year 6, there was a girl in my class called Annie, and Annie had very cool hair. In the mid-year break, my parents took me to a hairdresser and I carefully described what I wanted, in order that I would look like Annie.

The structure, texture and density of Annie's hair, I now know, were absolutely nothing like mine. Annie's hair was fine, thin and naturally pin-straight. Mine is dense, wavy and unruly. To my utter devastation, I did not come out of that haircut looking anything like Annie.

There had been a glitch before the property one, which Marie had missed. She had opened our appointment by saying, 'Just so you know, I am neurotypical.'

I had said, 'Oh, I'm sorry.' As in: *my condolences*. As in: let's take the piss together, for a moment, by pretending that it is you, and not me, who is the strange and unlucky one in this situation, which is clearly not true because (here, at least) you are the professional and I am the assessed.

Marie had said, 'There is no need to be sorry! I like to work with autistic people.'

Berlant writes:

> Any work on relationality would do well to consider the joke… If one is lucky, and in on the joke, the reciprocity is technical, a performance of a sudden interestedness and solidarity. Or, a joke can provoke a painful attachment-break.

'Let's begin,' said Marie, though of course we already had.

In Year 8, the popular girls all got mullets. These were not the naturally textured, androgynous mullets of the current moment, which I love unreservedly, but long, heat-straightened hair with waxed spikes on the crown. Closer to David Bowie in Labyrinth *than to Courtney Barnett.*

I begged Mum to take me to a hairdresser.

My mullet did not go down well. I'm still not sure if this was because I was not a member of the group that was allowed to get mullets, or because there was something different about my mullet when compared to other people's. It's possible that the sharp uptick in bullying I received at this time was a coincidence and had nothing to do with my hair. But I started to be physically blocked out of chatting circles of girls at lunchtimes. Once, it happened in class and a teacher saw and said, 'Lilian, make some room for Caitlin, please.' This was humiliating, obviously, and Lilian did not make room, because Lilian had more power than the teacher did in this scenario. The teacher seemed to recognise this, and moved on.

Someone in my year level set up a burner account to email me and tell me that the jumper I always wore to casual clothes days was ugly and so was my hair, and that everyone thought it was annoying how I started twirling my hair whenever anyone complimented someone else's haircut. I realised, retrospectively analysing group conversations I'd been in, that girls had been loudly complimenting each other's hair in front of me, presumably to make fun of this hair-twirling behaviour. I hadn't noticed; I just play with my hair when I'm stressed.

'It's funny how many autistic people end up doing PhDs,' says Marie. Then she looks up at me. 'I mean, it's not... *funny* funny. Not *literally* funny.' I nod to assure her that I understand, and that I agree.

I tell Marie I work remotely, and that I like the independence. Yes, it does get a bit isolating sometimes, but overall it suits me better than working in an office, so I take what I can get.

'The good and the bad,' says Marie.

'Yes,' I say.

There is a pause in the conversation while Marie types on the keyboard she has sitting on her lap. Then she looks up at me and says, 'You didn't know what to say.'

'When?'

'Just then. I said, "The good and the bad," and you just said, "Yes."'

'Should I have said something else?'

'It could have been a conversation,' says Marie, going back to her typing. *CAITLIN MAY NOT KNOW WHAT TO SAY IN A CONVERSATION AND THEN MAY FEEL UNCOMFORTABLE AND FEEL THAT SOMETHING IS WRONG.*

Months passed, and everyone grew their mullets out. Once, in the toilets at the same time as two of the other girls, I overheard them making fun of themselves. 'We looked like pineapples,' they said.

I realised: we had all looked silly. But they had looked silly together, and now they could laugh and be laughed at safely.

If one is lucky, and in on the joke.

No-one could bring up my mullet for years without my face burning with shame. A painful attachment-break.

I have been asked about autism, and in response I'm writing an essay about hair. This is not to say that my hair is autistic or that my autism is hairy, though both are probably true.

I am saying one thing and meaning another.

(I thought I should mention the fact that I like dogs in case there were sometimes people who didn't, and I wanted to be clear that as far as I was concerned Henrietta could come and go as she pleased. So, I suppose there was a subtext, it's just that it wasn't identified correctly.)

But I am also – and this is important – telling you about my actual hair.

Or perhaps – *IN RESPONDING TO QUESTIONS OR COMMENTS IN CONVERSATION CAITLIN MAY NOT KNOW THE INFORMATION TO SHARE UNLESS IT IS DIRECTLY AND EXPLICITLY ASKED FOR* – I am simply misunderstanding the assignment.

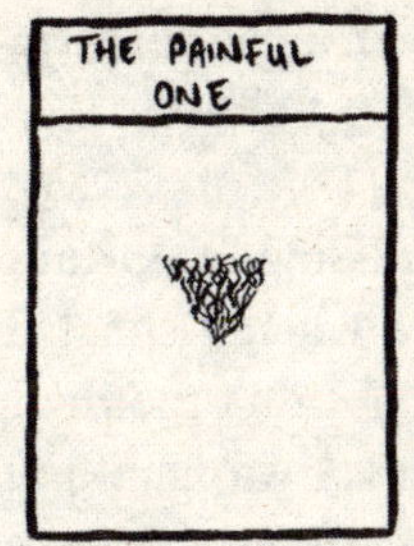

The first person I ever dated was a leery boy – well, a man technically/legally – four years older than me. I was fourteen and I met him while I was working my weekend retail job at a chain store.

This guy met the one criterion I had at the time for dateworthiness: he was interested in me.

*At one point, he texted me to ask whether I had any pubic hair (*R u hairy? lol*). I lied, and he wrote back,* Good! Hairy girls are gross haha.

This lie created a dilemma, which I attempted to solve by placing a crappy disposable leg razor against my pubes and dragging it straight through them.

Marie tells me that even *she* finds it very difficult to understand autistic people, sometimes. She knows an autistic woman who nearly got married to a man that she never even really liked!

I say I don't find that hard to understand at all.

Marie makes a note.

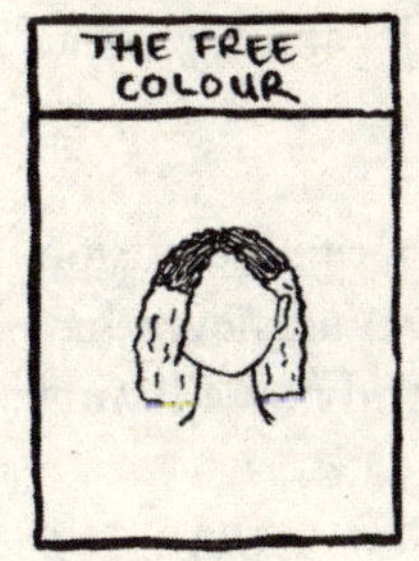

Towards the start of 2020, I realised that about the only colour my hair hadn't been in the last fourteen years was its natural one. The lockdowns had started and my hair was blonde, which is the only colour I still prefer to leave to a hairdresser. Now was as good a time as any, I decided, to grow it out.

It was not the shimmering copper of my four-year-old self. I was old, and it was brown. I bought some copper tint online, but didn't use it; it felt like a worthwhile challenge to leave it as it was for a bit.

After nearly two decades of dyeing my hair non-stop, I was stunned that the colour of the hair growing out of my head didn't need any maintenance. It was, I kept telling people incredulously, a free hair colour.

Another glitch, of sorts: Marie tells me I am missing important non-verbal cues in our conversation, because when I speak I look at the walls instead of at her directly. 'You didn't see this,' she says, 'but I was nodding, and sometimes I was making movements with my hands in response to the things you were saying.'

I tell her I did see her movements, and that I had in fact been watching her reactions quite closely. I explain the concept of peripheral vision.

'I didn't know you were doing that,' she says. 'You didn't tell me!'

I do not refer her to Hans Asperger, whose work her profession is largely based on, for two reasons: one, his work is abhorrent to me; and two, I understand this may embarrass Marie and be interpreted as rude. He did, however, write in 1944 that 'autistic children do not look with a firmly fixed glance at anything, but rather, seem to perceive mainly with their peripheral field of vision. Thus, it is occasionally revealed that they have perceived a surprisingly large amount of the world around them.'[2]

Instead I say, 'You didn't ask,' and she laughs and says, 'See? Differences in communication!'

I do see.

'It's useful for me to know that, about the peripheral vision,' she goes on. 'If you hadn't told me that, I would never have known you were taking that information in. And now I'll know to ask the next autistic person I see!'

I DID NOTE THAT SHE IS PROCESSING NON-VERBAL CUES THROUGH HER PERIPHERAL VISION AS OPPOSED TO THE NEUROTYPICAL WAY OF LOOKING TOWARDS THE OBJECT OF ATTENTION.

(Here, at least, you are the professional and I am the assessed, but whose expertise do you deal in, really?)

Because my parents wouldn't let me dye my hair, and because I was convinced that doing so was the key to my happiness, my friend Alex bought a box of dark-brown hair dye for me from the supermarket. I swapped her a ten-dollar note for it on the bus ride to school.

Once I finally mustered the courage, I hid in the bathroom and initiated myself into a ritual that would eventually become second nature: don gloves, mix the colour with the developer, inhale the ammonia, section and coat hair, wait, rinse. I emerged transformed. My parents didn't notice.

I explain to Marie that when I was growing up I'd spend time at night analysing the conversations I'd been in that day, trying to work out why they'd made me feel some sort of way, or how I might have embarrassed myself. *Their conduct, manner of speech and, not least, often grotesque demeanour cries out to be ridiculed.*[3]

'That sounds exhausting,' says Marie.

'It wasn't very efficient,' I say.

I am trying to be light-hearted and self-deprecating, but Marie flags another glitch. 'I was making an emotional offer, by saying that must have been exhausting for you,' she says. 'But instead of accepting my offer of empathy, you said' – and here she puts on a gruff voice, presumably to imitate my emotionlessness – '"*It's not very efficient*".' (Their conduct, manner of speech—)

When I was in Year 1, I was sent to the Year 3/4 class for English lessons. In this 3/4 class was a girl named Tessa. Tessa was assigned the role of looking after me on the afternoons I came to English class, which she fulfilled by repeatedly threatening to chop off what she referred to as my 'pumpkin' with her little red pair of scissors.

My mum had had my hair cut into a tapered bob – longer at the front, shorter at the back – and my hairline grew along the nape of my neck in such a way that there was a longer, pointed section of hair in the centre. This piece of hair, said Tessa, was a pumpkin, and it should be removed immediately.

I was both deeply ashamed of this pumpkin and terrified that Tessa would follow through with her threat.

Marie says she knows a lot of autistic people, both through her work and outside of it. Her brother-in-law is autistic, she tells me, although he doesn't think so. 'He says other people aren't clear in their communication, like *they're* the problem!' And then – I am almost certain – she says this: 'I have a lot of autistic people in my private life. It's because I like smart people, and *it's the downside of that*.' I double-check later: yes, this comment is in my notes. But maybe, surely, I misheard.

Once my hair had outgrown its pumpkin bob, my mother would brush my hair and tie it up in a ponytail each morning before school. This was excruciating, but I learnt not to wince. 'Crooked as a dog's hind leg,' my mother would say when it was done. 'But it will have to do.'

Marie shows me a series of photos. Each one has a person, or people, in some kind of situation: three people with backpacks on, waiting at a bus stop; a child standing in the middle of a messy room with their hands on their head; a group of adults sitting around a dinner table. I am to tell Marie what I think is happening in each photo, and how I think the people might be feeling.

The people are clearly actors, so the task is to interpret not genuine emotion but the ones being intentionally projected.

I don't point this out. I say that these people are waiting for a bus; they might be bored, or they could just be tired. This kid might be overwhelmed by the mess in his room, but he could also be stressed because he's been asked to clean it. And the people having dinner might be genuinely having a nice time, or they could be overperforming their enjoyment because dinner parties come with social expectations of civility.

Marie makes a note.

'What does this exercise tell you about people?'

She keeps typing while she explains. 'Neurotypical people don't give so many options,' she says. 'You thought about different possibilities and gave them to me, like you were second-guessing your first instinct.' *He made life hard for himself by his awkwardness and endless hesitations.*[4]

'I just look and know my instinct is right,' she adds. *A NEUROTYPICAL SOCIAL COMMUNICATOR 'KNOWS' AN EMOTIONAL STATE WITHIN A SCENE WITH A CERTAIN AMOUNT OF CONFIDENCE AND IS NOT USING THE OVERLAY OF 'THINKING' ABOUT THE SCENE OR THE EMOTIONS PRESENTED.* I ask her how she could possibly know this. 'Because we have a lifetime of being right. And if we're wrong sometimes, we don't care.'

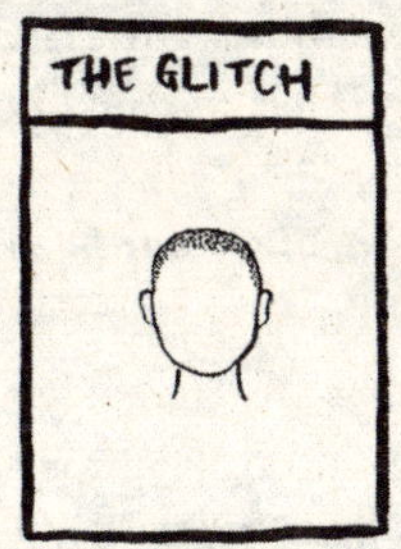

Shortly before my eight-year-old son started at his new school, I asked him if he'd like a haircut. 'Would you like me to shave it, since it's been so hot?' He said yes. I shaved his whole head, and when he realised what I had done he burst into tears. 'Why did you shave all of it?' He had thought I was only going to shave the underside of his bowl cut.

I told him I was sorry, and my partner and I consoled him with all the platitudes I'd heard myself countless times – it's only hair, it will grow back, it looks good even though it's not what you were expecting – and we helped him into the shower.

Once he was out of earshot, I howled. My partner repeated the platitudes to me – it's only hair, it will grow back, it looks good even though it's not what he was expecting – and I struggled to explain the horror, the potentially everlasting trauma of what I had just done.

He was fine.

We have reached the end of our allotted two hours. 'I will send you an invoice,' says Marie, who will charge me $600. 'And once you have paid that, I will send you your report. But, in the meantime, you can tell your psychologist, "Marie says yes."'

'Yes, you think I'm autistic?'

'Yes, I think you're autistic. But you already knew that, didn't you?'

I turned thirty while writing this essay. I've been cutting my own hair since I was sixteen. I never use a hairdryer (too loud), I avoid salons altogether (too loud, too bright, too many confusing social interactions), and I do a better job than any professional ever has. Maybe that's because I'm no good at communicating what I want to anyone else. Maybe it's because I know my own hair really well. Or maybe I'm just good at it.

The hair at my temples, I noticed the other morning, has been lifting to a light copper.

Sources

1. Berlant, L 2022, *On the Inconvenience of Other People*, Duke University Press, NC.
2. Asperger, H 1994/1991, '"Autistic psychopathy" in childhood', in U Frith (ed.), *Autism and Asperger Syndrome*, Cambridge University Press, pp. 37–92.

3. ibid.
4. Notes on case study of seven-year-old 'Ernst K' in Asperger, H, '"Autistic psychopathy" in childhood'.

BURNING OUT, AS AN AUTISTIC DOCTOR

LT

LT trained and worked as a medical doctor for five years before taking a break from the profession due to burnout. These days, they live a quieter life. They enjoy slow days, soft things, working with their hands and watching plants grow. Though it is not the life they thought they would live, it is a better one for them.

At medical school, autism was taught in the form of generalisations, statistics, dot points and slides: all rather dry and removed from reality, as most lectures were. I'm sure there was a section on the DSM-5 criteria for autism, all of them deficit-based and observed from the outside. Phrases like 'abnormal social approach' and 'reduced sharing of interests'. We didn't learn about autism from the inside – how autistic people experience and inhabit their lives. If we had, I might have connected the dots and realised I was autistic sooner.

I left medical school not knowing much about autism, let alone that I was autistic myself. When I eventually did read about autism from the inside, it was much more enlightening than serious-sounding statistics, though some of those were both revealing and alarming.

I suppose I understood that autistic people suffered worse health outcomes, but I was astounded when I found out by how much. No doubt, the figures would have occupied a single dot point on a slide in my course.

Autistic people have a twenty-year gap in life expectancy compared to the general population.[1]

We are also nine times more likely to die by suicide.[2]

As an autistic doctor, I find this doubly horrifying. We need to do better. We deserve better.

I've heard so many stories of autistic people who were not listened to, not believed, brushed off, misunderstood. In each of them, I see a bit of myself.

When I went through my burnout, when I sat on the other side of the desk as the patient, there was such a gulf in understanding that it felt like I was speaking a foreign language. My GP at the time had only met me twice. As a young, otherwise healthy person, the main reason I attended the clinic was for routine vaccinations.

Like many other autistic people, I struggled with executive function, including booking health and dental appointments.

My GP said something I couldn't forget: 'Your level of functioning is so far from where you should be, and I don't know why.'

'Neither do I,' I replied. 'Isn't it strange?'

I was heavily masking at the time. I'm sure I seemed very pleasant, calm, even cheerful. When speaking about my struggles, I always adopted an upbeat air, minimising myself and diminishing my symptoms. I dreaded attention, even when I was actively seeking help. Though I tried my hardest to communicate, my body wouldn't let me. I couldn't bear to show my true self.

There are so many examples of people being mistreated or misunderstood by the profession. My story is one of them: an undiagnosed autistic doctor who struggled, triumphed to finish her qualifications and start practising as a GP, then eventually distanced herself from a system that so often overworks its people and stretches them to breaking point. In which colleagues who call in sick are looked down on and blamed when the team has to pick up the slack. A system in which lunch and bathroom breaks are luxuries, and evenings and weekends are free game. In which perfectionist, idealistic students from medical school are moulded into self-sacrificing healthcare workers who would do anything for their patients.

If we struggle, it is on us to make changes. We are told to meditate, get better at 'time management', start antidepressants, get better sleep (despite the shift work and being on call). When the onus is on the individual, suffering equals failure. No wonder most of us don't seek help.

Let's start at the beginning.

We were immigrants from Asia, so you might think my parents pushed me into medicine. They didn't. In fact, my father was against it – though his reasons weren't quite politically correct. He thought that being a doctor was too hard for a woman and I should have a more relaxed life. At the time, I thought a career in medicine would marry a couple of my strong persisting interests. (Special interests, you might say – though I never really took to the term. It sounds a little childish, though that's the way with many terms relating to autism; so much of the discourse is about children.)

I have always been interested in science, psychology and how humans work. I had to be. Like many autistic girls and women, I developed this interest in psychology and human behaviour – which seemed fascinating and foreign – to survive. I observed and read books on social interactions and practised the art of being human. This was fraught with trial and error. The problem with not having any close friends is the absence of feedback. No-one to tell you if you make some social mistake, no-one to give you pointers. I didn't get bullied too badly, so I must have done alright – but my academically inclined school didn't seem prone to bullying anyway. No teachers pulled my parents aside to share concerns. I flew under the radar.

I listed medicine, along with psychology and medical science, as my preferred options for university study. For some reason, I never made the connection that studying medicine would mean becoming a doctor and treating patients. Uncharacteristically, I didn't plan every detail in a spreadsheet, I didn't do my due diligence, I didn't create a timeline and scope out all my career prospects. Perhaps I was wiser about embracing the uncertainty of life back then. I was never gung-ho about medicine, so I read through my acceptance letter with an attitude of, *ehh, okay.*

They say going through medical school is like being on train tracks. Once you leave a station, you can't get off until the next one, at least not without risking bodily harm. It's study, exams, placement, study, exams, placement. This worked for me, with its strict, in-built routine. There were limited demands on socialising, and most of the time we discussed the common topic of our study. This worked for me too.

While it wasn't easy, I struggled less during university than I did in the years that followed. After medical school, new graduates are allocated to a hospital for two years to gain experience under supervision. This was when my various autistic traits really started to rub up against reality.

To become well rounded, we rotated between several departments over the year. It meant that just as I was settling into one role I would go off into a different environment: a different team with different kinds of patients and new collections of medical conditions. There were new names to keep track of, new consultants to learn about, a new dynamic to fit into. The constant change and lack of control didn't work well with my desire for sameness and predictability. But it was bearable.

The worst aspect was navigating the social sphere. I couldn't just focus on gaining experience and practising safely. I had to ensure I was in the good graces of the seniors who would assess me. Any wrong step could be a threat to my career.

Ever since childhood, I've presented as an agreeable, passive person. I learnt early on that safety lay in not being noticed. It was easier to hide the problematic parts of myself – which seemed to be most of me. On some rotations during my medical training, I had to turn this up a notch. I have laughed at inappropriate sexual comments. I have pretended to have bigoted opinions I didn't share. There was bullying, a strict hierarchy and constant pressure to keep up. Somehow, I survived it with only a few hiccups.

The shift work was frequent and punishing. Healthcare doesn't sleep. There were the day shifts, the evenings, the after-hours, the nights, the weekends. I needed good sleep: nine hours minimum. Perhaps I needed the extra rest to recover from all the masking, but, whatever the case, I hated, *hated* shift work. But who didn't? I once made the mistake of trying to engage in small talk with a senior. 'Do you like night shifts?' I asked. Another junior just laughed. 'What a question,' they said. I could feel my rapport points slipping. I had meltdowns even then, before the burnout, though I didn't recognise them as that. I thought everyone cried. It seemed the logical response to the conditions.

I had to escape the hospital, so I left for general practice after my second year.

I was less enamoured with being a GP than attracted by the opportunities for flexibility and a shorter training pathway. It took only two years of full-time further training to become a qualified GP, compared to five years or more for most hospital specialties. I did like the potential for practising preventative health, as well as the possibility of sub-specialising in mental health.

I still think becoming a GP was the right choice. But the next few years presented my biggest challenges. By now, everything I'd experienced in my medical training was building on itself: trauma over trauma.

'You never know what comes through the door,' a GP said in one of our lectures. 'It's exciting and challenging.' Sure – but the uncertainty of it caused huge waves of anxiety. I needed control. I needed information, too. Just seeing a patient without preparation seemed impossible.

Before work every day, I would go through the list of patients scheduled and review their backgrounds, their medications, their previous visits, their pathology and imaging, and their specialist letters and come up with a potential reason they might be back. Sometimes I got it right. Mostly, though, I was way off. Then there was setting my own agenda as their doctor. Did they have screening tests that were due? Were there abnormal results from previous tests that might need addressing? Were their medications all appropriate? There were so many aspects to my preparation that others didn't seem to need. It was inefficient and sometimes a complete waste of time, but not doing it would've gone against my very nature. Worst of all was when an easy, predictable follow-up was cancelled and a new, mysterious patient popped up – who I hadn't had the chance to pre-review.

The intense time pressure of having to manage complex issues in only ten or fifteen minutes was terrible, too.

There's this concept of top-down and bottom-up thinking. Top-down thinking is like thinking of a recipe, figuring out what ingredients you need, purchasing what you need and then making the meal. The big picture is formed first, then worked with to identify the details. Bottom-up thinking is like looking in the fridge to see what you've already got, then piecing together a meal from what you have. That is, you start with the details, then build up. Autistic people tend to favour the latter. I certainly do. It's how I process everything, from cooking, to social interactions, to planning for retirement, to working with patients. It's a big energy drain.

Everything is evidence to be gathered. Only once the puzzle is almost complete do I understand what I'm looking at. Sometimes the picture is glaringly obvious, but I only see it after the patient leaves the room and I've had the time and energy to put the puzzle pieces together. There were times when I found I'd given the wrong advice, or that additional investigation was required. In those cases, it would have been wrong to leave it. So, I'd call the patient, explain myself and spend more time discussing this new scenario. This meant I was thorough, but not efficient in the way my colleagues were.

Sometimes I would run over time. Then it would be worse, because the rules of the appointment state that a 9:00 am slot is seen at 9:00 am, not an arbitrary time after that. (Though this rarely happens in practice for many doctors.) I was very rigid about this. Running over time meant people were waiting for me. It meant less (or no) time for lunch. No bathroom breaks, no time for water. It meant staying back an hour or longer to catch up – when I desperately needed that time to recover. I saw it as a personal failure.

They tell you, when you're a doctor, that you have to make time for yourself. That a tired doctor is worse for the patient. I'm now realising perhaps this wasn't meant literally, that it may be something that's just thrown out there, like saying everything's fine even when it's not. We want to live in a society where everyone has the opportunity to look after themselves, but many don't have this luxury. I couldn't sacrifice my patients' quality of care, so I had to sacrifice myself.

I did all this while creating the perfect persona for each patient: putting effort into understanding their body language, their tone of voice, and trying to mirror the right responses back. At times, I was too good a listener. All my formative years spent cultivating the skill of continuing a conversation meant I had never practised ending one. I'd sit with a patient for forty minutes, an hour, because they'd finally found someone with an open ear.

I spoke to a psychologist about the energy I needed for all this, before I had my formal diagnosis. 'Why can't you just go with the flow?' they asked. Remarkably unhelpful. It's like telling a drowning person they'd be better off relaxing and not flailing around – without knowing they have sandbags tied to their feet. The psychologist didn't know that what I needed was different.

It didn't help that COVID-19 had just emerged. Perhaps that was what pushed me over the edge, though the rumblings had started well before that. I resorted to harmful stims such as scratching my skin and pulling out my eyelashes between patients in order to distract myself, to make it through the day. I stayed in my room and didn't eat lunch with the others, to preserve my energy. I was miserable at home. I spent the few days I had off dreading my return.

Not all days were bad, but that's all they were: not bad. It was an exceedingly confusing time. Breakdowns, panic attacks, and intense periods of stress and dread were becoming more frequent. Yet, at times, I felt perfectly fine.

I once came across a collection of images, generated by an artificial intelligence program, meant to depict autistic people.

I wasn't surprised they were all pictures of white men and boys, but it was stark how sad they all looked, too. Not a single happy face.

Artificial intelligence thinks autistic people are sad because society thinks so. Autism = suffering. Isn't that baked into the DSM-5? You literally can't be diagnosed as autistic unless your autism is causing impairment.

One particularly bad day, I had my worst meltdown yet. I was on the floor, hitting my head, crying, having an intense out-of-body reaction. A part of me was breaking down and another part was carefully assessing if I was crazy enough to be admitted to a mental health institution. I decided not everyone felt like this. I was finally impaired enough to be autistic.

What a joy it has been to find a lexicon for myself. To define something is to bring it to light, to make it visible. I came across the concept of alexithymia early in my search. Like many autistic people, I have difficulty recognising emotions until they are out of control. This meant I felt fine until I really, *really* wasn't. I could push through until I couldn't. This, combined with high expectations (based on what I'd already accomplished), and my innate desire for optimisation and planning, was dangerous. I was always teetering on the edge of destruction.

Burnout and stress crept up on me less like a burglar and more like a conman. I didn't know it had ambushed me until it was too late. I dropped down to part-time work. I saw my GP. I attended those psychology sessions. But I never felt understood, because I didn't yet understand myself. I just knew that what I'd been doing hadn't been working. I was grateful for the times I broke down so completely I lost control, when I hit my head and body. The meltdowns and burnout were evidence of my suffering. Without the spectacle, it would be less real.

My official diagnosis gave me permission to look after myself. We shouldn't need someone else to tell us we're worthwhile. I shouldn't have needed to pay to have someone tell me something

I already knew. It was a relief though. For a long time, I was worried I was making it all up, that I'd become delusional in my pursuit of something, anything, that would excuse my failings. It was a relief to know I hadn't gone mad – though I still experience periods of autistic imposter syndrome one year on.

The lens of autism has helped to reframe much of my past and present, but it's made the future more uncertain. The process of discovering yourself, of unmasking after living someone else's life for so long, feels less like waking up and more like being born again: weak, frail, needing care.

My identity is in flux, my previous self shattered. We all change every day, but somehow other people seem to have a continuity to them, a grounded surety that I lack. So far.

The struggle with identity is a common theme among late-diagnosed autistic people. It's a different kind of gap, dealing not with mortality and death but with years of self-actualised potential.

Can I afford another adolescence of self-discovery when bills are stacking up and piles of laundry need to be folded? Would things be different if I had received my diagnosis at four, or even twenty-four? Would I have had a happier, healthier life?

Perhaps one day I'll find joy and meaning in medicine again. Finding other autistic doctors online gave me hope I can learn new skills and advocate for my needs. But I'm a bit too tired and a bit too worn out for that right now. I'm taking a break from medicine.

Perhaps I'll become a mushroom farmer or run in-house hydroponics and supply bok choy and salad leaves to my neighbours. Perhaps I can delve into research and contribute to expanding our understanding of neurodiversity in all its forms.

My identity is still undergoing the process of being broken down atom by atom, before it can be built again. From the bottom up. Who am I now? I am an autistic adult, newly diagnosed, trained to be a doctor and a GP, burnt out from a multitude of factors but still passionate about so much more.

Most importantly, I'm someone ready to depart on the journey of my new adolescence. Now that I know more about who I am and what makes me that way, I have control over how my life will come together.

My new knowledge has given me power.

Sources

1. Commonwealth of Australia 2022, *Senate Select Committee on Autism: Services, support and life outcomes for autistic Australians*, Parliament of Australia, Canberra.
2. Richdale, A, Haschek, A, Lawson, L, Hayward, S & Abdullahi, I 2020, 'Supporting mental health: What young Australian autistic adults tell us', La Trobe University.

WHY TEACHING ENGLISH AS A SECOND LANGUAGE MAKES ME FEEL KNOWN

Adele Dumont

ADELE DUMONT is a writer and critic. Her latest book is *The Pulling.* When she's not reading or writing, she likes baking, cycling along Sydney's backstreets and eavesdropping.

'One never realises an emotion at the time,' wrote Virginia Woolf. 'It expands later, and thus we don't have complete emotions about the present, only about the past.'[1] I can't help but think this is doubly true for people of my kind, who are so prone to slight misinterpretation and misunderstanding, who are frequently swamped by feeling but struggle to name what these feelings are or to trust in their validity and their authority.

I began teaching English as a second language over a decade ago, and from the start I had the clear but mysterious impression that this was nothing short of a vocation. It's only recently, though, that I've been able to properly parse my feelings around this particular role. It's easy to frame the classroom as a highly constructed and artificial environment, cut off from what people like to call the 'real world'. Maybe this is why, for many years, I dismissed the happiness I experienced as a classroom teacher. Or rather, I didn't believe this feeling was quite *real*. If I flourished in front of a whiteboard but panicked at the thought of after-work drinks, then maybe I wasn't a proper person: only a strange, scripted one.

When I was doing my teacher training, my instructors couldn't believe I hadn't ever taught before; I was just so 'natural', they kept telling me. One of the first principles we were taught – which a lot of beginning teachers struggle with – is to avoid talking too much: students' brains can only process so much, and the goal should be getting students to produce language themselves. Another important skill was to grade our language, so that it aligned to the students' level but in such a way that our speech was still natural and didn't come across as patronising.

This mode came very easily to me, thanks to my acute self-consciousness. I was used to speaking minimally and always measuring my words, incapable of just freely speaking my mind or casual 'chatting'. I was also inclined to what people call 'overthinking'. But I saw the other beginner teachers pile convoluted explanation upon explanation, tying themselves in knots. The students in their charge would be flummoxed and mute.

Over my subsequent teaching career, again and again I was surprised at how much my students seemed to *like* me, trust me and grow attached to me. I was used to people finding me aloof, or a bit of a loner. I had a window, for the first time in my life, into what it was like to be popular. My students saw me as bright and confident, cheerful and patient. (Occasionally I might describe myself as shy and they'd assume they'd misunderstood the word.) I never tired of helping them and being in their company, and I knew that they could feel this. Learning a new language can be a very vulnerable process. Students who are not usually shy can turn so. I was so intimately accustomed to being awkward and anxious that I could detect in an instant when students felt these things, and I knew, instinctively, how to reassure them and make them feel safe.

There was also my attention to detail and the swift speed I read at, so that I could detect errors in a page of handwriting almost automatically, even from the upside-down angle at which I read it while walking past a student's desk. My lifelong habits of observing and listening to people intently, detecting the most subtle of patterns, equipped me to facilitate lessons in which my students felt properly guided and understood. I knew precisely the limits of their vocabulary and the particular grammatical mistakes each individual student was likely to make. My students would often comment that sometimes they forgot I wasn't speaking to them in their language, so perfectly could they follow the substance and logic of my lessons.

All of this stood in stark contrast to my social shortcomings outside the classroom walls. I struggled to participate in any of the staffroom chitchat. Once, I heard a teacher arrange to meet up with another teacher for coffee after class. I didn't know this was something you could *do*. I would feel sorry for whoever was trying to make conversation with me. The invariable cliques and alliances and tensions that develop in any workplace mostly went over my head. If I was liked by my fellow teachers, it was in part, I suspect, because I was a neutral party.

People would coax me to come along to after-work drinks and weekend gatherings, but without fail these left me utterly drained. Friday afternoon drinks and pizza in the office – when other teachers seemed to loosen up – left me rigid with panic. I remember once escaping to the bathroom, sneaking my way to the lift and then leaving the building without any of my belongings. The prospect of a weekend without my wallet, my house keys or my phone (all still sitting on my desk) was preferable to having to face my colleagues again and invent an excuse to leave, which simply felt beyond my capacity.

I always felt much closer to and more comfortable with my students than with my co-teachers. They were my main source of company and entertainment. They gave me a sense of belonging. I don't mean only at work but in my life as a whole: I used to feel embarrassed by this fact. Occasionally, I'd accompany them on excursions or for a drink to celebrate the completion of a unit. But when the usual classroom parameters no longer prevailed, once again I felt myself withdraw.

I spent countless lunch hours hidden in a bathroom cubicle, tearing my hair out. (I do not mean this figuratively.) I know now that repetitive behaviours like hair-pulling are relatively common among autistic people, especially as a response to stress or anxiety. I began pulling as a teenager and have bitten my nails since I was a young child. (I try my best not to ever let my students see my nails, because I'm afraid the sight might scare them.)

Aside from their repetitive nature, these behaviours have a strong sensory component: people tend to focus on sites rich in nerve endings, like hands, feet, mouth and scalp. Depending on the person, this can be highly stimulating or alternatively, as in my own case, incredibly soothing. Back when I spent my lunch hours overcome by my compulsions, I hadn't yet come across concepts like 'overstimulation' or 'self-soothing' or 'masking'. At some level, I guess I sensed I needed a break from people, to recalibrate, but I didn't know how to go about this. At the time, all I knew was that I wasn't 'normal' and that I needed to keep this from being discovered at all costs.

Along with my bodily compulsions, I have a tendency to read compulsively. It's this habit that led me to discover, first, that what I did with my hair had a name – trichotillomania – and, second, that the emotional struggle *behind* it also had a name – autism. I didn't share either of these two morsels of knowledge with anyone for the longest time, but I secretly devoured any information about them I could get my hands on.

That I felt so uneasy around people in general but so at ease around my students struck me as a paradox for the longest time. But learning about autism has helped me begin to comprehend it.

What makes me feel so at ease in the classroom, I think, is that my social role there is pre-set and well-defined. Some people say you need to be a 'people person' (which I most definitely am not) to be a good teacher, but my experience of teaching is that I'm able to simultaneously be with people and also be independent. Part of a group but also separate from it.

In teaching, there are clear rules about who speaks when, about what topic and to whom. I determine the topics of our discussions and dissect them in advance. The bread-and-butter of my line of work – the mechanics of English grammar, linguistic patterns, detailed error-correction, the ability to explain semantic subtleties – remains endlessly fascinating to me. Because I'm in this predictable and safe territory, I feel more present, less focused on myself and better able to engage with the other people in my company.

Some teachers, even very experienced ones, struggle with the lower levels of English-language learners, where communication is so restricted. For my part, I cherish this space, where all my words have to be carefully selected, and where the students are often near-silent. To me, there is something so precious and calming about it. But also, I have the feeling among such students that they *can't tell*. Can't tell what? There comes a point with most people I meet (and the higher up the English levels I go) where I can sense they've clocked there's something a bit curious about me. If I had to put it into words, I might say it's that I'm socially awkward, painfully shy and solitary, but others have used words like *different* or *special* or *unusual*.

Another paradox, though, is that sometimes I have the feeling my students can see me *better* than others. The more rudimentary their English, the truer I feel this to be. My theory is that with such restricted access to the linguistic, we are forced to rely on – and therefore to become more attuned to – other dimensions of the self.

I'm not talking about something as straightforward as body language or facial expression. According to the tests I took as part of my diagnosis, I have below-average ability in these basic skills, and numerous therapists have noted my blankness of facial expression. I guess what I'm talking about here is something more instinctive and ineffable. Something to do with a person's nature, or spirit; something that manages to transcend culture and language. I still think watching someone intently, being in their wordless presence, is a grossly underappreciated form of understanding.

I get why some might regard the classroom as an artificial space, on account of its rules and boundaries, its instructions and clear expectations. Why they might see the outside world as more 'authentic'. But I don't see such a rigid division.

Interactions beyond the classroom walls are also governed by rules, albeit more subtle, unwritten ones. Most people learn these implicitly (in the same way native speakers of a language will speak fluently and accurately, without necessarily being able to articulate its grammar). It's only now, through therapy, that I am learning some of these, in all their intricacy: how to initiate and sustain a conversation with someone; how much eye contact is appropriate; how to enter a conversation already in flow; how to know what to talk about next; how to end a conversation, and how to exit a conversation you're not being included in; how to signal that you need a few moments to yourself and don't want to be approached, without being rude.

I have heard other teachers describe having to 'act' a certain way in the classroom, or 'perform', or put on a 'mask'. I relate to the sentiment. For me, though, these feelings are more applicable to the world beyond the classroom walls. Often, mid-teaching, I catch myself feeling so capable, so connected. And I wonder: is this what other people are used to feeling?

Sources

1. Woolf, V 2023, *The Diary of Virginia Woolf, Volume Three: 1925–1930*, Granta Books, UK.

SCHOOL SYSTEM REJECT

Sienna Macalister

SIENNA MACALISTER (they/them) is an emerging screenwriter and influencer. Sienna is multiply neurodivergent and lives with chronic illness. They believe the way to inclusivity is through education and understanding. They are passionate about authentic representation of people with all support needs in the media. To do this, Sienna is pursuing a writing career to elevate stories that represent their communities. One of their short films, *One Closed Door* (2019), was a semi-finalist in the Changing Face International Film Festival and the Eurasia International Film Festival. Over 34,000 followers engage with Sienna's TikTok. You can find them at Sienna.Stims on TikTok and Instagram, and Sienna_Stims on YouTube.

'So, do you actually, like... get periods? Like the rest of us?'

I paused. We were standing beside my private school's indoor heated swimming pool – the private school that my parents had done everything they could to send me to because they thought it would give me better opportunities and more support. The private school that spent quite a lot of that money on unnecessary things: new MacBooks each year, building renovations... even my bathers had the school's logo on them. Bathers that I shivered in as a gust of cool air caused a sudden temperature change.

The girl addressing me stood with six others, all dressed in uniform as they held notes that excused them from swimming that day. Behind them sat another three girls, transfixed by their phones – also in uniform, notes having also excused them from swimming. Given that our class of twenty had swimming lessons every week, it was statistically unlikely that ten girls would be on their periods. It should be closer to five. But then, there were always more than five girls not swimming – and most of those girls seemed to have their period every week when it came to swimming classes—

'Well, do you?'

To this day, I don't know if she was being unkind. Maybe she was genuinely curious. Most of my peers knew that there was something 'wrong' with me: they discussed it openly in front of me. But I don't think a single person knew that I was Autistic. I doubt it crossed their minds – they didn't think Autistic kids could go to mainstream schools. And on the off-chance they did know, I highly doubt that they were asking me because Autistic people are more likely to have endocrine disorders. I mean, we did have health and human development class – but, at that point, I don't think we'd been taught that some people are intersex. We'd just learnt the basics around periods and, of course, how to put a condom on a banana penis. (You know the ones; we all had them in school. The dick-bit was covered with a plastic banana skin. You slid the skin off and hey, presto, there was a plastic phallus.)

I shivered in my bathers again, before nodding. Of course I did.

The girl looked shocked, I think. Then, she turned back to her friends. She pulled out her phone and as they sat down they started typing and laughing. I assumed that it wasn't to do with me – in hindsight, there was a solid chance it was – so I went over to the dive blocks. As I slid under, I let the silence of the water surround me. Here, I didn't need to engage with anyone: the only thing I needed to do was keep making the same, repetitive strokes. It was calm. It was nice. I was good at swimming.

There really wasn't much in the way of neuro-affirming care or therapy twenty years ago, or even ten. Or five. I mean, I guess you *could* find it if you looked for it – after all, activists like the late Rosemary Crossley were working in the field – but it was rare. You either had to be extremely lucky to get the right treating professional at the very start, or had to be educated enough (and have enough time) to seek your own information. And that information wasn't easy to come by – it's important to remember that platforms like X (Twitter) and Facebook didn't exist. Neurodiversity-affirming groups – whether neurodivergent- or parent-led – quite literally didn't exist.

Consequently – though, maybe it is generational as well – a lot of parents just listened to the professionals in front of them. Because why wouldn't they? New information was limited and hard to access, and a lot of professionals used scare tactics like 'unless we get onto this soon, your child will never speak / go to school / have friends / use the toilet / [insert something else every parent wants their kid to be able to do]'.

So, parents were coerced into accepting the first solution presented to them, and, as I wrote earlier – therapy was not neuro-affirming. It was compliance training. It aimed to cure, to make me 'normal' – not to assist me with life. Just like every other kid, I wanted to be praised by my parents, so wanted nothing more than to comply – to make everyone proud of my achievements – but somehow, I just ended up feeling more like of a failure. Plus, I now have a persistent need to please other people.

So, there's a common misconception about early diagnosed neurodivergence – that diagnosis and therapy helped you understand yourself.

Oh, and the 'accommodations' weren't great either.

I started Prep at a very small, mainstream Catholic primary school. My kinder actually suggested that I start school a year late – but we didn't do that. This school had also been picked on the belief that its size would offer me more individual attention. And the theory had been spot-on – almost. In a class of only seventeen, the teachers definitely had time to give more attention to each student. But they only picked certain students – and they weren't the ones who needed it. They were the ones whose parents had social capital: sat on the school board, were involved in the parish or donated their services to the school. Not the ones with disability.

On NAPLAN days – trauma for many, I know – the school went as far as trying to send disabled kids home, so we couldn't lower their scores. When I did sit NAPLAN, 'Language background other than English' suddenly appeared on my record. While I do have a Culturally and Linguistically Diverse background, I was born in Australia and we only ever spoke English at home. My background was purely cultural – so the 'Language background other than English' was a lie my primary school used to justify my lower scores. Interestingly, my brother's NAPLAN didn't have this label.

But one of the biggest things the school did – which I now know is not legal – was to adjust my education and behavioural plans without my parents' knowledge or consent. This included the addition of 'planned ignoring'. Planned ignoring is a behaviourism tactic that falls under the umbrella of negative reinforcement. It sets out to deliberately ignore 'problem behaviours' as an 'extinction' tactic: don't pay attention to the behaviour and, hopefully, it dies out. However, these behaviours almost always – if not always – hold meaning. In my case, the 'problem behaviours' were meltdowns. The instruction was to leave me alone in the corner of the room. Once, we had a scheduled lesson in another room. First, the other students filed out, and then the teacher turned off the light, left and locked the door behind her. She left me alone for a few minutes before returning to collect me.

I was terrified.

Planned ignoring has been determined to be harmful to a child's psychology. It tells the child that they and their emotions do not matter, and it makes no effort to understand the underlying reason for the 'problem behaviour'. These extinction plans are often put in place when a child is doing something socially undesirable – whether that's calling out, walking around the classroom when they should be still, or even biting – but what is never addressed is *why* the child is doing this. Are they frustrated? Are they hungry? Are they overstimulated? But because this behaviour must now be deliberately ignored – and every teacher must adhere to the directive – no-one can actually address the behaviour and help the child feel better.

And this is with a child who already struggles with communication. Ignoring a communication attempt – even if it isn't 'socially acceptable' – just makes the child feel even more isolated and frustrated. So, even when the behaviour stops, the child's needs are still unmet. No-one has worked out what the child actually wanted, and no-one has helped the child to find a better way to communicate the issue. And, so, the cycle continues.

I didn't have the social awareness to realise that the other girls refusing to let me play with them was bullying. I didn't have the social awareness to realise that them making me sit alone and actively stopping other kids from coming near me was bullying. I didn't have the social awareness to realise that when they did let me into their group, for brief periods, it was only so they could laugh at my speech and mannerisms. I did not realise that an adult refusing to let me on the netball team with every other girl in my class – even if I was terrible – was not right. I did not even realise that the physical shoving, being tripped up and hit with backpacks was bullying.

I did not have the words to tell my parents that I was being bullied. I did not have the verbal language to communicate what was happening in my day; this was due to my difficulties in communicating what was happening, as well as my literal lack of vocabulary to explain that I was being bullied – but also due to the fact that *I genuinely did not realise that I was being bullied.* The lack of self-awareness to express that I was dreadfully unhappy at school. The lack of any other form of communication to express that I was terrified. The fact that I did not even have the social awareness to *realise that I was actually being bullied.* I was trapped, so I just shut down, became overly compliant and attended school without complaint.

I did not realise that being made to feel horrible, every single day – was not okay. That meant it went on for four years.

When I did become aware, I was nearing the end of Year 3. I managed to vocalise it to my parents – and as soon as they started asking the right, specific questions, they were horrified.

They contacted the school.

I can assure you, we have a strong no-bullying policy. We can only act on it if we see it happening.

The very next day, I saw – I *saw* – the principal witness it through his office window. I saw him watch a girl push me into a bush. I saw him.

I caught his eye and he turned away. He did nothing.

My parents called again.

We need to see it to believe it.

*

Unfortunately, no-one thought to ask the school for my records when I left, and it shut down only a few years later. The paper records for all the students were transferred to an offsite facility and seem to be poorly organised. I asked for them eighteen months ago under the FOI Act and am still sporadically receiving pages – many of which prove the school knew what was happening and that they neglected multiple responsibilities in their duty of care.

I was moved to a private girls' school. The private school had to be better. You pay good fees to go there.

They did a lot more to stop bullying. The teachers looked out for it, and I was regularly asked both at home and school if anything was happening. Other girls also had a strong sense of justice and called it out when they saw it.

One day, I had finished my lunch, which was very unusual for me. My mum commented on it and I responded, 'I forgot that I was at my new school and I am allowed to play with the other kids. So, I sat on the bench all of lunch time.' That day, my teacher had been away, and no-one had helped me to find a group to play with. Mum started using this as a way to keep track – if I finished my lunch, something might be wrong.

A few weeks later, I had finished my lunch again. So, she questioned me.

'Oh. I was in [principal's] office with [bully].'

Mum didn't understand – why would she? She'd had no call from the school. 'Did something happen today?'

'No, it was one of the normal weekly sessions.'

Normal weekly sessions?

These sessions occurred during lunch, once a week, and were run by the principal – not by a registered psychologist (which the school had). According to the school, they had the potential to 'rehabilitate' the relationship between me and the other girl (which was never going to happen) and, more importantly, would provide me with much needed 'social skills training'. Both the school and her parents saw her participation as an act of charity – in fact, I think she was rewarded in some capacity.

So, we read between the lines and called it for what it was: a social experiment. Not only did the school blame the bullying on my lack of social skills, a core feature of autism, they also stripped me of my lunches and forced me to spend them with a girl who had been tormenting me for a year to talk about our emotions. We had to do Positive Minus Interesting charts about each other.

And this was at a school with no detention.

In hindsight, I believe that they were also trying to create some general plan of action for when Autistic students were being bullied. But that's what seminars, lectures and workshops are for. You don't have to do an experiment on your resident Autistic student. I don't know how many students like me were punished for things that weren't our fault – how many were blamed for the actions of others. How many bullies got away with it because, instead of being held accountable for their actions, they were reassured that the 'abnormal' child was to blame, because no-one would blame them for treating us badly.

And I'd like to say that it's stopped now, that students with diagnoses are protected – but it simply isn't the case. Too often, Autistic students are still told that it is *our* lack of abilities that causes us to be bullied – which does a number on our confidence.

The other issue was that the school did not allow me to do any of the extension activities. I was in a remedial class for spelling and handwriting, and when I was younger I was behind in reading. I was, however, always good at maths.

But I was never allowed to do the maths extension work, even though it was nothing but worksheets. The official justification was that being remedial in one area was stress enough; I couldn't have the extension work on top of it. But that's just what they told us – I'm sure that the real reason was glossed over, because the school knew that it wouldn't sound good. And that real reason was that the stigma of my disabilities meant they weren't even going to give me the opportunity to demonstrate and develop my strengths. They had a label and would not look past it.

This, too, is unfortunately far too common for students who start school with a diagnosed disability. All too often we are not given the opportunity to prove our capabilities in the classroom. Instead, our education is limited – often severely. And, once you fall behind, it becomes a self-fulfilling prophecy.

This is a documented phenomenon. Disabled students being pushed into classrooms and education plans that will limit their learning from day one because they are *perceived* as incapable – only to later prove themselves. These are students who have been denied access to the curriculum for decades – only to catch up to their peers *within a year* when they are finally given access. People might tell you that those students are one in a million, but they aren't. It's just that someone finally saw past their disability and presumed competence in them. The supports that the United Nations *requires* schools to give students – whether that's an aide to help them stay on task, or even the ability to learn in their own way – were finally provided and, for the first time, these students were able to succeed in the classroom.

At some point, I once again managed to put my feelings into words – 'Mum, I want to go to a school where the teachers actually care.'

So, I moved school again, this time to a forward-thinking alternative school staffed by dedicated and caring educators where I was finally understood. There were no year levels – so, if you were 'behind' or 'ahead' in a subject, you could be in a class that suited you – and there were dozens of non-academic programs. These catered for students who didn't find strength in academia, but they also taught critical skills that many mainstream schools do not teach.

For the first time, I had a leadership role – first in the animals program, where I was Head of Reptiles.

These programs did more to develop my social skills than any of the *direct* social skills programs I'd been forced to take in the past.

I also ended up school co-captain.

I'd found my people.

For a while, I continued working with the school to support Autistic students. I now advocate for diversity and inclusion – especially in the early, formative schooling years. I have seen how inadequate workplaces are – even ones that claim to be 'inclusive' – when it comes to including neurodiversity. And this is fuelled by the segregation of disabled and non-disabled children in school. I still have PTSD from my childhood experiences.

It's going to be a long time before we have a system where disabled children are not at significant risk of abuse – but we're headed in the right direction: a direction in which all children are respected and valued in the school environment, where no child will miss out on opportunities due to their diagnosis. Where supports are provided.

I imagine what that could look like: schools where kids aren't made to sit at restrictive desks but can move freely through the classroom to regulate themselves. Schools where fidgets are not banned but provided. Schools where alternative seating arrangements are available, clear and visual instructions are offered, and the curriculum is individualised to the student. I imagine growing up in a school like this and feel the confidence building. I can see myself not being broken down. And I see the other kids too; no longer fearful of difference, they now see inclusion as the norm.

Building a richer world for all of us.

AN AUTISTIC TRANS MAN TRAVELS BACK TO THE NINETIES TO GIVE HIS YOUNGER SELF SOME ADVICE

Kai Ash

KAI ASH (he/him) is a writer from Yuggera Country (Brisbane region, Queensland). His work has been shortlisted for The Ampersand Prize, Adaptable, the Lane Cove Literary Awards and the Melbourne Lord Mayor's Creative Writing Awards, and he was a mentee in the ASA/CA Award Mentorship Program. Kai has lived in many different places in and outside of Australia, including New Zealand, Scotland, Spain, Czechia and the Palestinian Territories. He has degrees in psychology, law, and gender and cultural studies.

Listen, son. Listen, little man. Yes, I'm talking to you.

It's time to stop doubting, to stop dillydallying. I am hereby giving you permission to leap into maleness, deep dive into white socks and trans-man jocks. You don't need to pretend anymore.

What's a trans man? you ask.

A trans man is you! Or, it will be you. For now, you're a trans boy, which is like a regular boy, except harder. People will insist on calling you a girl, but you know better. Trust that feeling. It's not confusion. It's not sexism. It's not to say that being a boy is better than being a girl. Stuff all that rubbish. You are who you are and *you*, my lad, are a boy.

See how good that feels? See how the tension just eased from your shoulders. Notice that shiver of joy running up and down your body? That's called *gender euphoria*. Enjoy it.

Cast off the uniform dress and grab your brother's tie. Ignore the naysayers and the concerned well-meaners.

I am sorry to say that there is something of a countdown to this, and the clock is ticking. The faster you get people used to calling you 'he' and 'him', the more comfortable you'll feel in your own imperfect body. And the more comfortable you feel, the more you'll put yourself out there.

This is important, because it's the only way you'll get yourself known, the only way you'll find work, and you need work because you need money. Rough times are coming, and you need to prepare.

But I'm getting ahead of myself. You're ten. Jobs and money will come later.

For now, start with your name. Insist on Mickey at all times, not just among friends and family. You can change it later, but Mickey will do for now.

Note the spelling I'm using. None of that 'Micci' business,

not anymore. You need the Disney mouse seal of maleness that accompanies the M-I-C-K-E-Y.

Some people will get it wrong. They'll call you 'she' and spell your name with the feminine double-C. Be kind to them. Kindness won't always help – plenty of people will hate you anyway – but it'll save you a bruise or two and a hell of a lot of angst. What I'm talking about is *mitigation*, not *salvation*.

What do those words mean? Look them up. And get used to doing that. There are many new and confusing words in your future, starting with *transgender*.

Next, the medical business. I'm referring to puberty blockers and, later, testosterone. The stuff that'll stop your breasts from growing and give you a shaggy beard of your very own. The faster you get the blockers, the easier it'll be to blend in, to pass as male, to go *stealth*. Sounds cool, yeah? Well, it is. Way cool.

It's also a safety thing. The more male you look, the safer you'll be when taking a piss in the men's room.

The law around puberty blockers hasn't been set in stone yet. (That'll come later.) If you can find a sympathetic and proactive doctor, you'll be right.

That's the good news.

The bad news is that by the time you're sixteen and ready to start testosterone (the big T, the beard juice), the law will have changed, and you'll need to convince a Family Court judge. That means a diagnosis of gender dysphoria and a whole team of sympathetic medical and legal professionals. It'll be expensive and agonising and it'll happen right when you're meant to be putting your head down for your final years of school. But hey, at least you won't be aiming to study law anymore, so top grades aren't so important.

Why not law? you ask. Well, I'll tell you.

You're Autistic. No, I don't mean like that kid in *Mercury Rising*, and yeah, it's a good film, and yeah, Bruce Willis is cool. *Oi!* Pay attention.

You're Autistic, which means a whole lot of things that have nothing to do with numbers or trains, okay? Things like how you get dizzy when someone's cooking eggs or want to puke when someone's smoking nearby. Or how you feel like you're exploding inside when a plan changes, or how you get the shivers when two pieces of fabric rub together. Stuff like that, and way more besides.

You won't really understand what I'm getting at yet, or why it's important, but you will once you leave your Montessori school and go to a 'normal' high school. Then, when you find yourself starting to struggle, pop along to the council library and look up these words: *Autism* and *Asperger's syndrome*. You'll find a lot of rubbish (anything that suggests you're broken should be avoided) but some good stuff too, and it should help you get through it.

But – and this is very important – *you cannot tell anyone*. I'm only telling you you're Autistic now because knowing this will help you to avoid a decade of meltdowns and burnout in the future.

You're welcome.

But, sweet boy, tell no-one. Not for a few years yet. Wait until you're a legal adult and the court can't overrule your healthcare plans. Wait until you start hearing health professionals using the words *Autistic people* instead of *people with Autism* and *difference* instead of *deficit*. When that happens, you can take off the mask. When that happens, you can stop hiding.

For a little while.

A good few years before it starts getting bad again.

Seize those years. Make connections, build a community, revel in the glory of being fully recognised, supported and understood. It may be more sensible to avoid being tarred with the Autism brush, but your life will be filled with enough challenges, so I say seize this moment of joy and don't regret it if it comes back to bite you on the arse later, like when TERFs such as your (soon-to-be-ex-) favourite author start talking about 'vulnerable Autistic girls' and anti-trans ideologues take the opportunity to make a grab for your right to self-determination.

What's a TERF? you ask. You don't need to know about them yet.

What's self-determination? It's the right to make your own decisions about your own life and body. Pretty basic stuff. No, I don't understand why some people are against it. It's never made sense to me.

Talking about your (ex-)favourite author, I know you'll want to keep reading her books as they come out, and I'll give you a pass for that, because I know how much the stories will help you through your teen years.

But don't buy the books – or the merchandise. Check them out from the library. Not having them on your shelf as a physical reminder of the author's later betrayal will make it easier to cope with. Trust me.

Now, getting back to the why-not-law business.

You need to avoid jobs that require you to use a phone, sit in an office, have regular meetings and attend social events. It won't leave you many options and rules out pretty much all law-related jobs. Don't believe me? Research *sensory overload*, *executive function* and *auditory processing in Autistic people* and you'll understand.

Actually, you probably won't understand now, but by the time you're putting in your university preferences you should be able to. Understand these things, but don't seek professional help for them. At least, not yet. When you're asked why you're being weird, just say you're 'eccentric' or 'quirky'. You'll piss a lot of people off – they'll say you're just being difficult – but after almost two decades in the workforce, I still haven't worked out a better approach to take than this one.

Later, when it becomes briefly advantageous – or, at least, not seriously disadvantageous – to be Autistic, you can be more open about your difficulties. But until then, take note: you're eccentric and quirky, *not* Autistic. Got it? Good.

Work on being charming. Take lessons from your brother. And by 'lessons', I mean 'copy him'. It'll piss him off, but it'll be several years before he stops being permanently pissed off at you anyway, so don't worry about it.

(He does stop, though. Remember that and try to be kinder to him when he knocks on your door wanting to make up lost ground. You'll regret giving him the cold shoulder.)

Aim for contract work, self-employment and distance working arrangements. Pick university courses accordingly.

You'll hate it, but consider IT. It'll give you access to jobs where being Autistic is the norm. Ignore your cousin when he tries to put you off. He's still several years away from being someone whose advice you should listen to.

Since IT will be a drag, I recommend combining it with psychology. It'll feed your desire to understand people and hand you some tools to help change how doctors talk about Autism and gender. It won't be easy – they'll call your brain 'disordered', your traits 'deficits' and your maleness a 'psychopathology' – but you can do good there, you can give back to your communities, and I know you're stubborn enough to take the blows. You've never been afraid of an argument.

If you want to see the United States, go sooner rather than later, before a man called 'Trump' starts appearing everywhere. That's if you fancy it. Personally, I never bothered. Seems like a weird place.

Make some connections with New Zealand. Study abroad there. Make friends. A Kiwi bolthole will begin to look more attractive as the anti-trans lobby gains traction here.

What else? Ah, yes. The climate.

This millennium drought will end. Eventually. Then the floods will start. And the fires. You should always be prepared for something to go under or to go up in flames.

Climate change – that thing you're still calling global warming – is upon us. I would make a list of catastrophic events to watch out for, but there are so many that even the news barely reports them anymore. They're like school shootings in America: terrible for those immediately affected, but not unusual enough to entice consumers to pay attention, and I use the words 'consumers' and 'pay' with intent. The news is a business like any other. Take note of that. It'll be important later.

The 2003 Canberra bushfires will be a surprise, though. As will the Victorian ones in '09. The Queensland '11 floods too.

Get used to it. The planet's just getting started.

Pay off your HECS debt with all that money you'll be making while living your best Autistic trans life and avoiding all those meltdowns, burnouts and suicidal thoughts you would otherwise have struggled with throughout your twenties. (Once again, *you're welcome*.) The loans are indexed and indexation is not your friend. If you don't deal with it early, it'll get worse right around the time when the world begins to close in on you as an Autistic trans person, and your earning capacity will likely take a dive. Not to mention your mental health.

Put extra money into super for the same reason.

Learn Scottish Gaelic! You'll bloody love it. And put money aside to spend some time at the Gaelic college Sabhal Mòr Ostaig on the Isle of Skye in Scotland. You'll need to secure a trans-friendly GP there if you decide to do one of their longer courses, but it'll be so worth the challenge. Do it after the Scottish independence movement really kicks off. At that time, the Scots will decide they're going to be trans-friendly – mostly because it pisses off the English so much. Ride that nationalistic wave, lad.

But if you start hearing news coming out of Wuhan, China, about a novel coronavirus, then you've left it too late. No haggis for you.

When whispers of pandemic become hacking coughs, make sure you're settled somewhere with a good landlord – and don't underestimate how hard that will be to find. Make sure you have a good working arrangement with your GP and local chemist, because lockdowns and border closures are coming and everything's about to get far more complicated.

I know this sounds like a lot to take in, and it is. Let's take a moment to breathe. In. And out. Here, take this. They're prayer beads. No, I'm not religious, but fiddling with them can help us to calm down. It's called *stimming*. Embrace it, but until it's safe to be more open, do it sneakily. Rosary beads and that. Let people assume you're a proper Catholic. For whatever reason, being religious is not considered to be a mental health issue but being Autistic is. Go figure.

Look, for what it's worth, I am sorry. Sorry that I don't have better news. That I can't say everything gets better and then leave it at that. Unfortunately, reality is more roundabout than never-ending forward progress.

But, you know what? It does get better. Not forever, and maybe not for long, but it does get better, and you should know that.

So, here's my final piece of advice. Act now. Don't delay on the male thing. Don't deny yourself that. Claim your place among your brothers. Because the sooner you make this leap into the rest of your life, the further you'll glide before the ground hits you.

I'm telling you, lad, go for it!

Do it now.

Because the fact is, you're already falling. We all are. We just don't know it yet. The earth isn't firm beneath our feet. It never was. That story is a boomer illusion.

The ground is coming. The world is on fire. We're drowning in floodwater. Our houses collapse under the weight of the wind.

There's no time to hesitate. No time to waste.

Take that running leap as the ground rushes up to meet you.

We're getting sick. The water's running out. And our soil's full of salt.

Leap, lad. Leap and glide.

Reach your arms out wide, catch the air current, grasp joy, spread joy, be joy.

The ground is coming, and we'll all go splat, but don't just drop. Leap and glide.

Tell the ground you're coming, and that you'll meet it at the horizon, where the sun is bright orange, the sky's purple-pink and the clouds peek out from distant blue ranges.

WHAT IS A CAR? WRONG ANSWERS ONLY

Phoebe Lupton

PHOEBE LUPTON (she/her) is an Anglo-Celtic and Sinhalese essayist, editor and arts worker. She is autistic and queer. Phoebe lives as an uninvited guest on unceded Ngunnawal and Ngambri land, colonially known as Canberra. Her recent writing has been published in *The Big Issue*, *Overland*, *Antithesis Journal*, *Archer Magazine* and *Portside Review*, among others. Phoebe has acted as a member of the Australian War Memorial Access Advisory Group, participated in the Accessible Arts Ripple Internship program and been shortlisted for the Express Media Catalyse Nonfiction Prize. She is currently developing a collection of essays on invisibility.

1. An automobile

From *auto*, meaning 'self', and *mobile*, meaning 'easily moved'
I am the owner of an autistic body-mind that is mobile, but rarely in control of itself. Self-deprecating jokes about 'not really knowing how to walk' fly out of my brain and at neurotypicals. Intellectually, I know how to walk, but my body ignores my mind's instructions. In the autumn, I stroll through the deluge of leaves, stomping on all the acorns and shuffling on all the tiny rocks outside people's houses. Crunchiness beneath the feet is my go-to tactile stim. My mother walks ahead of me, her legs long and brain-body connection like steel. I supposedly have ownership over my legs, until I get angry and yell at them to go faster. They are unresponsive. I'm left at the bottom while Mum races to the top.

At the beginning of Year 5, I take up walking to strengthen my limbs and become used to the sensation of foot-on-concrete. My father drops me a block away from school, where I abandon the car's air-conditioned warmth, new-leather perfume and ABBA playlist, and I touch gravel for the first time for the day. I trudge down the hill past a sloped, jungle-like park and turn a corner to embark on another hill, where my classmates' parents have parked their cars.

A car whose owner I don't know zooms past. The driver, a random man, screams at me like a human-dinosaur hybrid. Twenty cars are lined up like chess pieces against the curb, with that human-dinosaur's car dancing around the road. I want to retreat to Dad's car: its safety, its warmth.

2. A metamorphosis

From the Ancient Greek *metamorphoun*, meaning 'to change shape'

My sister is a baby, and our car has broken down on Brown Mountain. It's a hot December, and sticky, dusty air is infiltrating our lungs. We wait for some time between ten minutes and two hours for the engine to push out enough steam to get us to the top of the mountain and back onto the freeway. My sister is crying. Mum reaches out to touch her tiny, jiggly feet. I dissociate and imagine a moth flying into the car. The moth lays eggs on my sister's head without her knowing and flies happily out of the window. I think it's returning to its little moth commune hidden in some crevice in the mountain, feasting on the dust and stickiness.

My sister is nearly eighteen now, and she can drive. She is not a moth but a beautiful, full-winged butterfly that once was a small caterpillar. I perceive her adolescence as more normal than mine, so I'm learning through her about child-adult metamorphosis. My sister drives to school, to work, to parties. She walks from her room to the car, keys in hand, while I wishfully think about a parallel universe in which my body-mind is free of sensory overwhelm. This is not a wish I always conjure for myself, and I would never ask to be cured of my autism, but when I look at my neurotypical sister, my self-esteem grows foggy.

I am twenty-five with a late diagnosis of autism, and I am unable to drive. When I am seventeen, without a diagnosis of autism, I try to be able to drive, but there are too many distractions pulling my brain apart. Research shows this is not every autistic young person's story. As of 2021, at least one-third of us receive our full licence by the age of twenty-one – but this is still a minority experience, and I am in the majority.[1]

To get your licence in the Australian Capital Territory, you have to read a booklet and pass a test. The booklet is illustrated with diagrams, step-by-step instructions and threats of legal action if you don't do everything the booklet says. You also have to attend a two-day course where you pretend to be drunk and watch simulations of car crashes. One of the car crashes I watch at the course, however, is not a simulation. It is a real-life woman who crashed a real-life car, lost her real-life friend and has real-life brain damage. I dissociate again. I picture myself driving, trying to figure out how to move my hands and feet in relation to the wheel and the brake, while missing stop signs and red lights, eventually impaled by a tree.

Canberra is a city of bad drivers. We are spoilt here. When Walter Burley Griffin designed our capital, he planned its roads with the meticulousness of a heart surgeon. There are no crowded Pacific Highways, and no diagonal CBD intersections. It is a perfect city in which to drive, but it is too perfect for drivers to handle. Mum drives me to a friend's house in the north of the city some months after my failure to get my licence, and a car on the road overtakes us when they're not supposed to. Mum flips the bird at the car, and says, 'Some people shouldn't be allowed to drive.' I agree and think, *That probably includes me.* I grimace. *If I cannot adequately manage my legs, how am I supposed to manage a vehicle?*

I do not think I should be driving, and Mum doesn't think I should be driving – but everybody else does. At Christmas, an aunt lectures me on the usefulness of driving, how brilliantly independent and competent having your licence makes you. *Phoebe, you should really do it before it's too late, before it's too late, before it's too late.* Before it's too late. Life is short. You only live once. It all comprises the cultural idea that metamorphosis should be quick – and if it's lagging, you need to do everything you can to speed it up. I learnt to toilet train later and with less ease than the other children at preschool. Aged four, I could not understand my body's inner ecosystem, much less the way it was supposed to expel waste. Now, I feel like I need to get my literal shit together before it's too late, *before it's too late, before it's too late.*

I now know my body-mind is autistic, and I dance to a different metronome. The pressure to accelerate metamorphosis is ableist. My advanced IQ belies my underdeveloped ability to read the signals of my own body, rendering my disability invisible. I have seen too many Marvel films involving car chases that go wrong. If I were to chase able-bodied standards of motor development, I worry I'd crash and burn, just like that woman in the driving-course video.

3. A gesture

From the Latin *gerere*, meaning 'to bear' and also 'to perform'
Able-bodied adulthood is got-it-togetherness. Got-it-togetherness is performative. Got-it-togetherness performers stage their acts using fifty-dollar blazers, iPhone Xs, black coffee, air kisses and cologne. The performers move within metal, which they manipulate in the direction of their workplace, or partner's place, or parents' place. They breathe independence, and when I ask them what makes them independent, they cite control over their bodies and where their bodies go. But when I watch these acts, I can't help asking: if you're so independent, why do you rely on an inanimate object to take you places? Of course, the answer is that these inanimate objects are convenient. But they are also dangerous. They have the potential for rapid movement, as well as murder. Rapid movement and murder: the substances that form the underbelly of adulthood.

Back in Year 5, I have been walking a short way to school for months and Mum suggests I walk to Sunday school, at a church that sits barely a block away from our house. I happily rev up my legs, and before long I've arrived at church – thanks to my little, old, undiagnosed-autistic body-mind. I meet my best friend, A, and her mum. They ask where *my* mum is, and I explain I'm a woman now. I am strong, I am safe, I am in control of my body. A's mum, like most church-going mums in the neighbourhood, is mansion-owning, intricately hairstyled and small-c conservative. She gives her daughter the side-eye and tuts. 'We'd better drop you back home,' she says. 'You shouldn't be walking all by yourself.' *All by yourself, all by yourself, all by yourself.*

It's like I've never been a child, and it's like I've never been a grown-up. Or, it's like I've always been a child and I've always been a grown-up, and I'll continue to be a child and a grown-up simultaneously until life catches up with me and runs me over.

I watch and understand Shakespeare film adaptations at the age of eight, while having the emotional regulation skills of a toddler. I study Virginia Woolf *pièces des résistance* and Wes Anderson films at university aged eighteen, while having Mum drive me to friends' houses in her old, smelly Mazda.

As an ambulatory eleven-year-old, I perform able-bodied adulthood to an audience of side-eyeing onlookers. As an ambulatory, sans-car legitimate adult in her twenties, my performance is no longer convincing. My audience side-eyes me for different reasons. I transgress the age binary in tasting bodily independence as a child, and I paradoxically transgress it in eschewing motorised independence as an adult.

A year after I begin walking solo, I receive a DVD of *Grease* for my twelfth birthday. While watching it, my associative brain can't stop making connections between cars and the coming-of-age genre. It's a movie musical, but it's also a coming-of-age car film. During the song 'Greased Lightning', Danny and his crew perform maintenance on a black car whose shiny coat makes my temples throb from just looking at it on the screen, and they boast about how 'the chicks'll cream' for them. Later, a bunch of kids from Rydell High go to a drive-in cinema, where Danny sexually assaults Sandy, and Rizzo confides in one of the other Pink Ladies about her fear that she's pregnant. Earlier in the film, during 'Summer Nights', the Rydell girls asked Sandy if Danny had 'a car'. I make these connections while watching the film, not knowing I'll never have a coming-of-age car story of my own.

4. An animal

From the Latin *animalis*, meaning 'having breath'

There is one time when I'm in the back seat of a car and I think I'm going to die. My dad, my sister and I are visiting family in Singapore. We visit Little India for a shopping session. My cousins have collected me from a restaurant where I've met my old church-going friend, A, who now lives here. Everyone else has travelled from lunch in a separate car. Me and my family end up in the same car on the way back to my great aunt's place. I am in the middle, no seatbelt, which surely can't be legal, but I don't die. I think I'm going to, though. Normally, the driving situation in Singapore is sensible. You can take a taxi there just like you take a bus in Australia – and most people do on a daily basis. If not for the country's free speech violations, legislated homophobia and anti-South Asian racism, I could get on in Singapore just fine. I could take a taxi from my apartment to work and back without spending all that much. After work, I could take another taxi to the shops and back, and maybe to a restaurant to have dinner with a friend and back.

Canberra is a city of bad drivers, but it's also great for driving. That's probably why, when I'm at uni talking to a new friend, G, and she asks where I live and I say, 'Narrabundah, in the south of Canberra. I take two buses and the light rail,' she looks at me like I'm terminally ill. Funny – this look is eerily similar to the one I get when I tell people I'm autistic. If driving is a sign of coming-of-age, then not-driving is a sign of age regression. But it could also be a sign of ageing too quickly.

My ninety-year-old grandmother acquires physical disabilities in her old age and her doctor advises her to stop driving. Grandma complains about this to Mum on the phone, while Mum and I are on our daily walk. As we're passing a street full of crunchy autumn leaves (I take the opportunity to stim), I hear Mum say, 'I mean, you really should not be driving, Mum.' It is a similar sentiment to the one she expressed when

I considered learning to drive. *You really should not be driving, you really should not be driving, you really should not be driving.* Luckily for Grandma, she has few reasons to drive. She lives in Bega, on the land of the Yuin-Monaro Nations. It is a piece of the world where you can walk from one side of the town to the other in less than an hour. Even then, Grandma barely leaves the house, unless she's going to book club or a Labor Party meeting.

I supposedly have many reasons to drive, but they all coalesce into one: you don't want to be taking public transport in Canberra. Sure, maybe not. I do not want to sit next to a sweaty man-spreader. I do not want to inhale potentially COVID-contaminated air. I do not want to have to navigate bus timetables, a TripView app that doesn't work and a map of the city that I can't read. Guess it sucks to be disabled, right? I suck, you suck, we all suck but… I'd rather be disabled on a bus than dead in a car from the silly driving mistakes I'd definitely make if I had a licence.

I watch an episode of *The X-Files* guest-starring Bryan Cranston, who plays a man with an affliction that causes head pressure so extreme it'll inevitably cause his head to explode, unless Mulder drives him west – non-stop. The accommodation for his particular disability is driving, or rather someone driving him. The accommodation for my disability is someone driving me. I wonder if my situation would make for a good sci-fi show.

5. A full stop

Symbol from the Greek grammatical system, originating in the third century BCE

I spend my undergrad lurking on the edges of a group that comprises a few students who live in a share house near uni. On Tuesday nights during the semester, we go to the uni bar's trivia night and get drunk on house cider that tastes like rain on dry earth and I don't drive home. Instead, I take Ubers, which costs money, but 'not as much as car rego', according to Mum.

During most Uber rides I call my dad, so the driver knows I'm a vulnerable young woman with a scary, powerful father and won't take advantage of me.

Despite this arrangement, through each Uber ride my mind plays a recurring fantasy/horror: the Uber swerves towards a divergent route, with the intention of kidnapping me like that poor woman in Emma Donoghue's *Room*. Mercifully, my fantasy/horror ends with Dad tracking the driver and calling the police. In reality, most Uber trips end with me asking to be dropped off at the stop sign outside the house. I do this, because we have two separate driveways and neither is at the front door, so people tend to struggle with placing themselves unless I give direct instructions.

Placing oneself is a conundrum. Most of the time, I am unaware of spatial or temporal contexts. It is only when I create these contexts myself that my body-mind's navigation system works like it's supposed to. Like my father driving me around the suburbs to entertain me when I was a baby. Even though I was a baby, and supposedly very stupid, I always turned my head seconds before turning the corner because I had already developed a photographic memory. Then I was two years old and hyperfixated on telephone poles. Then my mother drove me around the suburbs, because she worked from home and Dad worked long hours in the city. She played boring nursery rhymes, and I was moved by the marvellous symmetry of those tall planks of wood. Telephone poles placed me.

The road is its own language, its rules a grammatical system someone else made up – one no-one can ever explain to you. So, too, is the autistic body-mind. Like in high school French, when I asked my teacher the difference between *meilleur* and *mieux*. She blanked, unable to give me a straight answer, until years later I figured out it was the difference between better and best.

The car is the body that interacts, and the driver is the voice. Driving is an act of brain-body synergy, while autism is a disruption of brain-body synergy.

Sources

1. Drosey, B 2019, 'New grant awarded to study driving among autistic teens', Cornerstone Blog, Children's Hospital of Philadelphia Research Institute, 24 January, <research.chop.edu/cornerstone-blog/new-grant-awarded-to-study-driving-among-autistic-teens>.

BONES IN THE GROUND

Sarah Teresa Cook

SARAH TERESA COOK (she/they) is an autistic poet, essayist and trauma-informed creative mentor based in the Pacific Northwest. A former social worker, she now works one-on-one with writers and neurodivergent humans, and teaches through Unrestricted Interest. Her writing has appeared in *Hobart Pulp*, *Write or Die Magazine*, *So to Speak*, *Porter House Review* and *Spoon Knife*, among other places. She publishes *For the Birds*, a newsletter about creativity, neurodivergence and the more-than-human world. She is very fond of bugs and game shows. More at <sarahteresacook.com>.

I have these bones I keep on my altar, placed atop a dresser I've owned since childhood.

The dresser isn't pink, though I picture it that way. It's white with light wooden trim, the handles and seams tan, slightly marbled. I don't know where the intrusive colour is coming from, this colour like pale salmon. This colour like colouring-book skin.

I took the bones from the Oregon coast. They looked like they'd been there a while, that the death wasn't recent. (Certain things present; others absent.) I walked up and down a stretch of rocky shore, thinking and thinking and thinking about whether I should take them. My partner sat nearby on a sturdy piece of driftwood, reading a book.

'I'm taking two,' I finally said out loud, mostly to myself, 'but I won't advertise my decision.' As if trying to protect something. As if everything doesn't find its way to the page. As if writing isn't the sustained act of reflecting on personal choice, a constant marketing of the past self.

There's this thing people say about living in Maine: to be from there, you have to have bones in the ground.

No bones? Then you're 'from away'.

I was there for grad school, two fleeting and chaotic years, my presence destined to be flimsy, diaphanous. Torn easily and imperfectly, saran wrap on a grated edge. I had no buried bones there. I barely had a body there, the first quarter century of my life lived entirely on paper, which is to say: in my head.

What's this ground everyone is speaking of? How do I get there?

My therapist gives me words for this. 'Derealisation', 'depersonalisation', etc.

*

I've always loved cemeteries. And keeping flowers long after they've turned, when their colours mute and their petals crisp up. And looking at bones, those objects that symbolise fear and Halloween and yet which we carry inside us at all times, the literal structure of personhood.

For as long as I have been paying accurate attention to myself, I've noticed that I love such things.

Which is to say: not long.

My therapist gives me a word for this too. 'Trauma.' Not the preferences themselves, but the historic lack of attention.

In grad school, I'd walk to the bus stop every morning in downtown Orono, an Old Navy scarf – a chunky, knitted thing the colour of bright salmon – wrapped around my face three times. Heavy breathing. Winter is all encore in Maine. On campus I studied, learned Japanese, taught freshmen how to write basic academic papers and to read with care – Baldwin, Thoreau. Nobody got too excited. I pretended I wasn't terrified every moment: terrified of the esoteric lectures, of my brain's inability to understand what my peers obviously could. Of the institutionalised preference for certainty over curiosity, which nevertheless left me feeling constantly unstable. Of the fucking cold. Of the way literary arts – previously wild, feral – could be landscaped into a site of competition and dick-measuring.

Everything around me felt sharp. Everything inside me felt sharp too. Angular. Bones under taut skin. For years I could not see the thing inside me, only the painful shape it made when pressed against any surface. *Any* surface.

What do I call this thing inside me?

Not the credentialing, but the stuff beneath it.

Part of me can't believe anything's in there, that I contain the same things other people do: skull, pelvis, spine. Really? That I have anything in common with the dummies you see in doctors' offices in old movies.

Is this identity or passivity?

Certain things present. Others, absent.

Or rather, sometimes my attention goes everywhere, a kind of spilling. Too much of it, me. Too much of me in everything I see that (I could've sworn) isn't me.

More therapy words. This time they say, 'Neurodivergence.' Shortly thereafter, 'Autism.'

Waiting downtown, I'd watch unhoused folks hop off the bus and look around slowly, unsure what to do with themselves. I heard that Orono is the easternmost bus stop in the country, that crowded homeless shelters on the west coast used to hand out unspecified, prepaid bus tickets and send people on their way, to anywhere else.

Anywhere else became *as far as I can go*, which became, in this case, Maine.

The problem with *anywhere else* is that you still end up somewhere. Even when you're from away, that's where you are now.

Bones on the inside? Things are where they should be.

But bones on the outside? Something ghostly is afoot, a veil growing thin.

Some days I give in to the impulse and take a sweeping overview of the gains and losses of my life so far, try to itemise them, look at them side by side over time's shoulder and hope for good data about myself. Hope to spot improvement.

Other days I think, *Well, it's all the same*. It isn't despair, it's just that I care less and less about which column anything ends up in. Is this what maturity feels like? What I want, more than impressive tallying, is to hug the real ground with every single part of me that I can manage to lay flat. The soles of my feet. The backs of my thighs. One side of my face, followed shortly thereafter by the other.

To not have to go looking for myself again and again and again.

To not only find her on the page, but elsewhere too. Anywhere else.

Or to be able to tell which parts of me are because I'm a writer, and which parts of me are because of the trauma, and which parts of me are because of the brain-wiring, the cosmic-genetic-happenstance soup.

'I've never broken a bone,' I mention in casual conversation to someone I've just met.

What's this *small talk* everyone is speaking of? How do people know what to keep on the inside?

In some cultures, bones are read, thrown, divined with.

Mine stay put, placed precisely in a fluted glass jar I picked up from a thrift store near my home. There, they reside among other evidence of the once living: dried moss, airless and bright green; an unplanted acorn; a swath of orange fur from my cat.

I pay a lot of attention to these bones. Every so often I pick up the jar and twirl it around, admiring the organic diorama. Wondering if I'd look similar, were my skin made of glass. I picture someone – a reader, a stranger – lifting me off the ground, spinning me slowly, looking closely at all the things that, over long stretches of time, have found their place inside me.

My bones stay put, evidence of a reality I don't always feel.

Language is where we shape our perspectives, where we articulate our personal details, hoping they matter.

But before language: bones. The bones always matter. They're either in the ground already or they will be soon. Everybody's eligible.

For those without a dependable sense of self, it's a comfort to at least know something true about where we're headed, about how this body will end up. From there, maybe we can reverse engineer our way back to someone sturdy, some real living thing.

‘SHOW, DON’T TELL’ IS BROKEN – EMOTIONAL DEPTH DOESN’T HAVE TO MEAN FLUSHED CHEEKS

Naoise Dolan

NAOISE DOLAN (she/her) is a queer and autistic Irish writer born in Dublin. She studied at Trinity College, followed by a master's in Victorian literature at Oxford. She writes fiction, essays, criticism and features for publications including the *London Review of Books*, *The Guardian* and *Vogue*. Naoise's debut novel *Exciting Times* was published by W&N in the UK and by Ecco in the US in 2020, and became a *Sunday Times* bestseller, widely translated and optioned for TV. She has been shortlisted and longlisted for several prizes, including the Women's Prize for Fiction, the Dylan Thomas Prize and the *Sunday Times* Young Writer of the Year Award.

The most annoying question journalists ask me – and it's not even close – is how being autistic affects my writing. The answer I'm tempted to give is: 'First, you tell me how not being autistic affects yours.'

My neurology stays implicit in most of my work. When autism itself is not the topic, I see no need to hold readers' hands and break it to them gently that they're in communion with a lady of the spectrum. I would find it a hindrance and nuisance to continuously monitor whether my autism was showing, just as neurotypicals would find it unhelpful to constantly ask themselves: 'Am I coming across as emotionally incontinent and desperate for the validation of my peers?'

If this seems a cruel summary of neurotypical writing, please note how entirely normalised it is to describe autists' fiction as inhumanly aloof. Literary culture has a narrow definition of emotional depth, particularly when it comes to young women's writing. Certain readers seem to demand endless paragraphs on how the untimely death of a character's chihuahua made their stomach clench. Personally I'm far more moved by descriptions of emotion expressed through cognitive realism rather than somatic signs: the stomach cramps could equally be attributed to an ill-advised third cup of coffee, while zooming in on each pixel of a character's thought process can far more precisely reflect their experience.

It's not only that I theoretically value rigour over vibes – although I do. Clarity *is* an emotional experience for me. 'This is so fucking specific, fuck yes,' I think as I read someone like Vladimir Nabokov or Sayaka Murata or Mary Lavin. That's what loving a book feels like for me.

I enjoy descriptions of bodies when they're linked to concepts I find theoretically engaging or when the prose is stunning enough to become an object of interest in itself. (See: James

Baldwin.) Not all somatic writing is intellectually vacuous; I do not wish to reproduce the accusations of sentimentalism that have historically been weaponised against gay men and writers of colour who work in that tradition.

What I object to is:

1. the assumption that cognitive descriptions cannot equally produce emotional affect, and
2. the tyrannical expectation that all women should foreground bodies – and that if they don't, they're depriving the reader of something essential.

When a female character written by a woman has been romantically betrayed, she's not expected to analyse the language or the behavioural patterns or the accumulation of data as I would. She must instead direct the reader to her shaking hands or shallow breath. To me this shorthand seems coy, a cute way of containing systemised female rage. There is a power in the relentless pinpointing of facts that a focus on flushed cheeks seems designed to tame.

(Except when the cheeks are done well, of course. My only prescriptive stance is that more people should write well.)

The expectation to lead with blushing is a curse for autistic women writers. In our actual lives we're often concept-focused, not as a distraction from emotion but *as our way of feeling it*. This is not a deficit. We're not broken. We're just different.

There's one striking exception: Jane Austen. She has been grandfathered into perceived emotional heft despite offering little in the way of somatic detail – or indeed interior design or slobbering pets or any of the things women are supposedly meant to write about. She will name a furniture item or note that a dog is present. Her characters have bodies and use them. But the real action is verbal: the sentences her characters think in and the ones they exchange.

Austen is so clearly a genius that no one credible accuses her of emotional banality. Maybe that's the best hope for autistic women writing now: accept that in your lifetime you will be misconstrued as an ice queen for focusing on the elements of human experience that you yourself find most arresting and powerful and raw, but that maybe one day when enough dust has settled you'll be admired for your elegant restraint. It will still be a misreading of your burning cognitive intensity, just as it is of Austen's, but at least they'll stop calling you superficial. (I do think Austen herself was autistic, but that's another essay.)

I've focused on fiction here because it's where I feel most keenly the disconnect between how I want to write and what's expected.

Non-fiction can produce moments of similar disjuncture. 'Where's the *you* in this?' editors ask me. The whole thing is me! It's all my thoughts. There's an absence of relatability-based pandering in my essays, too, that probably reflects my being autistic. My ideal reader can cope without constant reassurance that I'm just like them. I don't bother with an 'I know I'm such a nerd for caring about these things' schtick, because the truth is that I don't find it untoward to have interests. All people do, though perhaps not everyone's revolve around comparing the degree to which the vocative case has declined in Irish versus Slovak. (I haven't actually written about that one yet, but since you're all so keen…)

On the whole, though, non-fiction is more implicitly masculine than fiction as a genre, so I feel freer to write however I want rather than reciting a gendered script. My fiction is often perceived as modishly empty, too cool for school, for deploying the exact same cognitive architecture that is accepted in my essays as deeply felt. I can write bodies by thinking about it – by forcing it out – but it's not the native grammar of my emotional perception. Reading over my published fiction, I can see all the points where I wanted to describe a character's analytical interiority but thought readers might prefer a quivering lip. Those sentences are not my best work.

Besides gender, the American-influenced creative writing MFA is another factor in this weird privileging of what are essentially stage directions over cognitive interiority. A worthy maxim ('think of all the senses when you write') has been turned, over the past few decades, into a tedious paint-by-numbers: 'Don't *tell* us they're embarrassed, *show* their face flush.' *Telling* us they're embarrassed could consist of gorgeously maximalist, David Foster Wallace-esque spiralling that details each aspect of the character's abashed inner monologue; *showing* their face flush could be just that, this vapid little curlicue that any hack could pen. Within the 'show, don't tell' framework, the latter emotion is still automatically more 'earned'. Trust Americans to make their metaphors economic.

(Neither DFW nor Jonathan Franzen has ever made much use of bodies as shorthand, by the way, and neither of them gets show-don't-telled by critics. They express emotion mainly through dialogue and transcription of their characters' thoughts. When they do write about bodies, it's as actual subject matter. Which I love, by the way. I adore somatic experience when it's actually investigated in its own right. *Ulysses* is a great example of this, or for a shorter one there's *Portnoy's Complaint* by Philip Roth – the protagonist's emotions are conveyed almost entirely through cognitive realism, and his masturbation gets enough airtime to wind up in the title. My point here is not: men get away with writing worse. It's: men benefit from a more generous conception of what it means for them to write well.)

In terms of its intrinsic scope to challenge me technically, fiction is my favourite form. It forces inventions and formal risks that essays don't, at least not for me. But regarding external reception, I think my non-fiction is more often understood for what it's actually trying to do.

Through writing this piece, I've settled on a promise to myself. From now on, whenever an editor asks me to insert X sort of somatic detail, I will reframe the note to myself as: bring out the characters' emotions in whatever way feels truthful.

To reiterate, I'm not telling anyone else how to write, beyond 'well'.

This essay was previously published via the author's Substack in May 2025.

IT ALLOWS KINSHIP – AN ESSAY IN FOUR VOICES

Dr Amanda Tink

DR AMANDA TINK is Postdoctoral Research Fellow at UniSA Creative, University of South Australia, and Adjunct Research Fellow at Western Sydney University's Writing and Society Research Centre. She is a proud disabled person with intense interests in Australian disabled authors, crip poetics and memoir, and the Nazi genocide of disabled people. Her writing can be found in publications such as *The Conversation*, *Overland*, *Wordgathering*, *Sydney Review of Books* and *Australian Literary Studies*. She lives in front of her laptop and braille display with good coffee nearby, and posts at @amandatink.

To Les and Alexander Murray, in thanks and solidarity

I would have this sense that there was this preverbal or nonverbal aspect of myself which I think of as an 'it'. Not in a bad way. It's just a stubborn, genderless, uncivilised pre-person: it. And it doesn't like this, and it wants to do that, and I can't push it too far. Yes – it. All those aspects of me that I hadn't found the language for, that I'd never been given the language for, and that I knew would get a 'What!' from my mum. Those were the it bits of me.[1]

Hugs have honesty and equality, even at different heights, and avert the imposition of lipstick, slobber or sharp hair, which precipitate the further imposition of having to respond to the offended adult who kissed you, and then the other adults in the room who side with them.[2]

Always feeling the odd one out and always sounding different. The way that I spoke English. The way that I used sentences. The way that I picked up certain words, probably from books or dictionaries that I was often reading intently, meant that I was almost treated like a foreigner, as though I had an accent. And I'm sure that that pushed me towards learning foreign languages, for one. Because I felt, perhaps unconsciously or consciously, that maybe I would stumble on my real native language… And also it made a writer of me because I think all writers in the end are looking to invent their own language, and looking to have a relationship to language in any event, that is very complex.[3]

I'd sit through lessons not taking anything in, and being unable to answer questions, because the dazzle of sunlight on a school desk caused me such discomfort.[4]

It took me at least five years to begin to articulate how deeply the poem affected me. The searing emotionality of it. Here was someone, an autistic someone, putting into words so many things that autistic children are taught to be ashamed of, and other things that we are never valued for. And the very first thing he says is that he values his relationship with his autistic son so much that he did not write the poem, or at least didn't make it public, until his son gave him permission. Reading it was like hearing him say 'all of you' (as in the whole of an individual autistic person) and 'all of you' (as in autistic people collectively) 'have a place in this poem and in poetry'. I wish I had had the words to tell him all this when I met him.[5]

At one time I got fascinated by *The Guinness Book of Records.* And so, I was making a book of the records in my own family – who could make the tallest coin pile and who lived the longest life. There was this feeling for order, for organisation, for compiling data.[6] When I was fifteen I still thought that 'don't take half an hour in there' meant that twenty-seven-and-a-half minutes would be okay.[7]

Numbers are a big part of my experience of language as well because, for as long as I can remember, numbers and words are, I don't know if I could say the same, but very similar in my perception. Both are forms of meaning. Both words and numbers express relationships to each other. And part of what makes their use so pleasurable is the exploration of those relationships. And the contradictions you find, you know. The fact that cat and caterpillar sound like they should belong but don't as objects and phenomena… or between the number 11 and the number 111. Or between 13 and 37, which are both prime numbers, and both have a lot of texture as numbers in my mind.[8]

I met him once. We got on like a house on fire... We looked in two different directions and we talked about our cats and it was one of the easiest conversations I've ever had. Most people in his position would talk as if they had a sense of their status and he never did.[9]

I remember there was one piece I wrote... It was incredibly detailed: there were lots and lots and lots of sentences, and it was all about tunnels, underground tunnels, and about towers that were incredibly tall. They went into the sky. So, it wasn't so much about social interaction. I think I wasn't old enough to understand social interaction at that point. I would have been about nine or ten. It was more about trying to convey emotion, the emotion of exploration, the emotion of obstacle and perhaps trying to overcome obstacle. The emotion of intensity, enormity; fear certainly would have been an emotion that was conveyed as well. Resilience perhaps as well. Courage of some kind.[10]

The graduation from bath to shower was a happy one for me, except for the sound of water drumming on the back of my ears. I still hate that.[11]

As a toddler in a pushchair, the scrape of the wheels on a certain supermarket floor made it feel like my bones and my brain were vibrating. At the same time, the bitter reek of disinfectant (I was close to the floor, remember) made even breathing feel horrible. The only thing I could do was start screaming and crying.[12]

One day coming across Les's work and just being completely blown away by the language, and feeling a sense of kinship which I hadn't felt with other poets, for all kinds of reasons. And really wanting to learn everything I could about this guy... This was the first time I felt, 'I have a role model.' *I do have a role model! It is possible!* For the first time I could form these words. It is possible to write and be me. And not just write a history essay and not just write a composition at primary school, but perhaps write creatively, imaginatively, and that was a revelation.[13]

When I was young, I didn't understand why everyone liked Friday so much when it had so many sharp angles. And I loved the joyfulness of lemon, with the bonus that it ended on an 'n' sound, but nobody else liked it. At first, I thought it was just that we had different relationships to words, but eventually I learnt that most people don't have relationships to words at all, only to concepts.[14]

I can't stand orange juice with bits in it.[15]

I continually argued for the equality of butter in the palette of spreads. It has as much flavour and texture as Vegemite or jam, whereas adults treated it as nothing more than a bread moistener.[16]

Les stayed with us and I found him very pleasant and easy to talk to – quite different from his reputation in some ways.[17]

People have used words about me, very flattering words in the past, media words, buzzwords, which I don't obviously identify with, words like genius and so on, but which always are nice enough to hear, you know, why not? Rather that than something else. You don't take it all that seriously, but it's so funny because when I was growing up and I was a kid I wasn't at all like that, because of the medication I had to take because of my seizures, because of the limitations of being brought up working class as well, no doubt, the lack of resources, I was quite late to learning how to read and write.[18]

I would say something because I liked the sound of it. I think I learnt quite early that I use language in an odd way.[19]

I struggled with brushing my teeth for a long time because of the sound. I hated the sound of the toothbrush.[20]

In the short time we spent together we just agreed on everything: the centrality of embodiment to writing; the annoyance of being interrupted for a photo; the joy of sharing silence together before his reading.[21]

Although no-one knew I was autistic, others did see I was different, and they called me different names. (I am not just referring to other children.)[22]

I distinctly remember learning how to write only at school… I was almost six when I began school. But I was late. I was late to a lot of things. It took me a long time to learn how to swim; it took me a long time to learn how to ride a bicycle. And just the whole thing about orientating myself in mental space. Because reading is not just learning how to acquire a code. I think it is also a spatial skill.[23]

I love to spin and spin and spin while listening to music alone. It's how I relax, celebrate, contemplate, grieve, process and dream. My family tell me I began this when I was two.[24]

We talked about difference more broadly and feeling like we were so different growing up and how writing was a way of finding our voice and making sense of our difference and making sense of our place in the world so that difference was not something that needed to be anything negative as such, but it could actually be something that allowed us to connect to other people.[25]

My feelings often fail to show in my face in a way that most people recognise, or, at least, they fail to show quickly enough.[26]

Throughout my childhood I spent time alone most weekdays, and hours on the weekends, trampolining or swinging or swimming, enjoying my silence surrounded by the clamouring world.[27]

With letters and words there was definitely a step up, and it took a moment of concentration and effort, which I don't remember having for numbers as such. The concept of counting, even of multiplication or division, it seems to me in hindsight, came to me more easily or more intuitively than something like how to spell or how to write a word on a page. Of course, once I did get past that, it became completely native to me, it became completely like second nature, but I do remember that there was a moment before it became second nature when it felt so, it felt kind of awesome! In both senses of the word: wonderful, and also a sense of awe, a sense almost of not quite fear but of intimidation, this is something that's going to change me. This is something that's very important.[28]

What Les said during the talk, in between poems, was something like: 'We auties [autistics] often find ourselves staying awake at night and reliving past conversations.' He didn't elaborate, but this struck me as articulating two things with which I identify as an autistic person. Firstly, the vividness of memory; secondly, the awareness that we are supposedly quite prone to making social gaffes. And, sometimes, this combination of memory plus social unease is a difficult one.[29]

I hate orange juice with bits in it too.[30]

Resting bitch face? Oh God, yeah! The first time I remember being aware of it was when I was seven years old. 'Smile!' said my teacher. 'You won't crack your jaw!' That was the year I began having nightmares about school.[31]

When I was twelve, we had a semester of learning German at school. And though German had never been part of my life before, it felt like a language I already knew. I didn't have to study; it just made sense to me.[32]

I think the first time that I read it, it was **so* intense. It was a little bit like when I would go to the cinema and feel overwhelmed by the film's images, and emotions conveyed by the images.[33]

Until around the age of twelve, I experienced an inexplicably heavy and somehow insurmountable self-consciousness over talking to others in the presence of my family. If I was being met at the school gates by a family member and another child spoke to me (in however friendly a way), I would behave as if she or he was not there.... I sense this had something to do with autism in a different way, of inhabiting just one aspect of my identity (or even self) at a time. Even now, it can sometimes take a lot of effort to overcome the feelings of chaos involved when introducing one of my friends to another for the first time.[34]

One tactic I used against bullies or other annoying people, which always worked, was to twist my fingers, hands and arms in to shapes that seemed painful or disgusting to them.[35]

That was how I grew up, with this fascination for words and numbers as objects in their own right, that I could play with, that I could explore for their relationships for what they could tell me about the world. And it was exploring them as objects before I learned perhaps consciously to understand them as social objects as well. That these are things that we share with each other as human beings. And their meaning and their value rose out of those exchanges that we have on a constant day-to-day level. And trying to find a way of reconciling my personal interaction with them, numbers and words, with how other people understand them. That was very important as well because I needed to feel that I could speak a language that was both meaningful for me but also for other people.[36]

He's not just following his son around with a notebook… He's not exhibiting his son; he's displaying empathy for his son. And there's a huge difference between the two.[37]

I cried from both fear and joy, from the physical pain of them. As a child I didn't know how to explain this, and other people rarely understood. Dogs did though.[38]

Being British, I like my fruit cooked (apple crumble, banana in porridge).[39]

When I was ten I discovered that I did not like dodgem cars – one discombobulating jolt after another – and spent the entire probably three-minute round yelling, 'Beep beep! Get out the way! Get out the way!' The family friend driving me around did not know what to do.[40]

People always assume that I would have been an ace at maths because of my relationship with numbers, but not at all. I was very strong in primary school when it was mostly arithmetic, but by the time I went to secondary school and I had to learn about algebra and all this sort of stuff, calculus and geometry, those things interested me much less, and I didn't have any particular talent for them.[41]

My preference for sameness is such that I have rarely been able to share daily life with 'a partner'. It also means that, as yet, I have never truly wanted to do so. Every day has been somehow enough in itself.[42]

As a kid, I jumped at any opportunity to tag along when any of my family visited our doctor. Adjoined to the reception area was a kids' playroom. It was always in a huge mess, and I delighted in tidying it.[43]

I just love colour. My response to it is almost tactile. There's a certain green that I can't look at without tasting Granny Smith apples. I experience blue as a hug. I feel I could fall onto blue. And I love the rainbow – I seek out the spectrum at make-up counters, in art shops, in the towel displays at John Lewis. They all make me ridiculously happy.[44]

I wrote a poem for him as well, which came out in my little book of poems that I got published sometime later. And he said, 'Oh, thank you for that peach of a poem.' He was definitely like a mentor to me as well. He was very happy to play that role, to encourage, I mean not in any sort of really effusive way. That wasn't in his nature. But he definitely found the words, the few words that needed to be said to let me know that what I was doing made sense to him as a writer, as a professional writer, that there was something there and I should definitely keep going.[45]

Sources

1. Joanne Limburg, 14 March 2023, Zoom interview with Amanda Tink for her 'Learning My First Language: Blindness, neurodivergence, and our creative writing practices' project (assisted by the Australian Government through Creative Australia, its arts funding and advisory body).
2. Amanda Tink, reflections motivated by 'It Allows a Portrait in Line Scan at Fifteen' by Les Murray.
3. Daniel Tammet, 26 June 2023, Zoom interview for 'Learning My First Language'.
4. James McGrath; Gensic, J 2020, 'Autism Interview #128: Dr. James McGrath on representation, transition supports, and reframing the autism identity narrative', *Learn From Autistics*, 5 May, <learnfromautistics.com/autism-interview-128-dr-james-mcgrath-on-representation-transition-supports-and-reframing-the-autism-identity-narrative>.

5. Tink, reflections.
6. Tammet, interview.
7. Tink, reflections.
8. Tammet, interview.
9. Limburg, on meeting Les Murray, interview.
10. Tammet, interview.
11. Tink, reflections.
12. McGrath; Gensic, J, 'Autism Interview #128'.
13. Tammet, interview.
14. Tink, reflections.
15. Limburg, interview.
16. Tink, reflections.
17. McGrath, on meeting Les Murray, 26 April 2021, email to Amanda Tink.
18. Tammet, interview.
19. Limburg, interview.
20. Tammet, interview.
21. Tink, reflections on meeting Les Murray.
22. McGrath, J 2017, *Naming Adult Autism: Culture, science, identity*, Rowman & Littlefield International, London.
23. Tammet, interview.
24. Tink, reflections.
25. Tammet, on meeting Les Murray, interview.
26. Limburg; Brown, H 2021, 'Joanne Limburg: "Autistic women don't simper. We have no interest in making a man feel big"', *The Independent*, 7 July, <independent.co.uk/arts-entertainment/books/features/joanne-limburg-interview-letters-to-my-weird-sister-autism-b1878250.html>.
27. Tink, reflections.
28. Tammet, interview.
29. McGrath, email.
30. Tink, reflections.
31. Limburg; Brown, H, 'Joanne Limburg'.
32. Tink, reflections.
33. Tammet, on reading 'It Allows a Portrait in Line Scan at Fifteen' by Les Murray; Johnson, M 2017, *Two Poets*, BBC Radio 4, podcast, 16 February, <bbc.co.uk/programmes/b08dr5r4>.

34. McGrath; McGrath, J, *Naming Adult Autism*.
35. Tink, reflections.
36. Tammet, interview.
37. Limburg, on 'It Allows a Portrait in Line Scan at Fifteen' by Les Murray, interview.
38. Tink, reflections.
39. Tammet, 25 January 2024, email to Amanda Tink.
40. Tink, reflections.
41. Tammet, interview.
42. McGrath; McGrath, J, *Naming Adult Autism*.
43. Tink, reflections.
44. Limburg; Brown, H, 'Joanne Limburg'.
45. Tammet, on Les Murray, interview.

ECHOES IN A WHITE ROOM

Ange Crawford

ANGE CRAWFORD (she/her) is a writer, editor and PhD candidate living on unceded Wurundjeri land. Her debut young adult novel, *How to Be Normal*, won the inaugural Walker Books Manuscript Prize. Her writing is driven by curiosity and experimentation, and as a result meanders across genres and styles but is often connected by her enduring interests in queerness, art, storytelling, place(lessness) and language. Apart from writing and editing, she is a fan of cats and synthesisers, and can often be found with an armful of books in a local independent bookstore.

Unfurnished

I return to being fourteen, tapping. The keys demand deep pressure – each tap is a deliberate part of the rhythm. And the sound, the feedback, is part of the meditation. A fantasy novel is taking shape here on the aged CRT monitor, and I know I am no Isobelle Carmody, but I'm furnishing from my daydreams a place for me to go when nothing around me makes sense and the world feels too much. Which is often. Only, the place is not so furnished. Example: a scene, early in the novel, where a pair of magical creatures fly with the reluctant heroine over the ocean at night – the wind does not buffet-shriek
her ears do not ring-rush
though she is held by her arms, there is no vertigo-ache,
and in this intense hyperfocus, I am all mind, all fantasy, no body, cannot imagine how any of this would feel, cannot say why.

One day, years from now, I will be told that this novel is afflicted with white room syndrome. It's as though the characters are floating in a blank space and the setting does not exist. There is no sense of the world around them. Despite my best efforts, for years, I write myself into a white room.

And in another time, I am in the worn chair underneath my creaking study-bunk, where I perch, entwining my fingers in Blu Tack, moulding, melting, because my mind is stuck.

hummmmmmmmmmmmmmmmmmmmmm. I am younger here. Young enough that, despite my lifelong obsession with writing, I have only just come across the universal writerly principle of 'show don't tell' – my writing is too direct, too monologuing, too inclined to turn everything into a lecture, when the audience wants to be shown all these actions! Sensory details!

tap, tap, tap   Sideways glances across the room: I glare into my bedroom mirror and ask myself what of this constriction in my chest surfaces on the outside – *don't tell me the moon is shining; show me the glint of light on broken glass*, says Anton Chekhov, says the nascent internet – but all the glass around me is stubbornly whole and so it reflects everything, everything, everything, and at the same time, my body says nothing.

I turn away from my notes on the second-year sensation and perception class – at nineteen, I am studying psychology, hoping I will one day pick up on the language of the social world, the way I do with literary language – but still nothing captivates me like writing, so I am returning. This university teaches almost no arts courses, but there is one shelf here in the library filled with screenwriting texts. Among them is my new favourite book of all time: *The Writer's Journey* by Christopher Vogler.[1] Beneath its bubble contact covering, it feels like the mysteries of the literary universe are revealed to me – archetypical characters that recur across generations and cultures, twelve steps to a universally relatable plotline. This simplicity makes my heart race faster.

clock-tick   I always return to it, rewarding myself with little dips into the formula. I sit at a desk closest to the shelf, overlooking the artificial lake with its pretentious fountain – a repetition that appears universally liked, water going nowhere. Despite the craft book's pleadings to do no such thing, I turn it into a checklist before I graduate. I add a note to myself – don't forget s-e-t-t-i-n-g – and I worry that all these processes mean I am not creative and therefore not a creative writer, but the comfort of these coffee-stained pages is unparalleled.

tap, tap, tap

I build a shelter with my writing, and it is enough to hold me, so I am always going back. *The eternal return.*[2] The pairing of creation and destruction. The necessity of repetition. The building and re-building of structures. I am building and re-building now, as I always have, and probably always will.

Spotlight

In my late twenties, I am writing, sitting in	bang, bang, bang
my car in the semi-darkness in our covered	
parking space beneath the apartment, between	bang, bang, bang
my noise-cancelling headphones comes the	
free remote Iowa Writers' Workshop session	
and someone is talking about objects – things	
are never just things; they are also symbols,	ringgggggggggg
when you take a character's perspective. I am	thump, thump,
still not good at setting. I am old enough to	thump, thump
worry whether this is my whiteness showing:	
a colonial tendency to see places as blank	clang
spaces unless they are owned, unless they are	bang, bang, bang
productive. Even though I have always felt a	
secret sort-of animistic connection to the	thump, thump,
objects around me (apologising to the	thump, thump
smoking oven, sheltering the worn-out socks),	crash
the written objects sink stubbornly into this	
digital page, where they refuse to symbolise	thump, thump,
anything other than the great distance	thump, thump
between me and the Iowa Writers' Workshop	clunk
and whatever kind of insight will break me	thump, thump,
thump out of this constraint.	

Eden Arefaine,
describing
monotropism in
autism, called
attention *the beam*
of light shining down
the tunnel.[3] Maybe
because the world
feels so intense for us,
one natural response is
narrowing attention, so
the amount of input is
less overwhelming. *This*
light, while far-reaching,
is so bright that everything
not directly lit is unseen.[4] The
surroundings disappear.

The thing that I keep coming back to – the thing that worries me about story craft – is the way that each word sweeps over so many details like sandpaper and the filings get stuck to me. But I have learned to ignore their persistent impressions, turn everything else off, focus.

Floor, coverings

This table for one is slightly misaligned – or the floor is on an angle – and there is no centre of gravity here, facing this pillar in the middle of this bar in Mermaid Beach. Here, on the Gold Coast, where I grew up, I have always felt off-kilter like this – despite a deep affinity for the sand, ocean, sun – no matter how many window-shopping Sundays, plucked eyebrow hairs, faded nightclub stamps I bore. hover I am waiting here, and so I read to forget where I am. I'm twenty-four and wear black-framed hipster glasses; I am trying on a new idea of myself as someone who sips negronis and surveys crowds with a vague expression of disdain while wedging open the writing/craft/autobiographical book *Release the Bats* by DBC Pierre[5] between my thumb and pinkie… despite the strain.

breathe. And there are echoes of his tone in the atmosphere here – where people swap tales of drug-induced inspiration and shits and butterflies and women who walk like they wear high heels even when barefoot (toe-walking?) – but I am not yet aware that this approach to writing is far from universal, so I keep looking for myself in it, and wondering why I don't show up. And I don't yet know about toe-walking (though I do it when alone, my feet a little less on the floor, a little less in the room). This is my atmosphere – my setting – and my survival strategy has been to soak it up like a make-up sponge until it is

just another white

room and I am so heavy with all of it. *What would you write if you weren't afraid?* DBC Pierre asks in the numbered list of writing tips at the end of the book, all of which read profound when dipped in bitter Campari. *Write that.*

I can only return to this industrial-dark scene a little further back in time to this office, to the backstreets of Southport, to the shutter-light summery day after New Year's – Vogler or McKee[6] or Snyder[7] might call it an ordeal or a crisis or a dark night of the soul – but the reality just looks like a twenty-two-year-old office worker lying on the carpet pins-and-needles in an otherwise empty block and she is wordless, weighted down, like the musty carpet might shake off all the little paper fragments and envelop her. Her life is refusing to come together

heavy despite the earlier montage of a youth writing award, masterclasses, festivals, books, novels and cocktail bars and *promising* grades. She is only s-e-t-t-i-n-g, set-dressing, dressed for the setting, next to all these papers she started sorting to justify her salary today, because the laptop *on* button is much too much.

From a distance, nearly a decade, I return with Kelsey Allagood's essay 'Active protagonists are a tool of the patriarchy'[8] and words for this – autistic burnout. *It's much easier to tell a compelling story about a character striving to get what they want* – a universally relatable plotline – *I've been thinking about the kind of people in real life who are encouraged to be passive* – lying on the floor – women who walk like they always wear high heels – *It's always worthwhile to question what's widely considered good writing, and to ask who benefits from these 'rules'.*

If I let this room in, if I truly write as a body in this space, I fear that the words will just keep coming and they will stop making sense and flood out of me and writing will no longer shelter me.

Curled into the sofa, I write   blue, purple, pink
– my body an apostrophe, a comma, a silent connection,
a   caffeinated-shaking   pause for breath. I am in a
jaw-clenching   tunnel that I have
always been able to create for myself, focusing this spotlight – this time premeditated, a kind of hypnosis I *must* put myself in to meet a novel contest deadline every   flaring   morning for the next three weeks. There's a not-right feeling, but I don't have the words to spare for it. Here, at the end of my twenties, all I know is that this hyperfocused state was once a private ritual comfort and now feels so p-r-o-d-u-c-t-i-v-e – this straight-A force I can still exert over myself. I am darkly pleased with myself to be this effective. Vogler says: the (active) hero must enter the special world and face great obstacles to obtain the elixir.[9] There is no story without conflict. And, there is that quiet voice in my mind asking the question I don't want to hear after twenty years of this recurrence – what if I need despair

to write – everything good I've ever expressed has come out as a way to process how

everything

everything is – so in this productive edition of my lifelong monotropism, I am missing clues about what will happen next in this story (and setting!) I am carefully constructing – editing – self-editing – editing myself, until I get it done clamour

but not well not

well not well enough my body reasserts itself

and the setting follows.

stretched out in the scraggly park opposite my office

shivering in the shadow of the corporate-lobby sculpture gasping in the detergent aisle of Coles dozing in the sunny corner of my bedroom shrinking away from others' shoulders on the city train crying in the YouTube blue light

Walls

I am reading Jenny Odell's *How to Do Nothing.*[10] I am doing nothing.

I've also learned thul patterns of attention – what we choose to notice and what we do not – are how we render reality for ourselves, and thus have a direct bearing on what we feel is possible at any given time. Noticing never felt optional to me. But I am thinking of the choice I do have – what to do with all this noticing.

Editing comes more naturally to me than writing. I take pleasure in returning – again and again – to what I have written before, casting out the bits that are *too much*. I love this editorial mindset, curating these writing memories for you. But their impressions remain on my body. They eternally recur.

In *Save the Cat! Writes a Novel*, Jessica Brody writes that, after it seems that all is lost, the hero *is allowed to move* backward, *instead of forward.*[11] A *return to the familiar.* I return to a scratchy memory – I am contained in this loft above a café in the Brisbane CBD – above a soprano-steam spiralling blue staircase. I am twelve years old and mapping a fantasy world in a class with the first author I have ever met. The task is to imagine what happened here in this fictional place I have created – why the land looks like this, how this situatedness would impact the people who would grow from it, in it, of it. I am growing from, in, of this plasterboard that surrounds me, that holds me up, which is covered – here – in the scratching bumpy inky haiku and microfictions and asides left by other attendees. The words spring from and in and of every corner here. A literal echo of those structures I want, but am yet, to build. I am thinking about how stories have always felt like houses with their beginning-doorway middle-roof ending-doorway – a construction within which we can shelter

bibliosmia! In the

lunchbreak, the bright orange spill of tomato soup on the author's shirt – the

skin-prickling dryer in the bathroom as she tried her best to clean it all away, the whispers under her breath about this failure of containment. I knew already that I was someone who noticed details and got stuck distracted

flushing and that this sort of detail does not belong in a story of self-discovery and she tried so hard to make her clothing perfect again, like I wanted to make my words, so I averted my eyes, but the stain persisted and so did the details in the writing

tasted like tomatoes.

And then twenty years later, in an art
writing program,
I cannot avert my eyes.
This time the floor is concrete and somehow stable
it is my brief to lie here. I am not these impressions –
alone in a Southport office. I am in a psychedelic, screaming
Melbourne contemporary art gallery all around
among the woven and discarded and seeping-piercing-aching-
fragmented and blanketing works of queer
artist Paul Yore. I am here to write rainbows
about it all,[12] and it is all so very, very all.
Slurs and textures and tones and echoes and glints and stains.
World-building. This time I am joyous-static-ghostly-
comforting, confronting, naming this sensory
overwhelm
(not like that time in Southport)
because it is my brief to name what I know –
I am failing at this – and because
Jack Halberstam writes that
the queer art of failure turns on the impossible, the
improbable, the unlikely, and the unremarkable.[13] The
other writers reading and discussing this – safe amongst
all that constant, flashing neon-LED
muchness – so I turned to this book detours
and tried to keep … up.
Only to be told to lose. The queer art of failure *quietly loses, and*
in losing it imagines other goals for life, for love, for art, and for
being.[14] I untangle these sensations from here
on the floor in this gallery-white cube, incoherent-clicking
where I recur each visit, because being stuck
floored has been my experience – and writing
has to come from experience. On this
floor I realise I am drawn to ekphrasis –
this form of writing that is all response –
because in writing about art, everything can be / surface, but

not surface as
opposed to deep, but surfacing as in surfacing,
as in reaching and gasping,
as in sometimes it feels like speaking is just survival,
like the words get away from me because of all these sensations,
but fingers can type, fingers can grasp, weaving something
from all this real,
and turn all these details into tapestry and
I am in my body surfacing.

Inside, outside

All these memories are writing memories. Sensory memories. All these memories, to which I've returned while writing this piece, are from before I discovered that I'm autistic. But all these memories are still autistic. All the sensitivity, all the passion and depth, all the processes and processing, all the attempts to
cast out and
compartmentalise and edit out the bits that
didn't make sense,
everything
my body absorbed like a porous stack of paper, until the room appeared empty, blank, a white space. Which it never was. There is so much here.

Chloé Hayden, in her beautiful book *Different Not Less*, calls these joyful moments 'eye sparkles' – *those things that ignite a passion in us so deeply that it fills every crevice.*[15] Sideways glances across the room:
I stare into my bedroom mirror and ask myself what of this
eternal return and my eyes sparkle.

And although I love these formulas, these structures, and all the white space that sets out my work on the page… Sometimes

I need to cast it all off and walk away. Madeleine Watts says, *bodies were so absent in literature, whereas my own body was so present in my life.*[16] Literature, though, is present in my life and in my body. I had been editing out so many details (in my life and in my body), trying to make something coherent out of all the moments of overwhelm and confusion, absorbing everything into myself so that I could furnish a white room. But all those colourful little details sparkle for me. I could never see the forest for the trees. But I want you to see *this* tree:

Tapping – the sound, the feedback   tap, tap, tap
everything, everything, everything, and at the same time, my
body says
bubble contact covering,
          ringgggggggggg
                              so intense,
off-kilter like this   And there are echoes
          blue, purple, pink   – my body an apostrophe
                         in the shadow of the corporate-lobby
sculpture   all this noticing.
impressions   on my body.
               Plasterboard – echo
Slurs and textures and tones and echoes and glints and stains.
failure *quietly loses, and for art, and for being*
incoherent-clicking-stuck   writing
         surfacing,   and
                                                  surfacing.
my eyes sparkle.

I am holding

I am holding my phone out on the   light-smudged   Docklands
footpath and pointing it at a streamer that   sun-flecked
          someone has tied to a council bin – drifting in the winds,

howl-blasting inexplicably – and I am one of these office workers Bluetooth-magnified wandering – with inexplicable gazes fixed at some distant plexiglass-cragged point on the horizon where I might also be silhouetted but I – I am writing again in these ordinary places – taking in what Yuriko Saito[17] flowing flowing flowing has to say about everyday aesthetics and the beauty of the flowing flowing flowing laundry drifting on the clothesline on the cover of her electric second book about the aesthetics of the familiar – what Nicholson Baker meant by writing a whole book[18] about airless going up an escalator on one such office lunchbreak where walla-bounce so many weaving stories so many trees so many details could be found in annotations uncountable crannies in flecks in crevices that the eye might seek to skip this eye takes in all the setting this eye must look away or it all gets too much this eye might seek to skip but it has already taken in – aesthetics is about more than what can be found in the white room of an art gallery – that connection is more than eye contact – that there is no such thing as a white room – that this, too, is connection – that every coffee cup every siren every streamer is a sense impression – contact – meaning – everything impacts everything – meaning – it is everything to witness this – everything – and I am permeable sensitive here

sparkling

Sources – a big, earnest endnote infodump!

One of the great joys of literary wandering is when you get to the end of a short piece and find a long list of further reading. If you're feeling the urge to plunge into a topic or source referenced in this essay, I am so excited to present you with some deep-diving-boards from my own most enduring special interest – writing craft and its many, many related fields – and I hope you might find something in one (or more) of these places that makes your eyes sparkle.

1. Vogler, C 1992, *The Writer's Journey: Mythic structure for writers*, Michael Wiese Productions, United States; a book that inspired me to ask questions about what, if anything, is universal about story craft.
2. Cain, A 2022, *A Horse at Night: On writing*, Dorothy, United States; an exquisite book on writing and reading that I read and reread.
3. Arefaine, E 2023, 'Monotropism', staff writer, *Embrace Autism*, <embrace-autism.com/monotropism>; an interesting and readable look at this experience.
4. ibid.
5. Pierre, D 2016, *Release the Bats*, Faber, United Kingdom; a very voice-y craft book that gave me a push at a time when I needed it.
6. McKee, R 1997, *Story: Substance, structure, style, and the principles of screenwriting*, It Books, United States; an interesting text to read, think about, write from, write about, write against, perhaps.
7. Snyder, B 2005, *Save the Cat!: The last book on screenwriting that you'll ever need*, Michael Wiese Productions, United States; a craft book that has helped me at times of feeling stuck with structure, but that I've always found, for my own work, has served me best when viewed as a list of ideas, rather than a recipe book.
8. Allagood, K 2021, 'Active protagonists are a tool of the patriarchy', *Writer Unboxed*, 18 September, <writerunboxed.com/2021/09/18/active-protagonists-are-a-tool-of-the-patriarchy>; the title speaks for itself – made me rethink passivity as a porous and sensitive person.
9. Vogler, C, *The Writer's Journey*.
10. Odell, J (2019) *How to Do Nothing: Resisting the attention economy*, Melville House, United States; an amazing book for so many reasons, but I was especially inspired by the way Jenny Odell writes about attention and resistance, as this had unexpected resonances with my experience as an autistic person.
11. Brody, J 2018, *Save the Cat! Writes a Novel: The last book on novel writing that you'll ever need*, Clarkson Potter/Ten Speed, United States; an adaptation of Snyder's *Save the Cat!* formula to the novel form – same notes as above apply.
12. I participated in the 2022 ACCA/RMIT non/fictionLab program

Writing in the Expanded Field: Touching Feeling Writing, and it changed how I write. Publications from the program are available here: <touchingfeeling.acca.melbourne>.

13. Halberstam, J 2011, *The Queer Art of Failure*, Duke University Press, United States; a work of theory that is not only genuinely fascinating but also highly readable – and, honestly, embracing 'failure' is liberating.
14. Halberstam, J, *The Queer Art of Failure*.
15. Hayden, C 2023, *Different, Not Less: A neurodivergent's guide to embracing your true self and finding your happily ever after*, Murdoch Books, Sydney; there are many reasons to read this beautiful book, but perhaps a less obvious one is the central metaphor of a retold fairytale.
16. Watts, M (n.d.) 'Writing about the body with Madeline Watts', *KYD Online Writing Workshops*, <workshops.killyourdarlings.com.au/p/ writing-about-the-body-with-madeleine-watts-online-creative-writing-course>; I love writing courses and I especially loved this writing course.
17. Saito, Y 2010, *Everyday Aesthetics*, Oxford University Press, United Kingdom; because clotheslines can be beautiful and that matters.
18. Baker, N 2020, *The Mezzanine*, Granta, United Kingdom; a book that is well-known for its extensive and digressive notes, which gave me a great precedent for this little infodump!

KINDRED SPIRITS

Jo Case

JO CASE is a co-editor of *Someone Like Me*.

‘You named me after Jo March, didn’t you?’ I asked my mum recently, knowing she hadn’t. (My name is Joanne, not Josephine.)

‘If you want to tell people that, sure,’ she said breezily, deliberately not heeding my nonsense.

My practical, English-teacher mother didn’t name me after Jo March, but she did give me my first copy of *Little Women*. I don’t remember when I first read it, but nor do I remember a time when it wasn’t part of my vocabulary.

Mum encouraged my deep immersion in reading and writing, from as early as I can remember – despite these habits also encouraging what I now recognise, in retrospect, as a fanciful strangeness.

I can still picture the first thing I ever wrote – a book, made of stapled computer paper, that consisted of two stories. The first read, in full: ‘Joanne Peg found a worm in the dirt.’ It was titled ‘Joanne Peg’. The second story was about my best friend’s parents being killed in a car crash, and her coming to live with us as a result. On the last page was a drawing of us jumping on the bed together, with the word ‘Wheeeee!’ I was three years old.

I had a habit, in my primary-school years, of going to the houses of cousins – and even occasionally friends – and reading their books instead of playing with them. I have a vague memory of raiding a classmate’s shelves and sitting happily on the carpet with a stack of *Baby-Sitters Club* novels (which Mum didn’t buy me, as she thought they were trash) until it was time to go home.

Mortifyingly, I also remember reading stories I had written aloud to my cousins – just announcing it, not asking if they actually wanted to hear them. I was the oldest child of the oldest child on my mum’s side of the family, so I got away with a lot for a long time.

One mystifying time, my story-making helped rather than hindered one of my cousins. When my twin sisters were born, when I was seven, I was sent to stay with her family for a fortnight, including two weeks accompanying her to school. I was obsessed with the then-new film *Annie* and proposed a schoolyard game based on it, which was a huge hit. My cousin's whole class played it every lunchtime and I got to choose my role. For those two weeks, I had a brief, bewildering taste of what it would be like to be a popular kid.

By high school, I had grown into a precarious social awareness that meant I no longer raided my friends' bookshelves when visiting their homes. (I don't think I did, anyway.) But central to all my teenage friendships was our habit of writing and swapping long, illustrated letters and stories about our classmates and crushes. In my spare time at home, I filled exercise books with fledgling novels. I was never not writing.

It has never seemed surprising that my favourite childhood books included *Little Women*, the *Anne of Green Gables* series and *Harriet the Spy*: all beloved classics about girls and women who compulsively write. But it's only occurred to me in the past few years, well into my forties, that these books also share characters who are autistic headcanons.

A headcanon is something fans interpret or imagine about a story that doesn't appear on the page – so, autistic headcanons are characters who were not written as autistic, but can be read retrospectively as if they were, due to their constellation of autistic traits. I'm not the only one to claim Jo March, Anne Shirley and Harriet M Welsch in this way: the internet is studded with similar observations. These characters not only have autistic traits but have also always connected with something deep within me; their brain wiring has always seemed to mirror my own in crucial ways.

I believe they have an Australian sister too: Sybylla Melvyn, the prickly heroine of Miles Franklin's *My Brilliant Career*, who I didn't meet until my thirties. Her disconnection from, or confusion about, her own feelings and desires confused me when I first read the book, but it makes a kind of sense when viewed through the frame of an autistic woman. (Alexithymia, a difficulty experiencing, identifying and expressing emotions, is common in autistic people.) Like Jo March, Sybylla inhabits an awkward, artless – yet electric – physicality. And, like all these characters, she conspicuously neither thinks, acts nor looks like other women.

Little Women author Louisa May Alcott – who so resembled her most-loved heroine she sometimes called herself 'Jo' – was described even in early childhood as possessing 'unusual vivacity and forcefulness of spirit' and 'power, individuality and force'. Her father, Transcendentalist philosopher and (mostly unsuccessful) author Bronson Alcott, who was a better anthropologist of his children than provider for them, authored those descriptions.[1]

It's common knowledge the *Little Women* books are modelled on the life experiences of their author. But while this is broadly true, the reality of the Alcott family is darker, stranger and more complex. After reading about them, I added Louisa and her father to my treasury of autistic headcanons.

Little Women and its sequels are famously cosy novels. The Marches (whose name is a play on May, Louisa's mother Abigail's family name) are part of wider society, but on its fringes. This is partly due to their poverty but also because of their morals, which are less concerned with appearances than what they consider right. Like Marmee, the character modelled after her, Abigail Alcott regretted how much 'girls are taught to seem, to appear – not to be and do', according to Anne Boyd Rioux, author of *Meg, Jo, Beth, Amy: The story of Little Women and why it still matters.*[2] 'That the Alcotts were not like other people was a great part of their fascination for their neighbours, and central to their idea of themselves,' affirms Louisa's biographer, Harriet Reisen.[3]

My family, too, were not like our neighbours. My parents, who rarely drank and socialised mostly with our extended family, were considered uptight by our school friends (and, I presume, their parents) in Adelaide's northeastern outer suburbs. When I was in primary school, my parents had an ongoing feud with a neighbour who illegally rode his motorbike in the patch of creek and scrub across the road from our house. Dad would veer between calling the police on him and inviting him and his friends to play pool in our garage as a form of youth outreach. When the garage was vandalised, we suspected our neighbour.

Like Abigail, my mother believed surfaces were secondary. Or rather, she didn't believe in courting popularity (social or romantic), though she did believe in correctness: being neatly groomed and wearing the right school uniform. As an adult, I once caught her telling my son to respect John Howard, 'because he's the prime minister'. In contrast, I had recently stuck his impassioned poem about Howard locking up children on our fridge.

My father, like Bronson, did not care about social rules for their own sake (nor did he expect us to respect John Howard). He modelled inhabiting your idiosyncratic self, rather than forcing yourself into an ill-fitting mould, in a way I intuited from early childhood. When my son was diagnosed as autistic, the first thing most of us thought about was how this explained my father.

Early in *Little Women*, the family's poverty is explained by Mr March having 'lost his property in trying to help an unfortunate friend'.[4] Louisa's father had been against both owning property and working for a wage since his experimental school dwindled to six paying students when she was young. The family often went hungry and were frequently supported by loans, monetary gifts and property courtesy of Abigail's relatives and Bronson's friends, including Transcendentalist writers Ralph Waldo Emerson and Henry David Thoreau. Emerson and Thoreau (along with German poet-philosopher Goethe, whose work Emerson introduced Louisa to) even served as composite models for Jo March's eventual romantic match, philosophy professor Friedrich Bhaer.

Louisa modelled much of *Little Women* on her time in Concord, Massachusetts, where she spent the 'happiest years' of her life.[5] The family's time at Fruitlands, a short-lived commune Bronson co-founded, did not make it into *Little Women* or its sequels – and would not have been nearly so relatable. At Fruitlands, the family of six shared two bedrooms between them, co-habiting with at least one other family, sometimes more. They restricted their vegetarian diet to exclude the 'too sensual' milk, butter and molasses and refrained from eating vegetables grown in the ground, only eating 'foods which would not give up their life force (i.e. are replenished on trees and vines)'.[6]

Even after the family abandoned Fruitlands, seven months into the experiment, the 'usual Alcott meal' would long remain 'a piece of bread, an apple and water, with frequent stretches of only bread and water', writes Reisen, who notes that Bronson didn't seem troubled by this. No wonder Abby, who would take over as head of the household (and organise the funds for their rescue and re-housing) after the Fruitlands disaster, was determined her daughters would have the means to support themselves.

Bronson's sayings, which Emerson tried to get published for him (despite admitting not liking them), included: 'Engage in nothing that cripples or degrades you. Your first duty is self-culture, self-exaltation; you may not violate this high trust. Your self is sacred, profane it not.'[7] Set against his family's destitution, it's a breathtaking moral declaration.

Bronson's head-in-the-clouds self-absorption was similarly reflected on a micro level. Boyd Rioux tells how Abigail once gave her husband ten dollars to buy her a winter shawl and he returned with a coveted book he'd seen in a shop window, having forgotten the shawl.[8] Louisa borrowed this as a moral lesson for newlywed Meg in *Good Wives* (swapping a shawl for a coat and a book for a silk dress) and had her repent, make amends and never do it again.

*

Jo and her creator – who often went by the boys' name Lu – would likely be called gender-queer today. From the opening pages of *Little Women*, Jo is adopting a 'gentlemanly manner', sharing her disappointment at not being a boy and declaring herself the 'man of the family'. At novel's end, Mr March praises her for having evolved from being his 'son Jo' into a woman.[9] At thirteen, Louisa wrote: 'I am old for my age, and don't care much for girls' things. People think I'm wild and queer.' She wrote to her younger neighbour Alf Whitman, one of a few confirmed models for Laurie, that she had a 'boy's spirit'.[10]

Katharine Hepburn, who played Jo in the 1933 film *Little Women*, similarly did not think of herself as female. As a child, she shaved her head, wore boys' clothes and adopted a boys' name, Jimmy. As an adult, she was famous for her signature trousers. A school friend remembered, 'There was something very different about her… She'd look at her girlfriends as if she didn't understand them, as if they were speaking a different language.' Hepburn's posthumous biographer, William Mann, who deconstructed Hepburn's many myths, wrote that she remained Jimmy in her heart all her life (as she privately documented). He wrote of her *Little Women* performance: 'Hepburn was playing herself, and it showed.'[11] Her brother and the director George Cukor, a close friend, both said she 'was Jo'.[12]

It's difficult, from today's perspective, to discern whether women like Alcott or Hepburn were trans or genderqueer, or simply adopting a gender identity that better fit their sense of self at a time when women were expected to perform a narrow femininity and gender roles were more highly restricted. Both interpretations, I think, are plausible.

Miles Franklin too, was reproached as a young woman for 'running around like a boy' and wrote to a former teacher about her 'anxiety at looming womanhood'.[13] Her character Sybylla is told she 'should have been a boy' and enjoys male friendship. But she also relishes her feminine makeover from her aunt Helen, who transforms her from plain to striking with the help of flattering dresses and careful grooming.[14] Similarly, *Anne of Green Gables*' Anne Shirley, while claiming the rights of a boy (particularly when it comes to education and intellectual competition) is an awkward misfit who longs to be beautiful and fashionable. Interestingly, in the 2017 Netflix adaptation, *Anne with an E*, the series creator imbues Anne, described by her original creator as 'feminine to the core', with a twenty-first-century feminism not in the books: for example, she declares she can do all the farm chores a boy can do.

Harriet M Welsch, heroine of *Harriet the Spy* (1964), is gloriously ungendered: she wears a unisex outfit of jeans, sneakers and customised tool belt. The book subverts gender in other ways, too. One of Harriet's two best friends, Janie Gibbs, is a fiercely shy aspiring scientist who 'plans one day to blow up the world'. The girls' mothers organise to send them to dance school, which they resist screamingly. 'I think you have to find out you're girls,' says Mrs Gibbs, a conspicuously foolish woman. Meanwhile, Sport, Harriet's other best friend, is the caretaker for his always-distracted author father, often dressed in an apron or planning nutritious meals; he takes on the parent role in the aftermath of divorce, as a daughter might be expected to.[15]

Harriet's creator, Louise Fitzhugh, like her literary predecessor Louisa Alcott, dressed as a boy and went by boys' names (including Peter and Sport) on and off throughout her life. Though she had a few relationships with men, most were technically unconsummated and when she broke up with her last male partner she said it was because she couldn't 'abide a male human being in my bed'.[16] She was also deeply immersed in Greenwich Village's gay scene of the 1950s and 1960s, with friends including Maurice Sendak and Marijane Meaker (who had a relationship with Patricia Highsmith, wrote young adult fiction as ME Kerr and believed Harriet was partly based on her own experience as a childhood spy – which she had told Fitzhugh about).

Meaker described her friend Louise as resembling 'a wonderful-looking little Victorian boy, running around in her boots and suits'. Fitzhugh had great tomboy style: her memorable outfits included a blue velvet pantsuit beneath a black cashmere cape. For a time, she would change her clothes depending on the company she was in, but after she received her first inheritance cheque following her grandmother's death she declared she would never wear women's clothes again.[17]

The fantasy of an odd, awkward, lonely outsider who is eventually embraced as their flawed, eccentric, essential self is at the heart of these stories.

I didn't think of myself as unusual for a long time – perhaps because, like Louisa, I grew up in an unusual family. When I finally noticed my difference from most of my peers, in my early teens, I assumed it was a result of my parents' out-of-step rules and restrictions, rather than who I was.

One thing I fixated on was my too-prim clothes. At my primary school, where there was no real uniform, Mum created one she thought appropriate, clothing me in skivvies and pinafores. When everyone was wearing ribbed denim skinny jeans, Mum thought they looked cheap and forbid them. 'Life is not a fashion parade,' was a frequent refrain. While she wanted me to look neat and cared for, she also valued my brain more than how I looked and wanted me to as well.

It's not the only reason I connected with Anne Shirley, whose longing for fashionable puffed sleeves rather than the ugly, serviceable clothes her mother figure made her wear, was a symbol of her longing to fit in. But when I recently rewatched the glorious 1985 television adaptation of *Anne of Green Gables* and the taciturn Matthew, who had one day observed that Anne was not dressed like the other girls, shyly presented the puffed sleeves Anne pined for, I cried along with Megan Follows's on-screen Anne. I confess, an irrational part of me still believes the perfect outfit could redress my lifelong inherent lack. It could make me appear, even if not 'like the other girls', the most competent version of my unique self.

Lucy Maud Montgomery, like Anne, was an orphan, whose mother died of illness when she was an infant – though Anne's father died soon after, while Montgomery's sent her to be raised by her maternal grandparents. Like Anne before life at Green Gables, Montgomery grew up a lonely child who invented imaginary friends for herself, including 'Katie Maurice', who lived behind the bookcase (and who she gifted to Anne). While she identified more with aspiring writer Emily in her *Emily of New Moon* series, and still more with 'queer', moody 'loner' Pat of *Pat of Silver Bush* ('spiritually she is I'), she also gifted Anne 'my imagination'.[18]

'But am I talking too much?' Anne asks Matthew Cuthbert, as he drives her from the train station to her new home. 'People are always telling me I do. Would you rather I didn't talk? If you say so, I'll stop. I can stop when I put my mind to it, although it's difficult.'[19] He admits, to his surprise, that he likes her talk. It's the first of many instances in which the people of Avonlea are charmed by Anne's odd, exuberant self – and Anne immediately declares him a 'kindred spirit'. Marilla, Matthew's sister, after an initial shock that she's not the boy they'd ordered to help with the farm work, concedes, 'She *is* kind of interesting as Matthew says.'[20]

And though Marilla worries about how 'such an odd girl' will get on with the other children, Anne is embraced by her classmates, especially her closest young neighbour, Diana. When she first meets Diana and her mother, Anne replies to the standard question 'how are you?' with: 'I am well in body, although considerably rumpled up in spirit, thank you, ma'am'.[21] The social faux pas of her response to implicitly scripted small talk – and the urge to honestly reply to 'how are you?' – will be intimately familiar to many a neurodivergent reader. 'You're a queer girl, Anne,' Diana tells her soon after. 'I heard before that you were queer. But I believe I'm going to like you real well.'[22]

This idea, of being embraced not just despite but *for* your unbridled, odd self – including spirited monologues and oblivion to social scripts – is a neurodivergent fantasy. I loathed Netflix's *Anne with an E* for spoiling it with a grim, 'realist' rewrite. Taking the logic that a traumatised orphan girl's vibrant oddness would rankle, not charm, it depicts Anne as being bullied rather than embraced for her novelty on her first day of school (and introduces age-inappropriate sexual talk to her schoolyard conversation). In this version, Diana awkwardly moves between isolated Anne and her own clique, and coaches her new friend on how to behave more appropriately ('don't talk so much'), cringing sympathetically when she missteps. Again, this kind of scenario will be intimately familiar to neurodivergent audiences – but the identification is painful, rather than soothing.

My two weeks of popularity as the inventor of the *Annie* game in my cousin's class was not representative of my normal life, where I was called a 'square' and a 'nerd' outside my friend circle, questioned about my regulation pale-blue socks and lace-up black shoes, and excluded from the Friday nights at Skateline that my parents wouldn't let me go to anyway. But I remember it because it was much more fun to think about and it buoyed my sense of self – and possibility – for years afterwards. I like it better as a story.

Harriet M Welsch loves 'doing everything every day in the same way'.[23] She has taken a tomato sandwich to school every day for five years. At three-forty, she has cake and milk. She would wear the same clothes every day if her lifelong nanny, Ole Golly, didn't stop her. And every day she follows the same neighbourhood spy route, including a wealthy couple who only come alive when showing off things they've bought and a poor, content birdcage maker who lives in two rooms with around twenty-five cats. 'Ole Golly told me if I was going to be a writer I better write down everything, so I'm a spy that writes down everything,' we learn.[24]

Then, Harriet's routine life is disrupted when Ole Golly, the one adult who understands her – Harriet's parents are pleasant, but distracted – leaves to get married. Soon, something worse happens: her classmates find and read her notebooks, which are full of mean observations. Sport cries when he reads: 'SOMETIMES I CAN'T STAND SPORT. WITH HIS WORRYING ALL THE TIME AND FUSSING OVER HIS FATHER, SOMETIMES HE'S LIKE A LITTLE OLD WOMAN.'[25]

Harriet becomes the enemy at school. And though she knows 'she shouldn't', she buys another notebook immediately. She writes in it: 'I WILL ALWAYS HAVE A NOTEBOOK.' It is a breathtaking declaration of artistic commitment. (And, yes, a fealty to routine.) When her mother later confiscates it, restricting its use, she struggles to process her thoughts. 'The thoughts came slowly, as though they had to squeeze through a tiny door to get to her, whereas when she wrote, they flowed out faster than she could put them down.'[26]

I was awestruck when I read *Harriet the Spy*, when I was about her age, ten. I don't remember if I carried notebooks before, but I have ever since. Like many other Harriet fans, I started a neighbourhood spy club: my brothers, a next-door neighbour and I met weekly in the park opposite my house to swap notes on what we'd seen.

Like Harriet, I think on the page. And like Harriet, I was unable to give up compulsively writing down my thoughts even after it led to disaster. More than once, my notes were found and read aloud at school, exposing my inner thoughts about my classmates, including my hopeless crushes. And in Year 12, Mum read my diaries to find out why I was acting strangely. Because of what she read, I was banned from seeing all my friends and was driven to school every day so I couldn't socialise on the bus. I bought a new diary and kept writing in it anyway.

'I AM CHANGING,' a distressed Harriet writes in a rare moment with her notebook during her period of restriction. 'I DON'T FEEL LIKE ME AT ALL.' Salvation comes through a letter from Ole Golly, with some sage advice: 'You have to lie… Little lies that make people feel better are not bad… But to yourself you must always tell the truth.'[27]

Harriet the Spy was lambasted by some horrified critics for this lesson,[28] though of course it's cemented in the unspoken social code. But it's a valuable one for autistic readers, not just for its advice on how to get by (to mask – which many of us eventually learn) but for its insistence on remaining true to yourself beneath the surface conformity. Don't change who you are, the book suggests, but perform as you need to in order to survive an often harsh, contradictory social world.

Fitzhugh, whose intensity amused the adults in her life, and who carried a sketchbook everywhere from the age of nine (and was furious when her stepmother called her 'crazy Louise' for the habit), was brought up to lubricate social relationships with 'small fibs'. But at the same time, after decades of therapy, she 'tried not to misjudge or delude herself'.

Her biographer reads a coded message of fellowship to queer kids into Harriet's conclusion, and into the moral she discovers: 'SOME PEOPLE ARE ONE WAY AND SOME PEOPLE ARE THE OTHER AND THAT'S THAT.' (Which mirrored Fitzhugh's personal philosophy.) I'm sure that's the case. But it's a fellowship that can be interpreted more broadly too, that speaks to any of us whose true selves are socially unacceptable – who long to be accepted as we are.

Fearing what she had seen of marriage, Louisa May Alcott was at ease only with men much older than her – like her father's friends Emerson and Thoreau – and younger, like Ladislas Wisniewski, a Polish man she befriended on her European travels and acknowledged as a model for Laurie, or weak and in need of comfort, like John Suhre, a soldier she nursed during the civil war. She once said, in her father's presence, 'It requires three women to take care of a philosopher, and when the philosopher is old, the three women are pretty well used up.'[29]

When Abigail Alcott died, Bronson was devastated, reading her letters, to realise his 'seeming incompetency' and 'utter inability to relieve the burdens laid upon her and my children during these years of helplessness'. Reisen concludes that this suggests he was 'far more debilitated by mental illness than anyone had guessed'.[30]

My own father, an English and literacy teacher when I was young, was unable to work for long periods, including most of my high school years, following a mental breakdown. While my mother also had a period of absence due to illness, I largely remember my father as a floating presence during this time, often absent even while physically there. When we got home from school, he'd often emerge from his study to ask us to do the dishes that had been in the sink all day. My husband nicknames Dad 'Philosopher Phil'; Dad has always encouraged and delighted in, rather than dismissed, 'overthinking'. We still have the long, rambling conversations about ideas that began in my teens.

I remember my mother as perpetually overwhelmed, always juggling her full-time job, endless marking, housework and raising five children who were nowhere near as helpful as the March (or Alcott) girls, with minimal daily practical assistance. As Abigail Alcott did, she instilled a deep work ethic, a sense that I can only rely on myself – and on her – to survive. Like sharks, the women in my family keep moving (keep working) no matter what.

'Love is a pretty myth,' says Sybylla, who toys with but ultimately resists marrying her 'one love', Harry Beacham, after accepting his marriage proposal with caveats and finally breaking the engagement. 'He offered me everything – but control,' she concludes.[31] If you've viewed your own parents' marriage as a trap, control might be hard to relinquish, particularly when gender inequality tips the scales against you.

In the opening pages of *My Brilliant Career*, Sybylla's mother tells her, 'your father has… no more idea of how to make a living than a cat'; she soon concludes marriage is 'the most horribly tied-down and unfair-to-women existence going'. Miles Franklin, of course, wrote these defiant words for her heroine at the age of nineteen – and, like Sybylla, she never married. Her biographer, Jill Roe, wrote that Franklin's 'final stance was that romantic love was illogical and human sexual energy was far in excess of all needs for propagating the species'.[32]

Lucy Maud Montgomery eventually married a Presbyterian minister in 1911, shortly after the death of the widowed grandmother she was living with. Her creation, Anne Shirley, would marry her soulmate, Gilbert Blythe, after initially refusing him (in a scene extremely like Laurie's doomed proposal to Jo in *Little Women*). But Montgomery's husband was not a kindred spirit. She hoped 'at first that I might find a friend in him', but they had little in common. He refused to help with raising the children or with the housework, and he was given to deep depressions.[33] She described his mind as 'medieval'.[34] When she died, a note was found on her bedside table that read: 'My position is too awful to endure and nobody realizes it. What an end to a life in which I tried always to do my best.'[35]

Louise Fitzhugh's parents' divorce was so acrimonious it made the news – and her millionaire father got sole custody of her from when she was two and a half. He would tell young Louise her mother was dead; she wouldn't realise otherwise until she was six and her stepmother urged him to tell the truth. Though her mother tried to connect with her, and they would remain peripherally in each other's lives from that point on, Louise never felt intimately linked to her. She grew up, like Harriet, feeling more attached to the household's servants than her parents.[36]

Fitzhugh, however, is the only one of these four writers who successfully invested in marriage-like relationships. She had a series of de facto relationships, at least two she considered marriages: a 'companionable marriage' to casting director Alixe Gordin and, later, to Lois Morehead, who was her 'wife' when she died, and whose daughter she considered herself 'a stepfather' to.[37] Biographer Leslie Brody writes that Louise was often looking for someone who would handle the day-to-day details of keeping a house going, while she concentrated on her art. In turn, she was happy to be the main financial support. In a traditional gendered sense of marriage, she wasn't the wife but the husband. She didn't have to relinquish control.

Sybylla tells Harry Beacham when she breaks off their years-long secret engagement: 'I am given to something which a man never pardons in a woman. You will draw away as though I am a snake when you hear… I am given to writing stories and literary people predict I will yet be an authoress!'[38] My first husband left me the year my first book, a memoir, was published, the Christmas before our seventh wedding anniversary. Among his reasons were that I was a nightmare to live with while writing my book. At literary Christmas parties that year, other women told me that my experience was a common one. 'You just have to tell him he's not allowed to leave you! That's what I did!' one formidably successful author told me. I was not the kind of woman who could do such a thing, nor would I have been listened to if I had.

'I'm homely and awkward and odd and old,' Jo March told Laurie when she refused him. 'You'd hate my scribbling, and I couldn't get on without it.'[39] Being homely and awkward and odd was another factor in the end of my marriage: my first husband had not liked my old-fashioned haircut or retro clothes or 'weird' friends and, following my provisional autism diagnosis, he often dismissed things about me that annoyed him as being 'because you're autistic'. I was poor at social lubrication and he hated my workaholism, which he accusingly said left him bored and forced to find his own things to do. (Which… I couldn't understand as a problem. Though I did understand I had made him feel alone, and lonely.) He did not like my fanciful strangeness.

The Christmas when my husband left, my mother drove to Melbourne to fetch me and my son back to Adelaide, where on Christmas morning I played The Beatles full blast in an attempt to be cheerful and she yelled at me for dancing around the kitchen while she was trying to clean. Back in Melbourne, she coordinated my house move, alternately telling off the movers and sending me to buy them chocolate milk and doughnuts. She sat with me while I cried, for days and months and years. As a parent, I know that was the hardest.

Eleven years later, I have two kindred spirits who don't mind my awkward oddness. The first is my neurodivergent writer best friend Mel, whose partner left at the same time as mine, and who became my significant other. She alternately indulges and calls me out on my overthinking; together we dissect and resolve life, while occasionally laughing at it. The other is my gloriously quirky, darkly handsome husband Luke, who I've spoken to every day since we spontaneously fooled random tourists into believing we were in a band together on our first date. On our third date, Luke emptied his bedroom cupboard to share the illustrated stories he'd written as a child. I introduced him to *Twin Peaks*, which we rewatch every year, and he introduced me to *Carnivale*: our favourite weird series about supernatural battles between good and evil. We relish routine, repetition and fanciful strangeness.

Coincidentally, I gave Mel the art deco diamond engagement ring it took me four years to give up (it's very beautiful) just eight days before I met Luke. She was best woman at our tiny backyard wedding. Mel and I talk for hours on the phone most weeks, sometimes multiple times a day, even though I hate talking on the phone. My son jokes that Mel, who attended his high school graduation with me, is his stepmother.

With Mel and Luke (and my son), I weave endless stories. We heed each other's nonsense.

They are my most kindred spirits.

Sources

1. Reisen, H 2009, *Louisa May Alcott: The woman behind Little Women*, Picador, United States.
2. Boyd Rioux, A 2008, *Meg, Jo, Beth, Amy: The story of Little Women and why it still matters*, WW Norton, United States.

3. Reisen, H, *Louisa May Alcott.*
4. May Alcott, L 1868 (2020), *Little Women*, Alma Classics, United Kingdom.
5. Reisen, H, *Louisa May Alcott.*
6. Bernier, N (n.d.), 'Fruitlands: The Alcott family and their search for utopia', *Orion Magazine*, <orionmagazine.org/article/fruitlands-the-alcott-family-and-their-search-for-utopia>.
7. Reisen, H, *Louisa May Alcott.*
8. Boyd Rioux, A, *Meg, Jo, Beth, Amy.*
9. Alcott, LM, *Little Women.*
10. Reisen, H, *Louisa May Alcott.*
11. Mann, WJ 2006, *Kate: The woman who was Katharine Hepburn*, Henry Holt and Company, United States.
12. Reisen, H, *Louisa May Alcott.*
13. Roe, J 2008, *Stella Miles Franklin: A biography*, Fourth Estate, Australia.
14. Franklin, M 1908 (2012), *My Brilliant Career*, Text Publishing, Australia.
15. Fitzhugh, L 1964, *Harriet the Spy*, Yearling, United States.
16. Brody, L 2020, *Sometimes You Have to Lie: The life and times of Louise Fitzhugh, renegade author of Harriet the Spy*, Seal Press, United States.
17. ibid.
18. Rubio, M 2008, *Lucy Maud Montgomery: The gift of wings*, Doubleday Canada, Canada.
19. Montgomery, LM 1908 (2015), *Anne of Green Gables*, Puffin Books, United Kingdom.
20. ibid.
21. ibid.
22. ibid.
23. Fitzhugh, L, *Harriet the Spy.*
24. ibid.
25. ibid.
26. ibid.
27. ibid.
28. Brody, L, *Sometimes You Have to Lie.*
29. Boyd Rioux, A, *Meg, Jo, Beth, Amy.*

30. Reisen, H, *Louisa May Alcott.*
31. Franklin, M, *My Brilliant Career.*
32. Roe, J, *Stella Miles Franklin.*
33. Brennan, JG 1995, 'The story of a classic: Anne and after', *The American Scholar*, vol. 64, no. 2, pp. 247–56.
34. Rubio, M, *Lucy Maud Montgomery.*
35. Ledwell, J & Mitchell, J (eds) 2013, *Anne Around the World: L.M. Montgomery and her classic*, McGill-Queen's Press, Canada.
36. Brody, L, *Sometimes You Have to Lie.*
37. Brody, L, *Sometimes You Have to Lie.*
38. Franklin, M, *My Brilliant Career.*
39. Alcott, LM, *Little Women.*

ACKNOWLEDGEMENTS

Eternal thanks to our publisher Aviva Tuffield, who eagerly embraced this book and was instrumental in helping us secure crucial funding to pay our contributors. She's been a passionate, wise and consultative collaborator every step of the way, and we are grateful for her work and for the team she's assembled at UQP.

Huge thanks, too, to Jenna Gordon and the team at VERVE Books, for not just publishing an international edition of our book, but taking on the big task of finding, adding and editing six new essays by UK and US autistic writers. We so appreciate your enthusiasm and expertise, and your detailed consultation over weeks and months.

Our editor Lauren Mitchell has been a dream to work with: meticulous, collaborative and kind. She's made our book infinitely better, asking excellent questions and helping us find the best solutions along the way. And she's made working with twenty-five authors at once look easy, though we know it's not.

Huge thanks, too, to the rest of the team at UQP (and freelance) working on this book. To Susan Le for our gorgeous cover, which we love, and for working with our vague concepts to come up with something better than we could imagine. To Kirstie Innes-Will for putting your considerable skills to work in proofreading our book. To UQP's marketing guru Jean Smith and savvy publicist Sarah Valle for working with us on how to get our book into the world.

We feel very lucky to have this team behind us and our book!

A big thanks too to Creative Australia for the funding to pay our contributors for their work, which has made this book possible.

Clem

It would not be possible to do what I do without the love and support of my family and friends. To Mum, Dad and Jane, Atti and Blazey, and to Ifer Moore, Rachel Short and Casey Holder, Alex Doenau, Adam Christou, Christos Tsiolkas and Casey Bennetto, 'Movie Club', James Wright, Talia Cain, Chris Tursi, Jess Pinney, Jenna Turner and Mike Skinner and Nell, I love youse all.

I'm very grateful to my friend and co-conspirator Dr Ali Schnabel for answering my many 'Hey, am I reading this research correctly…' messages at a moment's notice, then following up with some memes.

Thank you also to Leah Jing McIntosh, literary genius, for your friendship and sage advice regarding all things non-fiction, and to my colleagues Dr Radha O'Meara and Dr Cath Moore for your support and wisdom.

Big ups to my NDIS team, and may every politician who voted to cut NDIS funding never know a day's peace.

Thanks to every critical Autism studies and critical disability studies scholar whose work has expanded my mind.

And thank you once again to my dog and constant companion Milly, who sadly still can't read, but we'll get there one day.

Jo

Thank you to my eternally kind, supportive (and handsome!) husband Luke Sawford, a wonderful writer in his own right, who doesn't just tolerate but actively likes my unusual brain – and has listened to me talk about this book for years now. Thanks, too, for reading and providing crucial feedback on my essay.

And to my best friend Melissa Cranenburgh, my same person with different hair (except she needs noise, movement and change where I need quiet, stillness and sameness) for all of the above too – apart from the handsomeness.

To my son Felix for being the best person I know and the best company I could want, along with these two, and for your creative inspiration and company.

To my mum Jane and Nana Jean for showing me how to be in the world and catching me when I fall, and my dad Phil for his rolling conversations about ideas and example of how to be authentically yourself. And to my siblings, the ones who are in my life and those who aren't, for the love and support you've given me and my son. I will always be grateful for it.

To Rod and Aldona Sawford, for welcoming me into their family and for their incredible support. And to the Wilsons, Daina, Jason, (talented rising editor) Alex and Josh, for their love and company.

To my writer friends, especially Giselle au-Nhien Nguyen, Rochelle Siemienowicz, Mel Campbell (Writers Cum Friends), Rebekah Clarkson, Poppy Nwosu, Jane Howard, Tracy Crisp, Carol Lefevre (Adelaide crew), Maria Tumarkin (mentor and kindred spirit), Cristy Clark and Suzy Freeman-Greene. And my reader friends, especially my beloved Nikki Anderson.

And to Dr Janine Manjiviona, my first autism expert, for helping me understand myself and get through seemingly insurmountable difficulties, and Patrine Baptist, current keeper of my sanity, for her endlessly wise and kind counsel (and her dry wit).

Last but not least, to Louisa May Alcott and Jo March, and all the other writers who've kept me company over my lifetime, including everyone in this collection.

VERVE BOOKS

Launched in 2018, VERVE Books is an independent publisher of page-turning, diverse and original writing from fresh and impactful voices.

Our books are connected by rich storytelling, vividly imagined settings and unforgettable characters and narrators. The list is tightly curated by a small team of passionate booklovers whose hope is that if you love one VERVE book, you'll love them all!

VERVE Books is a separate entity run in parallel with Oldcastle Books, whose imprints include the iconic, award-winning crime fiction list No Exit Press.

WANT TO JOIN THE CONVERSATION AND FIND OUT MORE ABOUT WHAT WE DO?

Catch us on social media or sign up to our newsletter for all the latest news from VERVE HQ.

vervebooks.co.uk/signup

@VERVE_Books